72-5
123
164
183
188
213.

# SCREENING OUT THE PAST

To my mother and grandmother
who made me wonder,

for Lany
who made it possible.

# SCREENING OUT THE PAST

*The Birth of Mass Culture
and the Motion Picture Industry*

With a new Preface

LARY MAY

The University of Chicago Press
Chicago and London

This edition is reprinted by arrangement with
Oxford University Press, New York.

Copyright © 1980 by Lary May
Preface © 1983 by The University of Chicago
All rights reserved. Published 1980
University of Chicago Press edition 1983
Printed in the United States of America

90 89 88 87              3 4 5

**Library of Congress Cataloging in Publication Data**

May, Lary.
Screening out the past.

Reprint. Originally published: New York: Oxford
University Press, 1980.
Includes bibliographical references and index.
1. Moving-pictures—Social aspects—United States.
2. United States—Popular culture.   I. Title.
PN1995.9.S6M345   1983        302.2'343'0973        83-4927
ISBN 0-226-51173-1

# CONTENTS

# PREFACE

In the year that *Screening Out the Past* was published an unprecedented event occurred in America: a former movie star became president of the United States. As this investigation suggests, that should come as no surprise, for the connection between politics and Hollywood that surfaced during the 1970s had been there from the beginning. The election of Ronald Reagan was the logical culmination of a persistent trend that blended civic power and the film industry, politics and popular culture.

My study of the relationship between film and civic power, however, came through an unexpected convergence of interests. As is common with historians, I came to this subject with questions derived from prior investigations. Trying to understand how popular ideals of family and sexual roles evolved in the modern era, I turned to the movie industry, a new and influential entertainment that emerged as Victorianism faltered. It soon became obvious that sexual changes overlapped with larger cultural alterations, and that the producers of the new theater were acutely aware that this was a subject that they could exploit. Not only did the revolution in morals form the centerpiece of numerous productions, but the palatial movie houses, the star system, the fan magazines, and corporate Hollywood combined to integrate the imagery on the screen into the everyday lives of their audience.

Yet in the light of previous work, this discovery raised some troubling questions, for there was no accounting for it in the existing scholarly literature. Film studies had provided some excellent criticism, important biographies, and useful accounts of the industry. But their authors tended to isolate these subjects from one another, most often analyzing them as if they were divorced from the immediacy of popular experience. Correctly, these authors saw that cinema contained more than a mirror of reality, but they ignored the interdependency of form and content, of creativity and society. They ignored the fact that the continuing existence of the movie industry demanded a sympathetic and tangible relationship with audience views.

Recently some historians have begun to transcend the artificial divisions of previous scholarship and to integrate their studies with the movements of social change. Such efforts have not, however, offered an independent analysis of that change, nor have they offered fresh evidence to reinterpret the rise of the motion picture industry. Nonetheless, an abundance of new material demonstrates that a dynamic and essential relationship between the creators of American films and their viewers existed, and that this relationship offers a fundamental understanding of how films were created. Perhaps popular art in general, but certainly art as practiced by the creators of films in America, has been a cooperative enterprise between the artists and their audience, between those who create the images that give form to popular culture and those who choose which forms will endure.

Another difficulty was to comprehend the larger institutional framework in which this creativity occurred. If film studies had worked in a narrow context, scholars examining the emergence of mass culture and communications had erred in seeing it as passive before society. Writers working in a liberal tradition saw the subject matter of modern popular culture as primarily a response to private demands for escape; films were seen as divorced from the serious issues of everyday life. And those working with Marxist methodology, keenly interested in how capitalism surmounted periodic crises, stressed the power of big business to generate these fantasies for the purposes of social control. None of these interpretations made sense of my research findings which indicated that producers and their patrons looked to the movies, perhaps the most important of the newly emerging realms of informal leisure, to put new demands on the economy. During their formative years, films were neither isolated entertainment nor simple manipulating mechanisms controlled from above. On the contrary, they were important expressions of the independent desires of the urban folk channeled into a radically altered leisure realm.

When viewed in a context that includes the creators and the making of a popular institution, this experience offers a different vision of twentieth-century politics as well. For the new realms of leisure interacted with a revolution in sexual life that infused the reformist issues of the day, a finding that led me to reassess the key issues that absorbed historians of the Progressive era. The first step was to see that formerly separated investigations were tied together. Recent social historians have used innovative methods to show that there was a measurable change in morals among the urban middle classes between 1900 and 1920. Yet the convergence of that change with issues of power remained obscure. For example, the active communications and close relationship maintained between civic leaders and filmmakers, specifically with regard to the sexual revolution, was overlooked. Fearing that the rise of industrial empires threatened the traditional moral order, each believed that it was necessary to combat that threat. Nevertheless, by the 1920s urbanites had forged a new culture, a culture that was supported by all the modern institutions of leisure, sports, nightclubs, popular music, amusement parks, including the movies, to regenerate popular visions of progress and middle-class success.

The result was that a profound alteration in American identity was first born at the turn of the century. Movies were a key element in that transformation, helping to foster the shift from a producer's to a consumer's democracy. Centered in the large cities, the cultural revolution had an independent life. Of course, elites tried to control that process, but in spite of their efforts, filmmakers helped to reorient democratic individualism in an organized age and created models for a leisure realm that helped ease fears of social disruption. Though the promise of a richer life was often distorted in the tension, the strongest urge was to generate private fulfillment to counter an often alienating, bureaucratic society.

Precisely because consumerism supplied ideals for the political economy, producers tried to link their product to the democratic tradition by having politicians serve in the industry. Political leaders often accepted, hoping to link their programs to popular aspirations carried by the media, its leisure institutions and personalities. Much of that symbiosis has been a shadowy element, but it became overt in 1980. In the presidential campaign of that year Ronald Reagan promised to regenerate the modern American dream of consumption and economic growth, a dream that he dramatized on and off the screen for more than twenty years as a movie star. The political and artistic reality behind that synthesis has often eluded us, but this study suggests that it has been a powerful and permanent part of our culture since the turn of the century.

# ACKNOWLEDGMENTS

During the long process of creating this work, I have come to understand why the acknowledgments page precedes most scholarly endeavors: no man is an island unto himself. With this in mind, I would like to thank a number of people who lent their time, encouragement, and support. In its early stages, Professors Gary Nash, Stephan Thernstrom, and Richard Lehan read and criticized drafts in the roughest form. Throughout my efforts, Professor Alexander Saxton generously shared his insights and went over my writing with painstaking scrutiny. His kindness and scholarship have been a model I hope to emulate.

The staffs of the Museum of Modern Art, Library of Congress Film Archives, and Billy Rose Theatre Collection of the New York Public Library were all helpful. Roy W. Nicholson took all the photographs for me of those pictures from the New York Public Library Theater Arts Collection. I want to mention especially Mary Corliss and Charles Silver of the Museum of Modern Art and Monte Arnold of the Billy Rose Collection for their kind assistance. David Bradley and William Everson graciously allowed me to see films from their collections. Daisann McLane and Michael Davisson helped with the laborious task of researching and categorizing film plots, theaters, production companies, and movie personnel. Thanks also to Mark Woodard for the index.

Several people deserve special mention, for without their ideas and inspiration the project would have been impossible. A graduate seminar in my first year at UCLA with Donald Meyer ten years ago inspired some of the central themes of the work. Lois Banner and Eric Foner took time from their busy lives to read and criticize drafts precisely when I needed it most. I also wish to thank Sheldon Meyer of Oxford University Press for his constant encouragement and suggestions, as well as Victoria Bijur for her keen eye in editing an often imperfect manuscript. Most importantly, Lewis Erenberg offered his friendship, constant dialogue, and criticism during the entire project. Rudolph Schneider also helped me over the rough spots.

Lastly I wish to express my gratitude to Elaine Tyler May for her constant participation. On more levels than I can begin to fathom, she helped bring this project into the light of day. To her and two others this is lovingly dedicated.

*Minneapolis, Minnesota*                                              L. M.
*June 1980*

# INTRODUCTION

The motion picture presents our customs and daily life more
distinctly than any other medium, and therefore if we were to
come back a thousand years from today and try to find some
form of expression that clearly showed how we live today, it
would have to be the motion pictures. . . . In my opinion the
modern motion picture will not live forever as an artistic production, because its most important feature is currency—the
immediate fitting in with current thought.[1]

Irving Thalberg, Production Chief,
Metro Goldwyn Mayer Studios, 1927

Two years after the head of one of America's major motion picture
firms presented a college class with the above observations, Helen
and Robert Lynd studied Muncie, Indiana, and wrote their sociology classic, *Middletown* (1929). In examining how life in Muncie
had changed between the 1890s and the 1920s, these pioneering investigators of American life did indeed confirm Irving Thalberg's
perceptions. Four decades after Thomas Edison invented the camera, a new phenomenon had captivated the populace: movies.
Weekly attendance at the nine theaters in Muncie equaled three
times the entire population of the city. On Sunday, previously
characterized by strict Protestant mores and the absence of amusements, the movies gathered their largest audiences, outnumbering
the city's churchgoers. Surely this was a dramatic alteration in the
moral quality of their community. Yet Muncie's citizens saw even
greater evidence of change. In contrast to earlier recreations, the
viewers came from all classes and ethnic groups in the city, frank
testimony to the cinema as a mass medium. Nevertheless, while the
Lynds observed the impact of this new amusement, they gave only
passing attention to its connection to their other main concerns: the
alterations in work, leisure, and family that characterized the modern era.[2]

Others have perpetuated this oversight. Blind to the profound impact of the movies, scholars have failed to realize that the motion picture industry provides an ideal focal point for fathoming the birth of a new urban culture. When invented in 1889, and then displayed at the Chicago World's Fair of 1893, the kinetoscope showed little of its future promise. For nearly a decade, the device languished in obscurity until several small businessmen took it into the immigrant areas of the cities where it first began to spread. By 1902, a number of independent producers made hundreds of short films that showed in nickelodeons all over the urban North. Yet it was more than a decade before the producers widened the audience to include the middle classes, becoming by 1914 the first true mass amusement in American life. Despite former barriers of class and ethnicity, film innovators turned the once-crude peep show into a complex art form and a multi-million dollar business. From nearly a hundred small firms in 1912, eight major companies emerged in the twenties to centralize production, distribution, and exhibition. With this transition from an entrepreneurial to a corporate industry, the motion picture establishment generated the star system, lavish theater places, and Hollywood—a national symbol for the modern consumer lifestyle.

Right along with this development came the goose that lay the golden egg: films which gave immediacy to the rise of the affluent era. Audiences who thrilled to the artistry of D. W. Griffith, Mary Pickford, Douglas Fairbanks, Charles Chaplin, and Cecil B. De-Mille viewed talented innovators of the form. But millions of viewers came also because these performers and directors dramatized the central theme of the age: the change from Victorian to modern life that was at once so hopeful, so problematical, and so fearful. Viewers today immersed in a cult of nostalgia, or curious about silent films, might catch a glimpse of that turn-of-the-century world. Yet as they watch these early dramas unfold, they may find themselves identifying with the characters, since their problems still seem so close to home:[Mary Pickford breaking from the confines of a restrictive family life and entering the work force alone; bathing beauties in a Sennett comedy indulging in fun and rebelling against authority; Fairbanks enjoying boxing and gymnastics; Chaplin mocking modern forms of work and bureaucracy; Cecil B. DeMille searching for a family life that would include women's emancipation.] These issues, which seem relevant today, were certainly important for viewers at that time, when eternal mores no longer seemed so eternal.

Slowly that rebellion led to a synthesis that generated new ideals of success, even class, in America. By the 1920s, cinema personalities like Gloria Swanson, Rudolph Valentino, Harold Lloyd, and Greta Garbo no longer made distinctions between the styles of the rich and of the average American, on the screen or in their own Hollywood lives. For in the movie world, it appeared that the dominant messages of nineteenth-century popular culture had been turned upside down. Nothing characterized the urban press of the 1890s more than a disdain for the lavish, seemingly decadent behavior unfolding on New York's Fifth Avenue, Chicago's Lake Front, or the pleasure spas of Newport. As the Vanderbilts, Goulds, and other major industrialists squandered money, reformers equated their excess with the disorder of the larger society. With strikes spreading and the rich growing richer, moralists could easily observe that the greed of the robber barons spurred widespread discontent among farmers, unions, and small businessmen.

Yet by the twenties that same economy offered Americans the vision of affluence, and the older resentments of the rich gave way to admiration for big business. Although the work place remained regimented and hierarchical, and wealth remained unequally distributed, the trappings of luxury had come within the reach of the average consumer. Technology seemed to offer in small the material plenty formerly in the province of only the very wealthy. No doubt there remained a disjunction between the promise and the reality of the good life. But mass production had indeed brought a higher standard of living, and with it altered visions of success. In Muncie, Indiana, the new consumption desires absorbed the Lynds' attention. When looking for the most powerful influence generating notions of class sensibility, they looked not to old institutions, but to the modern mass communications system, particularly the movies. "It is perhaps impossible," they wrote, "to overestimate the role of motion pictures, advertising, and other forms of publicity in this rise in subjective standards. Week after week at the movies people in all walks of life enter, often with an intensity of emotion that is apparently one of the most potent means of reconditioning habits, into the intimacies of Fifth Avenue drawing rooms and English country houses, watching the habitual activities of a different cultural level."[3]

When we ask what caused this "revolution in morals" and its meaning for film making, the one clear answer is that it did not occur in a vacuum. A desire to understand the social basis for this phenomenon first came to me as a graduate student in the late 1960s. For it was during that decade when student activism and popular culture seemed to be intimately intertwined in a common alienation from the surrounding society. There was criticism of the Vietnam War, the Cold War, American race relations, sexual mores, and work patterns inherited from the previous era. Yet the critical edge lay in the realm of values, through which one questioned the status quo for its psychological repression, its power mania, and its injustice. The critique emerged in the form of a counter-culture promising love and harmony in a malevolent and commercial world. Music, movies, and other forms of leisure activities seemed to reinforce this rebellion, creating a widely noted youth phenomenon. Still this realm of excitement along with this political dynamic were quickly tamed, apparently absorbed by a consumer society. It struck me that this intense rebellion could not have been so quietly assimilated if the pattern had not had deeper roots in twentieth-century life. In a quest for finding its origins, I went back to the time when it all began in order to explore the beginning of mass culture in turn-of-the-century America.[4]

Clearly this trend had broad implications for politics as well as family life, and the rise of the motion picture industry provides a means for comprehending that historical problem. Above all, this calls for an examination of the way film makers were active participants in forging a leisure realm different from the past. To unravel the complexities of this process, I will examine the relationship among artists, their audiences, and the commercial energy of urban life. Like their viewers, movie makers inherited the expectations of Victorianism, and like all artists they responded in part to patrons' desires. Now, however, that determining force resided in an unprecedented mass audience centered in the growing cities. Between 1900 and 1920, producers had to be skilled not just at responding to the demands of this market, but at devising personal solutions to the major alterations in work, sexual roles, and consumption. In other words, only when we understand what meaning the larger social crisis had for individual artists can we begin to fathom the content and aesthetics of the films they created. Indeed, this mutual interaction determined the uniqueness of what we so often call "American" movies and of their habitat, Hollywood.

Because rebellion against Victorian styles and moral standards spurred so much creativity, the backdrop to the movie era is all-important. For film makers not only experienced personally the breakdown of the old order, but were sparked by the birth of a very modern phenomenon—mass culture. Middle-class Americans growing up in the 1890s knew that in the public, as in the private realm, formality ruled. Especially in entertainments, distinctions of class, sex, and ethnicity predominated. Every man knew that he could mingle in red light districts, pool halls, and gaming houses, but he kept this vice separate from his respectable life, and particularly from genteel women. Across the country, blue laws and temperance codes helped enforce these morals, and if these measures failed, periodic vice crusades ensued. In the years when the movie industry arose, however, this situation slowly changed. Now the middle-class men and women started to borrow music, dances, and even styles from blacks, Mediterranean Catholics, and other pre-industrial peoples. Why that moral experimentation should overlap with a crisis in economic, sexual, and political roles informs the opening section that follows. After a brief journey through the world before the movies, we then move on to the main epic.

# SCREENING OUT THE PAST

# Chapter One

# THE BACKDROP: VICTORIAN AMERICA AND AMUSEMENTS

> Our old town was not Athens, or Paris, or even Stratford. Yet
> so far as it went, a child's life there was rich and deep. He had
> by fourteen what anthropologists call *a* culture, which is quite
> different from *culture*. He had made himself by easy and natu-
> ral experience part of a conscious, an organized, a unified soci-
> ety.                                    HENRY SEIDEL CANBY, 1934

In 1934, Henry Seidel Canby, literary critic and editor of the *Saturday Review*, published a remarkable memoir. Looking back on the
passing of Victorian America he saw one apt symbol for that
change in his home town: the center of local society, the opera
house, had been turned into a movie theater open to all. But Canby
saw that this transition did not mark a total break with the past.
Rather, the values of nineteenth-century America remained alive,
in the town as well as on the screen. This strong holdover testifies
to the strength of Victorianism as a living reality that tied together
politics, work, sexual roles, parental values, and entertainment.
The middle-class Protestants who adhered to the code identified
with the creation of a northern Democratic society that grew out of
the industrial era. Families managed their own property, worked
long hours, and tried to control the habits of their workers through
laws against drinking, gambling, and ribald sports. And despite the
labor strife and political corruption of the age, they never questioned the inner core of their own values and the march of progress. In fact, the blacks, Indians, and Catholics who lived nearby
and worked for them only served to highlight their own sense of
civilization. As Canby noted, it was the "age of confidence," and

"the last time in living memory that everyone knew exactly what it meant to be an American."[1]

Canby's memoir is most useful because it helps clarify the internal reality of Victorian culture. All too often, this code of the nineteenth-century middle class is considered merely a stifling sexual ethic which pertained primarily to family life. The litany is familiar: Victorians resisted temptation and lived formal, even stuffy, lives. Presumably, they restrained their emotions and contained their sexual passions. Like all generalizations this does hold a measure of truth. But it fails to explain why people would place themselves under such repression, or the way in which the ethos related to the society at large. The beauty of Canby's *American Memoir* lies in its sensitive portrayal of bourgeois life in all its aspects. While scholars have looked at isolated facets of nineteenth-century culture, Canby describes its totality. He shows that Victorianism was a way of life that provided the glue for the community, and ramified through work, class exclusiveness, leisure, and childrearing. All of this was contained in a synthesis which bound together the values of entertainment and popular literature, and the practical aspects of everyday existence.

A set of traditions and folklore tied middle class groups together and upheld their world view. In a nation with no formal aristocracy, the "best people" had a profound sense of their own moral leadership. Unlike the immigrant workers or the Negro domestics in their midst, they had a sense of "ought" and a "concern for the future." In contrast to the Catholic laborer who "never went west and came back with fine clothes," the Protestant saw the economy as a place to exercise "pioneer training in self-dependence, his sense of room at the top, and his certainty that work can get him there." A life's career was more than an occupation, it was a calling. One learned that "only obedience and accuracy and a contempt for the pleasure of idleness could give a leg up the ladder of success." Fathers went to work at daylight, labored until dark, enforced the Sabbath and domestic discipline. Belief in the potential for mobility in the class order and in a frontier of expanding opportunities in the cities or in the West held the Protestant culture together. It was this popular value system that gave nineteenth century society its sense of classlessness, for all Americans could enter the respectable community provided they lived according to its norms. In this way it could bind together such diverse elements as the "transient micks," the Republican party, the steel mills, Andrew Carnegie, and temperance crusaders.[2]

Popular reading materials also directly informed the lives of the middle classes. It was not so much that in reading a western, a detective story, or a romance people were encountering things they themselves would do. Rather, despite their wide range of time and place, these stories held up a series of universal values which might be applied to everyday reality. With astute anthropological perception, Canby saw that the tales in magazines and dime novels were not something separate from "real life"; they were "what bards were to the tribe, a recalling, an enriching of memory." Authors such as Russell Conwell, Horatio Alger, and James Fenimore Cooper wrote sermons, success tracts, and novels with differing themes and contexts. But as Canby noted, they were all seen as "extensions without break from our own lives," from which "we drew an ethics of ideal conduct in emotional stress."

Not too surprisingly, these tracts often contained the values that entrepreneurs of good conscience and social responsibility carried into the market place. Each of these writers portrayed an ideal individual who was above all self-sufficient. Never did the autonomous hero, like Natty Bumppo of Cooper's famous *Leatherstocking Tales*, rely upon parental aid for getting ahead. Like Cooper's own father, who rose from meager circumstances to become a large landholder in the frontier province of New York, or the author's political idol, Andrew Jackson, who rose to become a "symbol for the age," the heroes in his novels were never deterred by circumstances. In a nation where the frontier was both myth and reality, they achieved on their own merits and merged their skills to America's historical destiny. Natty Bumppo, for example, cleared the land of savage Indians or the despotic and aristocratic Spanish. His allies then constituted a virtuous community of farmers, civic officials, soldiers, and businessmen. When the frontier was conquered by the 1890s, and Americans extended this manifest destiny into the Caribbean, the Philippines, and Asia, Canby found it nearly impossible to separate these tales from the imperialistic thrust of the Spanish-American War:

Certainly in our town where the past and future seemed to become romantic together at the turn of the century, I cannot separate in my own memory the bands and the cheering of ninety-eight, Hobson, Dewey and Manifest Destiny in an expectant world from the extravagant romanticism of the shallow, unphilosophical, unpsychological novels we had been reading.[3]

This reality did not emerge from a vacuum. Rather, it had antecedents in the religious and political enthusiasms that greeted the creation of a democratic culture in the first decades of the nineteenth century. Historians have begun to suggest that perhaps the most important development during the decades following the American Revolution was the shift from a traditional to a modern society. With the overthrow of British rule, many institutions disappeared that had made Europeans dependent upon one another for centuries: hereditary social or political ranks, primogeniture, and the unity of church and state. The lessening of hierarchical authority in America first appeared in the political arena. After 1800, the old property requirements for voting were shaved away. As the electorate expanded, the number of Congressmen who had relatives also serving in that body sharply declined. At the same time, Protestant sects emphasizing personal over traditional authority increased in number and variety. Yet democratization was most apparent in the economy. The opening up of the West and the first stages of industrialization brought an expansion of opportunity. In both the rural and urban frontiers, mobility was the order of the day. Everywhere, individualism was on the rise.[4]

The decline of public authority paralleled a similar alteration in family life. By 1830, a number of indicators point to the rise of an individualistically oriented domestic realm. In New England, fewer children were named after ancestors, suggesting fewer ties to the past; and in the North in general family size declined along with the birth rate.[5] Though the precise cause of this demographic transition remains vague, it does appear that it was related to the increasing mobility in the larger society. It was not so much that fewer children meant more time for parental pursuit of gain, or that more resources could be devoted to children's careers in a market economy. Rather, in a society where offspring were less dependent on their parents for land, status, or tradition, families could gear their children toward individualistic achievement and future opportunity. Echoing what a number of scholars have found concerning popular values of the period, Henry Canby recalled that, in the Victorian era, " 'God bless our home' never meant make our home a happy one. The blessing was asked upon those virtues more conducive to material success than happiness." In this context, sexual activity was repressed, for "except in sin or the reticence of marriage, sexual drives did not exist." The men thus carried over into their business life the standards of self-denial and endless striving that existed at home. The result was a community strictly divided between those who held to the code and those who did not. No mother had to speak of classes, "she merely let them be felt."[6]

Women were given a specific role in this milieu. To understand this, we need to examine male and female roles together. For the egalitarian polity and open economy had a strong effect on women as well as men. Before the Revolution, the household economy was the norm. Women participated in the canning of food, the making of clothes, tilling the soil, and educating the children. But in the nineteenth century, the spread of manufacturing destroyed the household economy by removing productive functions from the home. By the 1830s, a new pattern had evolved in urban areas: women were separated from the work world of men. Women of the laboring classes joined the work force, becoming factory operatives or domestic servants. Affluent women, however, would reign over homes isolated from the work place.[7]

Women responded to this in a number of ways, all of which fit a pattern of Victorian womanhood. One was to elevate and expand the ennobling function of the home. As early as the 1830s in the North, magazines, newspapers, and books carried articles telling women that they should act in a new way toward husbands, sons, and suitors. Love was to be an agent teaching self-control, for the urban economy demanded constant striving. Unlike the seasonal pace of farm work, or the pre-industrial rhythm of craft or mercantile pursuits, men now had to channel their energies into a ceaseless productive system, and pour profits back into the enterprise at the expense of consumption and leisure. Women fit into this scheme as partners in a millennial mission of progress. In this secularized Protestantism, women represented the spiritualizing force. As William Wasserstrom concluded in his study of popular romantic literature of the nineteenth century, "Unlike the European literature of love, American writing has identified women with society and suffused both with the Messianic ideal. Once we assume the burden of love, our literature says, we must assume the obligations imposed by history and remold the nation in order that it lead the way for all mankind." [8]

While spurring men on to success, women were also implored to control themselves, particularly their sensual natures. In other words, it was in this era that the proverbial American Puritan was created, rather than in the seventeenth century. Colonial Americans rarely condemned drinking or sexual pleasure; there were restrictions to be sure, but these pleasures were just one part of life to be enjoyed in proper bounds. But nineteenth-century Victorians vigorously tried to expurgate sensuality, games, and drink from both public and private life, seeing these joys as antithetical to personal and social order in a society dedicated to ceaseless work. Genteel women, however, were not born; they had to be made. Contemporary literature thus argued that while women taught men self-control, they too had to guard against "high spirits," for "fallen" women lost caste and could become contaminated with "disease." According to a recent study by Daniel Scott Smith, the rigors of this code reached far into the lives of Northerners. Premarital sexual activity did decline sharply between 1830 and 1860, suggesting that the code demanding rigid internalized controls over passions had an immediate effect on behavior. [9]

Beyond internalizing self-control, the woman's role also carried with it a social function of equal significance. In a society without traditional hierarchies, where mobility was the norm, the home was the center of the commercial order. Popular literature emphasized that the home stood in the center of a world in flux, balanced between decadent monopolists and disruptive laborers. Stage dramas stressed the importance of the domestic influence as well. Young heroes rose in society and furthered the nation's progress by protecting pure women from evil men. [10] Sweethearts and wives corroborated through their demeanor and household management, showing that their men could be trusted as solid citizens. For in a mobile world where entrepreneurs did not always know their potential buyers and borrowers, good women were the mark of good credit. Sarah Josepha Hale, editor of the era's most popular women's magazine, *Godey's Lady's Book*, exhorted women to be the "rational counterparts to their husbands." One of her ideal heroines had that "delicacy of affection for him which would not let her complain, or solicit assitance from others, lest some implication of bad management or neglect of family be cast upon her husband."[11]

At the same time the domestic role furthered enterprise, it also contained the potential for discontent. Evidence that females felt frustrated by their isolation appeared in the women's magazines of the day. "My enigma," explained one heroine in *Godey's*, "is that when I was poor there was excitement . . . now all is ennui. I have success. I married the man I chose. God knows I never loved him. I look around for an object unobtained. . . . I often envy the happiness of my maid servants." A female columnist offered one typical solution. In a country where "men's souls feed on ambition," shopping was "the chief delight of the inactive." Yet the endless advertisements spoke to more than mindless purchasing. Women were to be the exclusive bearers of aesthetic taste and refinement. As William Taylor in his study of Sarah Josepha Hale explained, the "role which she evolved for the American woman was a compensatory one. In America, she reasoned, where a man was forced to make his way and fulfill himself by the accumulation of property, the woman was left with a positive and dynamic function to play. She was destined to be the agent of culture and moral perfection."[12]

Moving beyond even this crucial function, women were also to extend the moralizing qualities of the home into the broader community. The Protestant church was one major force behind this process. One foreign observer noticed that "religion was the only activity outside the home which women might do without violating the proprieties." Accordingly, the great revivals sweeping across the towns and cities of the North encouraged women's involvement in their communities.[13] Rather than being concerned only with personal salvation, these outpourings of enthusiasm were aimed at reintegrating a community torn apart by the incipient industrial economy. As one study of Rochester in the 1830s and '40s has shown, religious awakenings converted individuals across class lines. Not only were women in the vanguard, but these crusades allowed businessmen to establish ties to the workers. Thereafter the owners of capital favored men who had temperance cards,

joined evangelical churches, and brought sober habits to work. Just
as participation in revivalistic churches gave a minority of workers
stability and the opportunity to move up the class order, so it
created ties of culture and sympathy between employer and employed. In all functional areas, from voting, to work, to family and
religion, there now seemed to be a unity of purpose for a significant minority of the Protestant community. It was the women
above all who constituted this cement; their new role as guardians
of the unfortunate brought them out of the home into churches and
voluntary groups.[14]

Nowhere can this reorientation be better charted than in the
careers of two noted women who popularized the new social
function for females, Catharine Beecher and her sister Harriet
Beecher Stowe. The Beecher family generated two great revivalist
ministers of the era, their father Lyman and brother Henry Ward.
The patriarch had crusaded against drink and social divisions, hoping that a religious awakening would bring the Millennium to
America. As Catharine later recalled, his was an "inspiring vision
to which all of his children were dedicated and to which some of
them might possibly belong." Catharine and Harriet wanted to
carry on their father's tradition and be useful citizens. But as
women they encountered a world where their productive function
was being undercut. Even though they might control the home
with strict temperance, or pursue status and prestige through
spending, they felt the female role to be stifling. In fact, Catharine
noted that the "disabilities and sufferings of her sex needed relief,"
for there was a "horrible decay of female health over the land."[15]

Certainly one of the most notable victims of this decay was
Catharine's sister Harriet. "Though she was blessed with comfort
and servants," Harriet Beecher Stowe wrote that she was "dismally
unhappy." At twenty she had married Calvin Stowe, a divinity
student in her father's seminary, and ever since "it has been hurry,
hurry, hurry and drive, drive, drive." In fact their life together was
"years of pain, confusion, anxiety, disappointment and suffering."
Ten years after their wedding she found her left side mysteriously
paralyzed. Giving clues to her malady, from the rest home where
she recuperated away from her family, she wrote Calvin that
"never again would I love with that blind, unwise love with which
I married, I love as truly tho more wisely." She also chastised her

husband's passions, telling him he had only "a few more traces of the earthly to be burned away with the fires of affliction," and had nearly achieved "the mastery of yourself in the most difficult point of all." Yet men could not master themselves alone. They needed the help of women, who were now encouraged to extend domestic discipline into the wider society. As Harriet and Catharine began to encourage females to be agents of social reform, they dedicated their book, *The American Woman's Home,* to the nation's females,

> in whose hands rest the destiny of the Republic . . . . While they sympathize with every honest endeavor to relieve the disabilities and sufferings of the sex, they are confident that the chief of these evils is the fact that the honor and duty of the family state are not fully appreciated.[16]

Advice of this kind was reinforced in perhaps the most influential novel of the day, Harriet Beecher Stowe's *Uncle Tom's Cabin.* Published in 1852, at a time when the North was alarmed at the possibility of slavery expanding into the western territories, Stowe's novel preached that the sins of human bondage could be erased by extending the power of true womanhood and the home into society. While it is not usually recognized as such, the central axis of the story revolves around the redeeming qualities of Mrs. Shelby, a "woman of high class, both intellectually and morally." As the mistress of the plantation, she embodies all the forces of Christian stewardship. Under her care is Eliza, a "mulatto slave who she protected from those temptations which make beauty so fatal an inheritance to a slave." Mrs. Shelby helped Eliza marry George Harris, a mulatto who achieved success in a large factory by inventing a machine to benefit humanity. While this showed that the home could be an agent for making free men of black slaves, Mrs. Shelby's son George has also been "well trained in religious things by his mother." Another dependent on the plantation, Uncle Tom, reinforced this by telling the lad,

> Now Mas'r George . . . ye must be a good boy 'n member how many hearts is sot on ye. Always keep close to your mother. Don't be gettin' into any of those fooling ways boys have of gettin' too big to mind their mothers. Tell ye Mas'r George, the Lord gives many things twice over, but he don't give you a mother but once. Ye'll never see

another such woman, Mas'r George, if you live to be a hundred years
ole. So now holds on to her, and grow up to be a comfort to her,
thar's a good boy—you will now, won't you.[17]

There is, however, one soul beyond the reach of Mrs. Shelby,
that of the plantation master, her husband. Despite his wish to get
into "heaven through the superabundance of his wife's saintly qualities," Mr. Shelby sells his slaves and sends them southward where
the geography of the slave trade corresponds to the spiritual realms
of heaven and hell. Tom's first master in the southern pit is Augus-
tine St. Clare, whose fall into Hades began when his "divine"
mother died at a young age. "If I had lived to grow up under her
care," he explains, "she might have stimulated me to I know not
what enthusiasms." But St. Clare was raised by his "born aristocratic" father, and he married a decadent, lazy female. Only his
daughter, "Little Eva," named after his mother, is capable of performing the task of true womanhood. As Eva dies, she exhorts her
father to free the slaves, and he undergoes a total conversion. Now
he rejects the indolent ways of his wife and reaffirms the work
ethic. Under slavery, he realizes, blacks would "never rise to do
much among us. The fact is we are too lazy and impractical ourselves, ever to give them much of an idea of that industry and
energy which is necessary to form them into men. They will have
to go North where labor is the fashion—the universal custom."[18]

Yet St. Clare is soon killed on a mission of mercy, and his
unregenerate wife sells Tom to a "superstitious" man who had
"dethroned God," Simon Legree. Spurning his mother who told
him to forsake gambling and drink, Legree "threw her senseless to
the floor and with brutal curses fled." He then went south where
his passions could run loose. There he takes a slave concubine,
Cassie, who had been raised in a convent where she learned
"music, French and embroidery." In brutalizing Cassie, he destroyed her potential as a true woman to uplift him and domes-
ticate the plantation. Indeed, "as time and debasing influence and
despair hardened womanhood within her, and waked the fires of
fiercer passions, she had become in a measure his mistress." Finally, salvation is restored as George Shelby, who upholds the
familial values of his mother, goes south to rescue Uncle Tom. But
when he finds that Legree has caused Tom's death, George "with
one indignant blow knocked Legree flat on his face, and as he stood

over him, blazing with wrath and defiance, he would have formed
no bad personification of his great namesake, triumphing over the
lion."[19]

The novel thus culminates with a moral victory based on the re-
silience of true womanhood. Each character reaps his just reward.
The author points out that she is not condemning commerce *per se*,
nor advocating a privatized domestic realm. Rather, she calls for a
moral family which will humanize an economic system based on
free enterprise. George Harris, the slave who invented a new machine for Northern factories, promises to build an African republic
of "hand picked men who by energy and self-education have in
many cases individually raised themselves above slavery." Rejecting from his African utopia slaves raised in Haiti under decadent
French Catholicism, George vows to use his energies in ways that
Protestants would approve: education, self-cultivation, and upward
mobility. All of these things were reinforced by his wife Eliza who,
like her former mistress Mrs. Shelby, would inspire him in the
proper path. Simon Legree, personification of all the chaos and
brutality in a buccaneer economic system run wild, received the
just punishment of a moral universe. "Excess," concludes Stowe,
"had brought on that frightful disease that seems to throw the lurid
shadows of coming retribution back into the present life."[20]

The same formula infused the literature and moral crusades of
the era. In fact, the function of true womanhood intensified. Beatrice Hofstadter's study of female novelists of the late nineteenth
century indicates that women began to create even more activist
heroines who spread familial ethics beyond the confines of the
home.[21] This theme also operated in the society itself, where two
of the most visible forms of female activity were Prohibition and
women's suffrage. Although female emancipation held the potential
for a new cultural style, its dominant civic thrust contained Victorian assumptions. Alan Grimes's study of women suffrage in the
West suggests that this movement was both an effort to broaden
the role of women and to further social order. Since literate,
middle-class women could be expected to vote more regularly than
working-class females, Protestant hegemony would be preserved.
"I noticed," explained a minister in Wyoming, the first state to give
women the vote, in 1869, "that a majority of women voted for men
of the most temperate habits, thus ensuring success to the party of

law and order." Similarly, prominent suffragette Susan B. Anthony wrote that votes for women would ensure control over vice:

> There is an enemy in the homes of the nation and that enemy is
> drink. Everyone connected with the gambling house, the brothel and
> the saloons works and votes solidly against the enfranchisement of
> women, and I say if you believe in honesty and integrity then do what
> the enemy wants you not to do, which is to take the necessary steps to
> put the ballot in the hands of women.[22]

When institutionalized for broader social purposes, these impulses defined much of the employment available to women in the nineteenth century. No doubt the central place where this occurred was public education. Starting in the 1830s, reformers such as Horace Mann and William Thayer argued that free schooling could serve as a means for assimilating outsiders and teaching the fundamentals of success. Working-class politicians of British stock supported these goals, and tax money was used to further educational efforts which taught literacy, temperance, and regularity. As Michael Katz noted in his study of early educational reform, " 'passionate' and 'sexual' became the two most pejorative words in educational discourse." By 1900 every state had a law requiring the teaching of temperance in the public schools; and the most widely read primer was written by a militant advocate of Prohibition, Dr. McGuffy. Women were the perfect teachers for this ethic. They could be cheaply hired and supervised by male administrators, and the Victorian moral code fit their defined role. In this way a young woman could earn money respectably. And in 1900, of all professional women 73 percent were school teachers.[23]

Women's new roles fit well into new institutions which promised to reward those who assimilated into Victorian norms. But since this often demanded a rejection of the pre-industrial culture of rural folk, workers, and recent immigrants, it generated sharp conflicts between native Protestants and outsiders. Foreign-born laborers, for example, scorned temperance in favor of their traditions of public festivals celebrated with dancing and drinking, and camaraderie at the corner saloon. They came from traditions where work went according to the task or season—not the regulation of the assembly line or the clock. When these groups retreated from public education to establish their own parochial schools, or used politics to protect their festivals and ethnic neighborhoods, it sparked an even more militant desire among the natives to outlaw the sports, games, and entertainments of the recently arrived immigrants. Nineteenth-century politics were often infused with these conflicts. In the Northern cities especially, Republicans were Protestant and Democrats were Catholic. Dramatizing these tensions in a novel published in 1896, *The Damnation of Theron Ware*, Harold Frederic had his hero strive for success and a moral home. Yet he felt these were threatened in the large cities where

> most of the poverty and drunkenness and crime and political corruption were due to the perverse qualities of a foreign people—qualities accentuated and emphasized in every evil direction by the baleful influence of a false and idolatrous religion. It is hardly too much to say that he never encountered a dissenting opinion on this point. . . . When he was at church seminary every member of his faculty was a Republican and every member of his class came from a Republican household. . . . He had never known a Democrat or had occasion to formulate even his own thoughts on the tacit race and religious aversions in which he had been bred.[24]

Frederic's fiction reflected the reality of Victorian life. No one saw this more clearly than Henry Canby, whose very upbringing was infused with similar values. In his home town, the schools were staffed by women, and "ethics breathed through every brick of it, except the boys' latrines." But they did not reach "the slum below the playground walls."[25] Catholic workers living in those poorer areas "represented the anarchy and the lawlessness that ever since the Civil War the country had been trying to subdue." For the immigrant, pre-industrial manners and festivals displayed the "reality of passion freely expressed." His fascination with the foreigners was the "disorganizing principle which aroused the opposite in us and made us believe there was something real in the precepts of our elders." It was thus imperative to extend Anglo-Saxon hegemony over these people, since "the immigrant need only be Americanized to make no trouble for the right-minded."[26]

Such ambivalence also stimulated fierce battles. Like the Western heroes they idolized, young men used force to subdue the savagery. On the way to class each boy would fight an Irish lad so that "the long walk to school each day was a replica in small of the journeys across the plains of three decades earlier." Only now the sons of the laborers had replaced the Indians: "Immigrants were the alien and had to be shown their place." Yet they could be tamed, for "this was America; if they would adopt our manner (such as our arrogance) we would tolerate them." An open class order depended on it. Provided the "alien" could shed his background and assimilate to Protestant asceticism, he could be accepted. This demanded, of course, adopting the proper code of sexual propriety.[27]

One of the more crucial areas for that code was in the realm of leisure. Victorians equated institutions of play with the mores of the larger society; both distinguished genteel individuals from outsiders. In the cities, great care was taken to ensure that entertainment beyond reading took place within private homes, or within the neighborhood churches. Women going to theater were carefully chaperoned, and plays followed the lines of *Uncle Tom's Cabin* and the genteel themes of Victorian writers. Managers ensured that this public arena would mirror the same values as well. Theater architecture was copied from Greece, Rome, or its Italian and French derivatives, for these styles radiated the clarity, balance and proportion desired in a Republican citizenry. Inside, the seating followed patterns that could have reflected an aristocratic as well as a democratic social order. The pit was for servants, the orchestra for the middle class, and the boxes for the upper orders. The balconies were for "colored" people and prostitutes. In essence, the formality of the seating reflected the dramatic themes on the stage.[28]

The wider realm of leisure reflected these divisions as well. Throughout the nineteenth century, there was an increasing spread of public entertainments. In one sense, politics could be looked upon as a pageant, with parades, music, and tremendous ritual activity. Minstrel shows, circuses, and vaudeville also contained the same democratic impulses, and drew men from all social levels. After the Civil War, boxing and baseball attracted large crowds, and the press glorified their heroes. Nevertheless, despite obvious egalitarian elements, and the drive of men like P.T. Barnum and numerous politicians to make these amusements respectable, there were still sharp social distinctions involved with these public events. Class and ethnic mingling might have occurred, but Victorians were always aware of the distance between their own genteel leisure pursuits and the raucous sports and festivities of those they considered beneath them. Most important of all, though politics and entertainment transcended social boundaries, Victorian women were excluded from these arenas. In other words, respectable females stayed away.

There were a few attempts to bring the sexes as well as the classes together in public. Perhaps the most notable of these were the parks springing up in urban areas. Starting in the middle of the century, elite reformers in cities like New York, San Francisco, and Boston tried to break some of the former patterns of separation. They built large scenic playgrounds for recreation, in an effort to harmonize society in an industrial civilization as well as to soften the city landscape. Led by the noted architect Frederick Law Olmsted, these planners envisaged the parks as a pastoral refuge for urban families. They also hoped that this environment would provide social uplift for the rougher elements, who might be influenced by the spiritual qualities of nature as well as by the example of their "betters." But there were problems with this ideal, as Olmsted realized when he built New York's Central Park. While there was potential for the spread of ethics from above, there was an equal possibility of non-genteel influences emanating from below. Olmsted and his elite allies feared that the "manly and tingling recreations" and "boistrous fun" of the immigrant males might corrupt the entire environment. In 1892, for example, a Tammany politician nudged through the state legislature a bill authorizing a race track in Central Park. Immediately Republican reformers mounted a successful counter-attack. Olmsted argued that such a track would lead to immorality and "anarchy," endangering the "security of every man to the enjoyment of his earnings."[29]

Much more dangerous than the parks, however, were those entertainments that combined drinking, dancing, and the presence of unchaperoned women. Every major city had vice districts which contained pool halls, ribald entertainment, brothels, and saloons. Victorians quietly sanctioned these outlets for male passions. "The higher sense of mankind," observed one female reformer, "says the family is the essential unit of the state. Our practice says that the family plus prostitution is the essential unit." Everyone knew about and tolerated New York's Bowery and Tenderloin, San Francisco's Barbary Coast, Chicago's South Side, and the New Orleans French Quarter where men could enjoy sexual liaisons separate from their business and family lives. Good women who visited these areas lost status, for it was feared that their chastity would be compromised. Even worse, they might mate with males who were socially beneath them, threatening their familial as well as economic status. In fact, middle-class observers rarely distinguished between these vices and the festivals and dances of the immigrants, where men and women often mingled freely. Both symbolized social and sexual anarchy.[30]

Urban amusements were thus divided by class and sex. By looking at the 1880 census, which for the first and last time listed all the theaters and saloons in the cities, we can discern the pattern. In general, small towns and southern cities had one public stage, the local "Opera House." Northern metropolises, on the other hand, had a wider variety catering to a more diverse population. New York City, for example, was divided into clearly demarcated entertainment zones containing twenty-five playhouses seating from 1,500 to 2,000. About half were in affluent neighborhoods and charged a dollar admission, four times more than other houses. In this way they excluded the "rabble" and catered to gentlemen and chaperoned ladies. Next were a series of concert halls attached to neighborhood churches, generally frequented by the Protestant middle classes. Below them and charging one-fourth as much as the high-priced theaters were the vaudeville, minstrel, and cheap melodrama playhouses. Then came the 7,000 saloons and beer gardens which either served an ethnic clientele of both sexes, or catered to males only. At the bottom were the vice districts reserved for male entertainment, where "no good woman would be caught dead."[31]

Within the Victorian "Opera Houses" the rituals of decorum mirrored the very values of home and family that the best people carried into their lives. Canby described how the annual ball in Wilmington, for example, juxtaposed these values against the festivals of the lower-class Catholics. Held in the local Opera House, the ball radiated the middle-class quest for refinement and security. Only one step removed from the "plain" people of the town, the aspiring elite tried to maintain "the pretense of being an aristocracy." With "the realm of making money . . . firmly shut out as the night behind the curtains," the aura of cultural superiority focused on the women. "We believed that every girl should for a moment at least of apotheosis, in the midst of a ball that had become hers, at the first utter opening of her petals, be not a lovely creature of seductive flesh, but a goddess manifest." Females embodied the highest values of the class order. That is why it was imperative that they exhibit the triumph of spirit over body: "We respected tradition and tradition dictated an immense respect for the women of our own class. A girl at a ball was a woman on show, a custodian of honor and the home who could flirt and be gay and tease and be teased, but one hint of the sexual made her 'common,' which was only one word above 'vulgar.' "[32]

Public decorum also extended into private life, particularly wedlock. No period of youthful experimentation was sanctioned for either sex. Women lived with their parents until they married, whether they worked or not. Once wed, those who held that marriage was for personal gratification or indulgence were compared "with the Negroes." Divorce was almost unknown, for unhappiness was no excuse to break up a home.[33] It was therefore very difficult to bring passion into married life. "We had learned to associate amorous ardors with the vulgar, or worse with the commonplace, and to disassociate them from romance. Our sensual emotions escaped from the control of our imaginations so that in love and marriage later we found it difficult to bring the two together again."[34]

With the split between higher and lower nature, males at least had one way out. They could turn to the implicitly sanctioned vice districts. Everybody in the town knew of houses of "ill fame." "Only fanatics," recalled Canby, "expected to abolish prostitution . . . but if the easy women could be banned as outcasts, the respectable society, so they thought, might be free of salacious desire." Appropriately, the prostitutes were usually immigrants. During the day, middle-class men demanded sobriety and regularity from their foreign workers; but at night some righteous employers were drawn to "chippies" in vice zones or amusement parks. Were it not for this safety valve, sensuality might invade the home and disrupt respectable society.[35]

Women in the "age of confidence," however, were not so lucky. Excluded from the economy and expected to uplift neighborhood life, they had no similar outlet for their libido. "Passion was bad for businessmen's wives," wrote Canby, "so their passion soon conformed to the kind of sexual relations which made for the least trouble." As Henry Adams observed in his *Education*, the American woman "had discarded all that men disliked; she must, like the man, marry machinery; already the American man sometimes felt surprised at having himself regarded as sexless; the American woman was often surprised at having herself regarded as sexual." Canby perceived that there were some women who chafed at this restraint. But they were condemned by their social peers. As he explained it,

> The girls of our own kind who were high sexed, and therefore amorous and desirous of the chase, were debased by this double standard in women. There was no compromise for them. Either they supressed their amativeness, trying to become good companions like the rest, but succeeding only in becoming coquettish to the edge of hysteria or morbidly sentimental; or they yielded just enough for too tight embraces in the dance or permitted fondlings and lost caste. The word "degenerate" was not in common use then, but that, most unfairly, was what we felt about them. And I remember that the men were more ruthless in characterizing them than were the girls.[36]

By the late nineteenth century, the restlessness that Canby was to perceive later infused the work of every major author. In Walt Whitman's *Democratic Vistas* (1871), for example, the poet saw that the society needed to be reinvigorated "from this daze, this fossil and unhealthy air which hangs about the word 'lady.' " This called for a "new birth, elevation, invigoration of women." Mark Twain, Theodore Dreiser, Henry James, and Henry Adams all focused on women who, in one form or another, rebelled from the confines of Victorianism. In Mark Twain's *The Gilded Age* (1873), the heroine acts on new familial and career assumptions. One of the main female characters in Henry James's *The Bostonians* (1886) calls for a rectification of "the gulf that already yawns between the sexes, since my plea is for a union far more intimate provided it be equal." Theodore Dreiser's heroine in *Sister Carrie* (1900) instinctively sought a new sexual style. Although these novels often ended tragically, they did show the breaking of old vessels. Even Harriet Beecher Stowe, after reading a European novel, realized the flaws in the culture she so deeply cherished:

> In America, feelings vehement and absorbing become deep, morbid and impassioned by the constant habits of self-government which the rigid forms of society demand. They are repressed, and they burn inward till they burn the very soul, leaving only dust and ashes.[37]

   Although all these writers were aware of the limitations inherent
in the ascetic separation of the sexes, they knew why Victorianism
had such staying power. For the propertied middle class, it offered
a comprehensive guide to behavior. The popular literature, home,
and neighborhood encouraged both sexes to weave a secularized
Protestantism into the social fabric. To fill the void caused by absent husbands and the loss of productive functions in the economy,
women formed social clubs, reform groups, and church organizations that promised to extend the cult of motherhood into public
life. There they encouraged the opposite sex to free itself from monopolists, slaveholders, and sensuality. Men would create a producer republic where the distribution of power and wealth would
be based on open opportunity and the work ethic. Only a fundamental alteration in values or the economy could question this
code of historical progress and national destiny for the middle
classes. When this occurred, Canby noticed a dramatic symbol of
the change. That is why the transformation of the local Opera
House into a movie theater, which collapsed the former divisions
between the classes and sexes, was such a profound event. How
this happened, and what anxieties it generated, informed the
following decades.[38]

*Collapse*
*Divisions.*

# Chapter Two

# THROUGH A LENS DARKLY:
# THE DECLINE OF PROGRESS

> I sometimes think that the descendents of the pioneers who
> mastered the plains are being conquered by the wilderness of
> leisure. Our constant cry is to make things easy for ourselves
> and our children, easier than for those whose only alarm clock
> was the war whoop of the savage.
>
> MRS. THOMAS EDISON, 1925 [1]

Shortly after the Chicago World's Fair of 1893, Thomas Edison's
chief photographic assistant wrote an article for the prestigious *Century* magazine, describing the latest wonder unveiled at that extravaganza summing up the achievements of the century. In this essay
and a pamphlet that followed, William Laurie Dickson explained
how he and "Mr. Edison" in 1888 had drawn on the international
advances in science to create the world's first motion picture camera, the kinetoscope. Dickson envisioned this new device not as a
form of mere entertainment or personal expression, but as the
"foremost" instrument of reason, for now people could actually see
empirical truth. No longer would history be tinged with the "exag-
gerations of the chroniclers' minds." Like the great classical buildings and imperial monuments built by Daniel Burnham at the Fair,
this signaled that the "resources of the world" were at the command of the democracy. To ensure mankind's liberation, Dickson
warned that the "utmost discrimination must be followed in the
selection of themes" for the films. He then asked rhetorically,

> What is the future of the kinetoscope? Ask rather from what conceiv-
> able phase of the future it can be debarred . . . the kinetoscope stands
> as the foremost among the creations of modern inventive genius. It is
> the crown and flower of nineteenth-century magic. In its wholesome,
> sunny and accessible laws are possibilities undreamt by the occult lore

of the East. . . . . It is the calling of the coming age, when the great
potentials of life shall no longer be in the keeping of cloister and
college, sword or money bag, but shall overflow the nethermost por-
tions of the earth at the command of the humblest heir of divine intelligence.[2]

Obviously, for Dickson and the select readers he addressed, the
Victorian synthesis was still intact; both saw invention and technology leading to improvement in all parts of the social realm. In
fact, this new piece of creative genius, the movie camera, testified
to the worth of a laissez-faire market place and a political democracy. For despite the fast pace of the economy, competition yielded
visible rewards. Had not the national wealth increased four times
in the last half of the nineteenth century, spreading opportunity
and the good life? Surely such a free and open society moved with
the "guiding hand" which classical economists thought guaranteed
national progress. It followed that the inventor was a national hero,
the spiritual generator; and the popular press celebrated American
superiority by boasting that more patents were registered here than
in any other country. In the words of one contemporary, these innovations would bring "back from Heaven's gate the application of
science to art," and symbolize the triumph of industry and democracy over the world's backward areas. Ironically, however, while
Edison personified the greatest achievements of the era, his later
life and the fate of his last great invention came to embody the
larger tensions erupting within Victorian culture.[3]

During most of his public career, Edison incarnated the character Americans associated with the self-made man. Repeatedly, the
popular press idealized him as a living Horatio Alger hero who rose
from modest origins in the Protestant Midwest to become
"America's greatest and most useful citizen." Skeptical of hierarchical institutions and emotional religion, Edison believed that only
through science could men discover the "divine intelligence."
Through inventions such as the electric light, phonograph, movie
camera, and telephone he felt he was "bringing out the secrets of
nature and applying them for the happiness of man." Even after
becoming a world-famous figure who was entertained by European
nobility, he remained a plainly dressed egalitarian who worked
long hours with his assistants, the self-styled "Edison Pioneers."
Forever the democrat, he still thought that the greatest event in

human history was the discovery of gunpowder, enabling stout-hearted yeomen to bring down mounted knights and equalize power.[4]

Like many men of his generation, Edison publicly proclaimed that the key to success was a strict home. From his parents he had learned early that men and women had separate, but mutually interdependent, roles. Thomas's father was a small businessman who scoured the Midwest searching for economic opportunity, while child-rearing duties fell almost exclusively to the mother. Living up to the popular ideal of the self-made man, Edison went to work at the age of twelve and would soon come to praise the source of the ambition that drove him to the top. "Every day I apply the advice and training given me by my mother." He married a woman of similar qualities. Mina Edison was the daughter of a pious businessman from Ohio. She was the model of temperance, serving in a number of church, social, and educational organizations devoted to Prohibition and the uplifting of the working classes, particularly Negroes. Mina also taught her sons to maintain "moral stamina" in business life, while Edison poured his energies into work, laboring "two shifts" a day, long into his old age.[5]

Given this exemplary career, it is no wonder that Edison attracted many disciples. One of the most dedicated was William Laurie Dickson, who helped him develop the motion picture camera. From his native England, the eighteen-year-old Dickson wrote to his idol,

> I have read of your life with the deepest interest and the lesson it has taught me of hopefulness, of firm endurance and determination. . . .
> I have no pride and would willingly begin at the lowest rungs of the ladder, and work patiently up, if by doing so I might hope to gain independence and repay my widowed mother for the care and affections she has lavished on me for so many years. I am sure you will not have cause to regret holding out a hand of friendship to a fatherless and friendless boy.

Though the youth had all the potential for self-elevation, Edison initially did not answer. Nevertheless, Dickson left his native England for the United States. After landing, he married a forty-year-old Virginia heiress, but not before securing her father's legal permission at the local courthouse. Perhaps it was his newly acquired

status that finally caught Edison's eye, for after another series of in-
quiries he was hired at Edison's research site in Menlo Park, New
Jersey, during the 1880s. Soon he was working on the "Wizard's"
latest project, the motion picture camera, and writing a laudatory
biography of his hero.[6]

The book was more than a biography of Edison. It described the
ideal character capable of perfecting civilization. Dickson's study was
the portrait of a man whose achievements were a "potent argument
in favor of total abstinence." Neither alcohol, drugs, nor the "foods
of rice-eating nations" had touched his lips. Nor had he spent his
youth reading "trashy or sensational fiction." He was able to
triumph over the "gross fixity of matter." "Floating in the billows
of divine life," Edison brought mankind closer to that "glorious
enfranchisement which is the heritage of the sons of God." Dickson
believed that when future generations look back on the passions of
previous ages, or the "wanton splendor of oriental and Latin
races," they will see only the "crooked paths" of "license, political
disintegration and declining intellectual power." Primitivism could
only be stamped out with the power of the moral home. When
"marriage shall be lifted from the slough of sensuality" and "freed
from the shackles of tyranny and oppression," then "jealousy and
strife will give way to union and cooperation." From this spirit
"shall be born new forms of social and political life such as are
undreamt of by the maimed and halting sections of humanity."
Purging lust and chaos from history would allow human will to
solve "every problem which has baffled the sundered halves of the
great human unit."[7]

While Edison's inventions might further these goals, Dickson
found that after his initial praise for the movie camera, an acute
ambivalence followed. Within Edison's vision, the phonograph and
kinetoscope would be used to improve education in the schools and
promote business efficiency. The man "who lighted Broadway"
never indulged in amusements. Rather, the "Wizard" saw his efforts culminating the mission of science and productivity: they
would be used in classrooms to teach skills, to help businessmen
sell goods, or to show more accurately the news of the day. Yet
Dickson soon realized that the experience of watching numerous
frames of celluloid spring through light and project on a large
screen challenged a clearly empirical view of the world. Images

were five times larger than life; they could defy time and space and distort reality. Commenting on one of the early showings at the laboratory, Dickson wrote of the invention he had just helped create:

> The effect of these somber draperies and the weird accompanying monotone of the electric motor attached to the projector are horribly impressive and one's sense of the supernatural is heightened when a figure suddenly springs into his path, walking with a vigor which leaves him totally unprepared for its mysterious vanishing.[8]

As a new device in 1889, the camera also failed to meet Edison's early expectations. Initially, when Edison tried to sell the camera and projector to the large investors and industrialists who had purchased his previous inventions, he found nobody interested. This was because of their unwillingness to open up a domestic market for mass-produced luxury or consumer goods. The nation's big financiers of Wall Street preferred to follow the lead of imperialists by sending "excess production," as they phrased it in the business journals of the day, abroad. Manufacturers held down wages and the purchasing power of their workers, and tried to moralize their labor force by suppressing sports, saloons, and pre-industrial customs such as saints' days, Blue Mondays, and drinking on the job.[9] Therefore, even though per capita income did go up for all groups, many financiers were "loathe to speculate" in new industries such as automobiles, cigarettes, and telephones.[10] Given Edison's reluctance to conceive of the movies as an amusement, along with the lack of investors, it is no wonder that he failed to take out a foreign patent, or to seek markets at home. Revealing his initial lack of enthusiasm, he wrote in 1893,

> I have constructed a little instrument which I call a Kinetoscope, with a nickel and slot attachment. Some twenty-five have been made, but I am very doubtful there is any commercial feature in it, and fear that they will not earn their cost. These zeotropic devices are of too sentimental a value to get the public to invest in.[11]

The "public" may have found the device too "sentimental"; but there were others who would readily gravitate to it. Much to Edison's surprise and chagrin, the camera fell into the hands of businessmen who realized the potential of the motion picture as entertainment. Among these was William Laurie Dickson who, after a nervous breakdown possibly due to frustration over Edison's reluctance to market the camera, left his idol to form the Biograph Company in 1895. Edison soon would try to limit such renegades by leasing his exclusive patent to his own men in the Edison company. But even then it was difficult to prevent newcomers from entering the field, for it took little capital to set up shop with an unpatented camera obtained from abroad. Several small businessmen began to display the camera as a curiosity device in New York City. By 1897 the novelty wore off, and these men took their films to vaudeville houses and projected them on a screen. Finally, to their dismay, they found that this did not yield much profit, since managers used them as musical, comic, or news shorts only, and demanded an exclusive set of films for each house.[12] Such a policy undercut the potential for mass production in the very nature of the film, since it could be endlessly duplicated. So by 1900, these American entrepreneurs began to find new markets in the rapidly expanding immigrant neighborhoods of the cities.

Even more surprising to the camera's creator, the device was not becoming the new tool for science and enlightenment. Rather, it was serving the desires of the "rabble." There were several reasons for this. One was the different cultural tradition of the thirteen million "new" immigrants flooding into the cities from southern and eastern Europe between 1900 and 1914. These newcomers and their children soon comprised the majority in many urban areas, with their elected officials holding local political power. This "machine" control, so widely condemned, often protected the amusements of the foreigners from crusaders eager to "clean up the city." Their labor leaders also saw that reform would lead to increased tensions, for the inventive genius of men like Edison created technology that made work more routinized. So pleasures became even more important when immigrants encountered mechanization. Workers thus pushed for higher wages and time off the job, not only to survive, but to find some relief from their ceaseless toil. Verifying this reality, one study of New York City in 1908 found that the laborers who raised their income above the subsistence level used much of the difference on leisure pursuits.[13] No savings

It was in this atmosphere that the early movies found their most receptive audience. Nickelodeons joined other amusements proliferating among the newcomers. In New York City, saloons in-

creased from 7,000 in 1890 to 9,000 in 1910, and cheap entertainments such as penny arcades and street shows rose from none in
1890 to 1,000 in 1910. Another and more infamous innovation was
the Raines Hotel. Managers opened saloons disguised as hotels
which skirted the state's Sunday closing laws. Though they were
condemned as brothels, they appealed to a clientele of both men
and women, who came to mingle, drink, and dance to music
played by black musicians who "ragged" favorite old-time melo-
dies with a pounding beat. Emerging on the outskirts of the cities
were large amusement parks such as Coney Island, Far Rockaway,
and Atlantic City. In these realms, immigrants and workers found
amusements which catered to men and women of all ethnic groups.
Here film makers began to find a market for their films of low life:
boxing, girlie shows, and stories that reflected much of this atmosphere.[14]

Yet when film makers tried to reach into middle-class markets,
they found themselves thwarted by the continuing strength of Victorian assumptions about amusements. Despite the fact that the increasing affluence of the period generated an expansion of leisure
time and pursuits for the bourgeois, the movies at the turn of the
century faced an almost insurmountable barrier in the class and
sexual divisions of respectable entertainment. A popular literature
of books and mass magazines that could be enjoyed in private had
spread over the nation; but it was limited by price and subject matter to the tastes of the affluent. Many of the most popular journals
had been founded by strict Protestant reformers who were hostile
to immigrant machine politicians, labor unions, and the "riotous"
sports of the workers. Magazines such as *Century*, *The Arena*, and
*Harper's* thus appealed to five million readers who thought they
were the most civilized people in a nation of eighty million.[15]
While the journals could be consumed at home, public amusements
for the Victorians remained in exclusive neighborhoods, usually
revolving around the church, or in theaters with a style and seating
arrangement that echoed the formal divisions of Victorian life.
Here, above all, women could be protected, far removed from the
wide-open amusements of the lower orders.

Nevertheless, the nineties brought the first glimmerings that the
social reality preserving this formal order was beginning to crack.
It was not just that massive strikes and agrarian revolt had spread

over the country. Rather, the structure of middle-class life was crumbling from within. To contemporaries, the most tangible expression of this anxiety was the fear that the frontier was gone. An expanding land mass had meant much more than the source of free territory and a farm; it had been the symbol that America was made up of "producers" who would be independent in economic and political life. The frontier meant that no matter how bad things looked in the East, the future offered freedom. Yet that physical reality had disappeared. Perhaps the most profound symbol of this came in the life of the pioneer citizen *par excellence*, Thomas Edison. By the 1890s, the Wizard had set up a factory and successfully resisted his workers' strikes for higher wages, and then tried to enforce strict temperance. But ultimately he succumbed to the forces that swallowed independence, and was forced to sell his firm to J. P. Morgan's General Electric Company. Writing to his lawyer, this "intensely competitive man" explained that "if you make this combination, my usefulness as an inventor is gone. . . . I can only invent under strong incentive."[16]

Edison's fate was part of a much larger process. It was in the cities that the economic basis of the frontier spirit was most vulnerable. Between 1870 and 1920, the urban areas grew from 28 percent to 52 percent of the population. As the historian Alfred Chandler has shown, here centered the rise of "big business." Key national industries had slowly begun to dominate supply, distribution, and production. In the long run the growth of horizontally and vertically integrated firms meant the steady decline in the prospects of the worker and farmer to achieve economic independence. Social mobility would continue to expand, but self-sufficiency was to be replaced by rising in the ranks. Even those who retained a measure of autonomy, petty proprietors and skilled workers, would find that decisions affecting their work rested in the corporate hierarchy. Furthermore, a rising standard of living was endangering self-denial. As the national product tripled, and per capita income doubled between 1870 and 1900, the work week declined. These changes were most dramatic in the northern cities which had a per capita income one third higher than the rural South and West.[17]

In these same areas, moreover, the traditional role of bourgeois women was altering. Victorian women had seen much of their productive function undercut by factories and public institutions.

In small towns where the rich and poor lived near each other, those
higher up the social ladder found a viable role as moral guardians of
the home, or uplifters of the poor. Yet in the late nineteenth century, even that function was dissolving. As major cities grew, they
became sharply divided along class and ethnic lines. With the poor
living in one section, the moderately successful in another,
women's communal and charity functions became more difficult.
Some might continue social guardianship in restricted neighborhoods through church work; others might seek to revitalize their
roles through settlement houses in poor neighborhoods. Still others
might turn to the opportunities opening up in the work world.
Perhaps because men did not want to assume the most menial and
routinized jobs in the corporations, businesses hired women as
clerks, secretaries, and sales personnel. For the first time, females
had money to spend, and the means to enjoy it.[18]

What would this mean for the Victorian tradition? In the early
stages a number of writers began to comment on the new world of
the cities. One of the most popular and revealing tracts was written
by a Congregational minister who had spent time in New York
City as head of the Evangelical Alliance. Running through Josiah
Strong's *Our Country* was an awareness that with the "frontier"
gone, the Anglo-Saxon pioneer was in a crisis. The men who
"worked more hours in a day, more days in a week, more weeks in
a year" than any people on earth were finding their independence
thwarted by the rise of routine work in large firms. On top of that,
our "wonderful prosperity" held a "decaying core." In the cities,
"Christian Stewards" of "God's Elect Nation" were turning excess
energy to hedonism and shopping, dangers that might return the
nation to feudal styles of life. A weakening of will would thus make
it impossible for Anglo-Saxon character to remain distinct from
immigrant culture of the cities. In order to restore the old character, Strong advocated a policy of imperialism, exporting "excess
production" abroad.[19]

Beneath Strong's anxiety was also the fear that the new position
of women was altering the family as well. Strong and like-minded
moralists rarely examined the psychological side of this phenomenon; however, novelists of the period did. One of the most penetrating efforts came when William Dean Howells asked his fellow
author, Harold Frederic, to write "of what you know best."

Frederic's resulting masterpiece, *The Damnation of Theron Ware*, takes place in the small New York town where Frederic grew up. His central character is a Methodist minister raised for a life of continual work. Yet he finds that the frontier is gone, and he is part of an organization prospering on the collapse of the old order. Slowly Ware feels a restlessness that turns him away from his wife and Protestant morals; he is lured to the Irish Catholics' festivals, church ceremonies, and women. All of this comes to focus on Ware's infatuation with Celia Madden, the daughter of the town's wealthiest Catholic. In order to win her approval, Ware buys her a piano at the town's department store, hated symbol of the new age because it offers mass-produced luxury goods and undercuts the independence of the small proprietors who comprised his congregation.

Ware's final damnation comes when he offers Celia his love, and the implicit promise to shed his ascetic past. But she answers in the tone of the new woman that this is "an old fashioned ideal . . . that women belong to somebody else as if they were curios, statues, or race horses. . . . You don't understand my friend that I have a different view . . . the notion that any human being could conceivably obtain the slightest property right in me is preposterous . . . as the notion of you being taken out with a chain and sold as a slave." In the face of this rejection Ware realizes that the new culture is beyond him. Consumed with guilt, he suffers a nervous breakdown. A female evangelist nourishes him back to health and vigor. Ware then hopes to revive the old life by going to Oregon. "Who knows," he muses, "I may turn up in Washington a full blown senator before I'm forty, stranger things have happened out west." Yet Frederic implies that with the frontier gone, this is no longer possible. Indeed, both Frederic and Strong were acutely aware that as both men and women began to question the older definitions of success and the home, they were reevaluating their relationship to foreign cultures.[20]

In the 1890s it was no secret where this change was most dramatic. All the major newspapers of New York City and Chicago were filled with the new behavior of the rich. These were the industrial titans who had the financial and social security for moral experimentation. Formerly, they had poured their energies into building huge industrial organizations. Now they could reap the

rewards of the corporate order they had ushered in. As one reformer phrased it, work for the rich had "lost some of its vital interest," and with "excess leisure and money" they began to build
lavish hotels, mansons, and museums along Fifth Avenue or the
Lake Front. These structures were testimony to their power and
hegemony: they would not be supplanted by local elites or the
laboring masses of the day. Yet even more important was the way
these public endeavors provided the wealthy with a platform for altering their older way of life. Behind the aristocratic façades, they
could indulge in games and parties that flew in the face of their ascetic pasts. Daughters married European nobles, or pioneered a
playful yet elegant style made famous in the magazines as the
"Gibson Girl." Likewise, young men in the Ivy League colleges
and clubs were "casting off the bonds that tied us to the censorious,
the utilitarian, practical bourgeois life with its emphasis on time
serving and being businesslike." [21]

The elaborate theaters that began to spread down Broadway,
"catering to the carriage crowd," as one producer phrased it, embodied the change of style. Successful producers such as Charles
Frohman and David Belasco each built grand edifices where the
"socially elect" could promenade. Belasco was most famous for developing the star system. Stage idols instructed viewers only a generation away from Victorian self-denial how to assume the trappings of aristocracy. A typical Belasco play might focus on a
titillating display of scandal among the rich, who triumphed over
their folly with grace. But the larger purpose was to show the audience how to indulge in high-level consumption in the numerous expensive restaurants and resorts of the city. As Theodore Dreiser
pointed out through his heroine in *Sister Carrie* (1900), this was particularly alluring for women:

> The matter of expense limited the patrons to the moneyed or plea-
> sure-loving class. Carrie had read of it often in the *Morning* or *Evening
> World*. She had seen notices of dances, parties and balls at Sherry's.
> . . . Every fine lady must be in the crowd on Broadway in the after-
> noon, in the theaters or at the matinees . . . she had not lived until
> something of this kind had come into her life. Women were spending
> money like water. [22]

Along with freeing themselves from frugality, the rich also
began incorporating some of the dances and music of non–Anglo-

Saxons.[23] This was most evident when vaudeville and minstrel shows were brought into the high-class theater district of Fifth Avenue and Broadway. The main producer, Tony Pastor, ensured that the price was high enough to keep out the "riff-raff." First he "washed out vaudeville's dirty ears, drawing it out of beer halls and gentlemen only dives where teasing soubrettes were awash with perfume and equal amounts of willingness." For entertainment there were real blacks, rather than people in blackface. Black chorus girls danced to exotic rhythms and displayed more of their bodies than would have been allowed of white women. In order to participate in this sensuality themselves, the rich began to hold masked balls which resembled the Mardi Gras. In New York City, there were no licensed balls in 1900; yet there were 1,000 by 1908.✓ The Vanderbilts went so far as to invite black dancers to their estate in order to teach the partygoers their "jungle rhythms." It seemed as if the atmosphere of the Raines Hotels had penetrated the top echelons of society. As one observer lamented,

> Society has decreed that ragtime and cakewalking are the thing, and one reads with amazement and disgust at the historical and aristocratic names joining in this sex dance, for the cakewalk is nothing but an African dance *du ventre*, a milder edition of African orgies.[24]

Private misbehavior began to explode at the high class cabarets, where women shed their cloistered demeanor. Formerly it was disgraceful for an unchaperoned woman to mingle in public, or drink and smoke with men in dance halls. But the new cabarets in the wealthy sections of cities broke down these barriers. New York City had none in 1905; but by World War I there were twenty, with such aristocratic names as Maxim's, Sans Souci, Chez Maurice, Jardin de Dance, and Café Madrid. A classic example was the Folies Bergères opened in 1911 by Jesse Lasky, a former vaudevillian. "Everything about the Folies," he wrote, "was unheard of in New York, including the prices." In order to provide a place where the rich would be willing to go, Lasky filled the insides with lavish furnishings. There a *maitre d'* met each customer at the door and—to cut down on the promiscuous mingling associated with vice zones—he seated each couple at a private table. Finally he added a tremendous allure by hiring black musicians who would play music for the cakewalk or ragtime. These dances were not formal as in the Victorian era, but filled with movement and energy.

Caught up in the rhythm, couples moved to such new dances as the Monkey Glide, the Fox Trot, the Bunny Hug, or the Grizzly Bear. But at the Folies, these beasts were tamed and carefully refined.[25]

In spite of its genteel veneer, cabaret dancing mirrored a type of female expressiveness appearing elsewhere as well. As early as the turn of the century, Ruth St. Denis and Isadora Duncan had pioneered modern dance and caught the attention of socialite women who sponsored them at salons and the Metropolitan Opera House. Both artists had drawn movements from exotic and far-away places, bringing sensuality into their creations. When Ruth St. Denis took her Hindu dances to Europe, the poet Hugo von Hofmannsthal caught the heart of what was different: she was "suffusing the European imagination with Asiatic beauty, going to the limits of the sensual and yet remaining chaste . . . nothing like it would have been possible a decade ago." A famous dance couple popularized this in the cabarets. Irene and Vernon Castle became the main headliners in New York by uplifting what Irene termed "nigger dances," bringing them through the refining air of "Paris." The husband and wife team then took the steps into parties and dance classes sponsored by the rich. Vernon's supposed aristocratic upbringing and Irene's cool, graceful air allowed them to radiate a genteel form of eroticism which appealed to the upper classes' desires for a release from convention.[26]

New York's elite did everything possible to make high-level consumption exclusive to their own group, utilizing the fruits of the economy to differentiate themselves from the masses. But their styles and behavior were quite noticeable, sparking a widespread commentary in the press. Gossip columnists in particular took a moralistic stance, echoing the outrage of their middle-class readers, providing them with a sense of superiority over the richest and most powerful people of the day. No doubt a number of famous scandals furthered this tendency, perhaps the most notorious being the Stanford White, Evelyn Nesbit, Harry Thaw love triangle. Thaw, a rich industrialist, killed White, the most noted architect of the day, in a café on the roof of Madison Square Garden. The cause was an affair between White and Thaw's wife, Evelyn Nesbit, a former chorus girl.[27] Moralists delighted in the sensation, and used it to illustrate the dangers of shedding propriety. Yet at the same time, it appeared that some of these same influences were spreading downward. "The immorality and degradation of the rapid life," wrote an editor of *The Arena* in 1900, "among the mushroom aristocracy is matched by the grosser manifestations of immorality in the social cellar . . . and the great middle class is caught in between."[28]

Nowhere was this scandalous behavior encroaching on the Victorian middle classes more forcefully than in the movie houses spreading through the cities after 1900. Initially it seemed that the motion pictures would die out after being released in the vaudeville houses. But that did not happen. Film makers stumbled on the expanding market for amusement in the immigrant neighborhoods, and opened a rash of nickelodeons, so called because it cost only a nickel to enter. New York's small theaters increased from 50 in 1900 to over 400 by 1908, showing movies to approximately 200,000 daily. Suddenly the middle-class press began to take notice. "In neighborhoods where innumerable foreigners congregate, the so-called nickelodeon has held sway for the last year," reported the *Independent* in 1908. Another journal declared that "the nickelodeon is cropping up in the crowded quarters of the city almost as quickly as the saloon. On one street in Harlem there are as many as five to a block, each one capable of showing to 1,000 people in an hour." The prestigious *Scientific American* claimed that there were fully 20,000 nickelodeons in the northern cities by 1910, and they seemed to be expanding daily. Commenting on why this amusement was spreading so rapidly in the midst of a mild business recession, Abraham Cahan, editor of the *Jewish Daily Forward*, wrote in 1906:

> Music halls have shut down. Yiddish theaters are badly hurt and candy stores have lost their customers. Yet the nickelodeon remains unhurt. For only a nickel or a dime you can see a show and hear a song and watch a dance. . . . Hundreds of people wait in line. A year ago there were about ten Jewish music halls in New York and Brooklyn. Now there are only two . . . the movies are not feeling the depression, for people must be entertained and five cents is little to pay. A movie lasts half an hour. If it isn't too busy you can see it several times. They open in the afternoon and customers, mostly men and women, eat fruits and have a good time.[29]

One of the reasons why this entertainment was spreading so rapidly was its potential for mass production. In the words of the time, it was "canned drama" which had the immense advantage of making costs low and profits much greater than either the high or low priced playhouses of the city. A producer shot his story once, then duplicated the film and distributed it to hundreds of theaters all over the city in exactly the same form. Exhibitors could then charge as little as five or ten cents admission, compared to $1.20 for a Broadway play, or sixty cents for a cheap melodrama, and still make a larger net profit. He paid only $25 for a license, while his theatrical competitors paid five hundred. Nor did he have to make sets or hire a stage crew and players. While it cost $2,500 a week to run a theater in New York in 1910, it only cost $500 for a nickelodeon. Moreover, a theater-owner was not limited to only one or two performances a day. Rather, he could run the story ten to fifteen times in a row. He had the further advantage of a silent product, which appealed to viewers who spoke various languages. Movies were clearly lucrative. As a reporter for *Success* magazine wrote in 1908, "Now that mechanical duplication is the secret in art, the motion picture revolution is coining money for all involved."[30]

Gradually observers began to notice that the movies also appealed to an audience that crossed class lines. A number of studies as well as police licenses showed that in New York City nickelodeons increased from less than fifty in 1900 to over 400 by 1908. These "common shows" which seated only 300 at first appealed to laborers in the poor parts of the city. But soon they began to spread into more affluent areas. The artist John Sloan depicted a movie house scene in 1905, showing what was truly new: young girls dressed in the most elaborate, expensive clothes were hovering over a nickelodeon enjoying the show. While this might appear to be merely an isolated observance of a rebel from Victorianism, others began to verify his portrait. The very obsession of the middle-class press with this new institution after 1906 testifies to its impact. One such reporter explained his own fascination with the movies: "It seems as if we who have this education, this culture, have had something taken from us. I wonder if we will ever get it back."[31]

By 1908, producers were learning that the movies might appeal to this quest for excitement. The *Nation* noted this mass attraction, calling film the "first democratic art." Stories were devoid of "high brow inclinations," and permeated with "the very ideas of the crowd in the streets." Over half of the 4,000 films released annually came from France, Germany, and Italy. Rarely was the American theme of rags to riches or the western motif portrayed.[32] More often themes ridiculed Victorian values. A gentleman in *Too Polite* (1908) tries to be "nice" to all mankind, but when he brings temperance to a small town, the commoners give him "many an unkind blow for his troubles." Another, *The Candidate* (1907), features a politician of comfortable circumstances running for office; but soon workers throw dirt on him after he makes a high-toned speech, and his wife beats him when he returns home, out of her sheer discontent. Female rebellion also permeated *Down with Women* (1907). It focuses on a well-dressed man condemning women's suffrage because the weaker sex in incompetent. On leaving the meeting, he meets a woman selling bread on the street, a female musician playing for children, another woman sweeping the road, and others driving cabs and trucks. Finally a woman saves his life, and when he is arrested a female lawyer defends him in court. So much for incompetence.[33]

Beyond these themes of rebellion, foreign films also reflected cultural values that were the antithesis of Protestant optimism. Rather, they depicted the foreign norms of immigrants from Catholic peasant backgrounds. Generally the backdrop was made up of the Virgin Mary or the Catholic Church. Unlike American themes of sexual restraint, these tales depicted pre-marital sex and even adultery as human weaknesses or even as something to be enjoyed. Rarely was sex condemned outright. (Interracial love affairs also received a sympathetic portrayal.) Often heroes and heroines were overwhelmed by circumstances or fate, culminating in tragic or pessimistic endings rather than triumphing over obstacles. When happy endings did appear, they did not have the puritanical tone of Victorian love stories. One typical ending celebrated the union of two lovers with a "fete on the public square where the girls are dancing nature dances while the men sit around and gamble."[34]

American producers imported many of these foreign films. But they also made their own with slightly off-color themes. Since they could not conceive of these stories as acceptable to a general audience, they geared them to the all-male crowd of the vice zones. Generally they appealed to the working-class market by having newsreels, boxing matches, vaudeville skits, and shorts. Slapstick

humor and serious films also attacked authority. For example, a
child in *Policeman's Dream* (1908) awakens a sleeping lawman by
setting him on fire. In the work of Edwin Porter, a Protestant
American film maker working for Edison, we find blatant attacks
on injustice. His most noted work was *The Great Train Robbery*
(1903) which pioneered a number of innovative techniques. Yet
along with the close-ups, parallel editing, and quick action of the
film, the plot showed lawmen who were just as ruthless as the
criminals in their pursuit of glory. Porter brought this theme to
fruition in the *Kleptomaniac* (1906). The film charts the story of two
women caught shoplifting. At the trial, the rich matron brings a
host of lawyers who argue that she is merely neurotic and should
be freed. As the judge dismisses her case, he jails the poor girl who
stole bread to feed her hungry family. The waif is led away, and
Porter focuses his camera on a figure of Justice. On one side of the
scale she holds gold, on the other side nothing. So the scale tips
toward money as the director shows a final close-up of the face of
Justice with dollar signs glittering in her eyes.[35]

Patrons from the "better" parts of town also saw a public arena
sharply juxtaposed to their own milieu. Theater owners decked out
their marquees "in plebian splendor of gilt and white, screeching
forth its welcome to every passerby." Though these styles emulated in small the façades of the luxury theaters uptown, one standard price admitted the public to an open auditorium with no
divided seating separating the classes. Along with this democratic
flavor, there was a sense of anarchy as the crowds came and went
at will, since the stories followed each other without a set time
sequence or schedule. Most alarming, however, was the fact that
amid this chaos, "girls drop in alone," as *Theater Magazine* explained, which "speaks well for that part of town . . . cheapness
reigns supreme in the nickelodeons." In that atmosphere there were
"opportunities for making chance acquaintances and familiarities of
one kind or another . . . the darkness takes away the feeling of responsibility." Yet it was this very atmosphere of excitement that
supplied a release for "monotonous" work, as the noted social
worker Jane Addams perceived. For "hundreds of young people
. . . going to the show is the only possible road to mystery and
romance." What was "seen and heard there becomes their sole
topic of conversation, forming the ground pattern of their social
life."[36]

The new medium itself heightened this captivating quality. Contemporaries were struck by the revolutionary nature of film. Movies were a dramatic break from older ways of seeing and perceiving. Within the darkened theater, action was defined not by the rise and fall of a curtain which interrupted the action, or by boundaries of an artificial stage with sets and backdrops. Rather, figures moving across the gigantic screen were larger than life, but they were real people in real surroundings. A kiss, for example, is rather benign in print. But magnified on the screen it carries a powerful emotional charge. As the *Evening World* reported in 1899, "For the first time in the history of the world it is possible to see what a kiss looks like . . . scientists say kisses are dangerous, but here everything is shown in startling directness. What the camera did not see did not exist. The real kiss is a revelation. The idea has unlimited possibilities." Directors could even emulate the mind's eye by moving across time and space at will. In fact, the viewer could be manipulated by the focus of the camera, creating a passive but receptive imagination. The "biggest attraction of the nickelodeon," noted a reporter in *Harper's Weekly*, "is that it makes no demands on the audience, requiring neither punctuality nor pattern, for it has no end, no sequence."[37]

The power of the medium also seemed capable of touching the "subconscious mind," operating almost like a dream. Viewers sitting in the darkness watching a standardized, mass-produced film were much more easily influenced than by reading or watching a stage production. First, the person watching the screen was shown what to see rather than choosing for himself. Next, he knew that he was watching a filmed story and thus was not evaluating the players giving a unique performance. He could relax the active part of his mind, and enjoy the "intimacy" of the silent medium. It is interesting to note that sound films were possible long before 1927. In fact, Edison's first demonstration in 1889 included sound. Film makers chose to keep the movies silent. The reasons are obscure, but it is likely that producers knew that silent movies could appeal to an audience of immigrants who spoke many languages. The result was an emotional communication through the universality of pictures.

Victorians were alarmed by this force, especially because the spread of "canned drama" knew no bounds. Anxiety was highest in small towns and rural areas, which had not yet been tainted by the urban amusements of large metropolitan centers. An article expressing these fears appeared in *Good Housekeeping* in 1907, written by a professor of philosophy at the University of Kansas. The professor warned that the motion picture was a danger worse than the games, sports, and amusements that good people had tried to repress in the past. As the movies spread over the small towns of his state, they drew boys and girls into the "atmosphere of a red light district" within the reach of "every home." Before the flickering lights, youth learned how to "flirt" and "deceive their mothers." The author realized that the danger was heightened by the emotional force of the medium: "Pictures are more degrading than the dime novel because they represent real flesh and blood characters and import moral lessons directly through the senses. The dime novel cannot lead the boy further than his limited imagination will allow, but the motion picture forces upon his view things that are new, they give firsthand experience."[38]

The main thrust of these worries focused upon youth. But beneath this moralizing was a deeper fear that no age group was immune to the forces of cultural change. Joseph R. Fulk, Nebraska's superintendent of schools, revealed this double-edged concern when he polled his fellow educators in 1912 to assess the impact of the movies on the "youth" of the day. His survey covered 64 towns of over 700 inhabitants, each containing at least one movie house. Fulk concluded that, since "free hours determine the morals of the nation," movies "engendered idleness and cultivated careless spending" at the "expense of earnest and persistent work." Whereas this was expected from laborers who "normally spend money for dancing and drinking," the movies mixed all groups together where the sensational and emotional was seen and not read. The power of the medium stirred up "primitive passion" and encouraged "daydreaming." Even more dangerous, "sacred and private" experiences were shown on the screen, fostering "too much familiarity between boys and girls" in unchaperoned theaters. Yet two-thirds of the audience he polled was comprised of adults. Was it possible that Edison's great invention might bring to the good people of Nebraska the atmosphere of urban decadence? If scandals among the rich and immorality among the poor ran rampant in the cities, Fulk feared that the movies might unleash dangerous passions among the entire population. Thus he meant more than "youth" when he wrote:

This constant playing on the emotions of the child and adolescent tends to overexcite and prevent the development of the emotional life, generating an overwhelming drive for something that stirs and thrills. This growing desire is apt to lead children and adolescents especially away from right ideals and morality. Here lies the greater danger of the motion picture drama.[39]

Still, some thought it might be possible to avoid this calamity and salvage the new medium, returning to the original aims of Dickson and Edison. An early advocate of this notion was Hugo Münsterberg, professor of psychology at Harvard and first president of the American Psychological Association. Devoted to behavioral psychology which he learned in his native Germany, Münsterberg argued that the "stimuli that brings sex to the mind and arouses the body" had to be controlled. In one of the earliest full-scale analyses of the film medium, *The Photoplay: A Psychological Study* (1916), Münsterberg perceived that cinema could not be understood in terms of any other art such as literature, theater, painting, or music.[40] Nevertheless, this heir to Western enlightenment idealism felt that film could ultimately realize the aims of traditional art, and further ethics and balance. This was especially crucial in the modern age, which eroded the Puritan past. Münsterberg believed that democratic order rested on removing "forbidden joys" from society; for sexual desire was the "great lure" that brought civilizations "downward." In the twentieth century, with the "influx of sensuous elements and expensive luxuries," the danger was especially acute. Women in particular had "fallen." As he explained,

The sexual elements in this wave of enjoyment become reinforced by the American position of the women outside the family care. Her contact with men has been multiplying, her right to seek enjoyment in every possible way has become the counterpoint of her independence, her position has become more exposed and dangerous.[41]

Although the movie industry contained all the elements Münsterberg feared, it also held the potential for regenerating Victorian values. The key lay in the power of the medium over the unconscious. As heir to the Germanic moral tradition of Kant, he saw the rhythmic force of the film working like a piece of good music that "emotionalized nature." Much as the human mind possessed an "inner freedom" to transcend time and space, movies could release the viewer from the limitations of the material world. A director might show a woman's face, her husband at work, an event from her childhood, and her fears for the future all in rapid succession. Through this visual manipulation of the environment, film could teach powerful moral lessons. As audiences watched vice being mastered, they might learn how to bring "desire to rest."[42]

To serve this end, the "best people" had to control film content. They would keep "unsavory French comedies" off the screen, which "poison the minds of youth." If not prevented, passionate romances and the sight of crime and vice would have disastrous results. "The possibilities of psychical infection cannot be overlooked . . . no psychologist can determine exactly how much the general spirit of righteous honesty, of sexual cleanliness, may be weakened by the unbridled influence of plays which lower moral standards." On the other hand, the photoplay could become an "incomparable power for remolding and upbuilding the national soul."[43] Rather than the fruits of progress eroding civilization, technological innovations like the movies might strengthen its moral core. Yet for Münsterberg's vision of the future to be realized, his concerns would have to penetrate deeper into civic institutions of power and politics.

*Chapter Three*

# RESCUING THE FAMILY:
# URBAN PROGRESSIVISM
# AND MODERN LEISURE

> From children's and divorce courts we hear of people going
> astray due to the movies. Therefore we need a law to step in
> and do for film what it did for meat and drug inspection, or
> the cinematographer will continue to inject into our social
> order an element of degrading principle.
>
> DARREL O. HIBBARD<br>BOYS' WORK DIRECTOR, YMCA<br>1921 [1]

On Christmas Day, 1908, the New York City police moved to
close the 550 movie houses and nickelodeons in the city. Each
officer performing his duty had orders not just from Chief of Police
Bingham but from the mayor, George B. McClellan, Jr. The week
before, McClellan had responded to the call of every Protestant de-
nomination in the city to use his licensing power to close theaters
that violated Sunday closing laws, which could "corrupt the minds
of children," as the Reverend Foster explained. No doubt one
source of righteous indignation was that Biograph had just released
*The Great Thaw Trial*, a film which showed in "graphic detail" the
scandal and famous love triangle of Harry Thaw, Evelyn Nesbit,
and Stanford White. In the wake of this controversy, vice crusaders such as Anthony Comstock and the Reverend Charles Parkhurst, as well as social workers and clergymen, asked for a public
hearing on the movies. The mayor took a walking tour of twenty
theaters and reported to the Bureau of Licenses that many movie
houses exited into saloons. The mayor then advised that all movies
would have to close and reapply for licenses, "in order to avert a
public calamity." [2]

Similar expressions of public anxiety erupted in other cities as
well. In Washington, D.C., a study commissioned by President
Theodore Roosevelt found that the films shown in the nation's capital encouraged "illicit lovemaking and iniquity." *Survey*, the journal of social work, called for regulation of movie houses in the nation's major cities. One of the journal's editors, Jane Addams,
explained that the "Five Cent Theaters" were in "undesirable localities" where men could offer "girls certain indignities." But the reformers did not speak for everyone.[3] As the New York *Tribune* reported, proprietors gathered to protest McClellan's closing of their
theaters. The protestors were "chubby Irishmen as well as Hun-
garians, Italians, Greeks and just a handful of Germans, but the
greater portion of the assembly were Jewish Americans." The controversy smacked of an older cultural war between native Protestants and ethnic Americans. The *Times*, the *World*, and the *Tribune*
all reported that Jacob Weinberg, a Jewish theater owner, had been
arrested for defying the closing order and showing a film that violated the proprieties. The Faust Brothers, a noted vaudeville team,
had also been arrested for making fun of the police in the midst of a
supposedly "educational lecture"—the only form of entertainment
permitted on Sunday. But the fervor of the outrage against the
movies indicates that this was not merely an extension of the Victorian battle against the rowdies. One "mother" applauded the
mayor's actions. In her plea, she disclosed the greatest fear associated with the new amusement:

> Thank God you have at last awakened to the horrors of those cheap
> motion picture dens. Being a cheap place my girls who earn their own
> money can go. Yet my heart has been broken by my own child spend-
> ing Sunday in those dreadful theaters. . . . Through the influence of
> some men she met, she ran away from home with another girl. When
> she came back she came to us ruined, and will never be the same child
> again. In the name of humanity stay firm against those places. Do not
> let it blow over as it usually does for a few dollars breaking our homes
> and hearts. I could give you the names of many more if I dared.[4]

The fervor over the movies was part of a larger movement of
crusading against vice that was stirring up the nation's cities. In the
numerous sex scandals and "white slavery" panics of the era, a
widespread fear surfaced that "good" women coming into the city
for work were being seduced into prostitution. Historians have

seen this as a major thrust of the Progressive reform movement. But they have failed to perceive its connection to new urban amusements. In general this has been seen as an extension of the various strains of Victorian uplift into the twentieth century: campaigns against sexual dissipation, nativist drives against immigrants, or efforts of patricians to reform the poor by expurgating their sports, festivals, and amusements. Some scholars have viewed the movement as another example of the attempt by the middle class to control the masses.[5] Yet we still do not really understand why the crusade against the "social evil" resulted in widespread legislation such as the Mann Act, Prohibition, and raising the age of consent, which were aimed at the entire population. Why was it that "good" men and women now appeared threatened by the immigrants' forms and places of entertainment? And how did the pariah institution of the movies manage to overcome this opposition to become a legitimate form of mass entertainment? To answer these questions, let us first take a look at those groups who never went to the movies but attempted to exert control over making them healthy.[6]

Unlike reformers of the previous era such as feminists or evangelists who were opposed to the ruling order, these modern vice crusaders constituted the leadership of their localities, with the backing and support of much of the citizenry. In Chicago, they were part of a business and professional elite who had come from small towns.[7] In New York, the most powerful vice group, the Committee of Fourteen, also came from among the city's leaders. Men such as Alexander Orr, president of New York Life Insurance; George F. Peabody, John Rhodes, and Edwin Seligman were typical in that they had college educations, held memberships in exclusive men's clubs, and their families were in the social register.[8] These cosmopolitan Republicans were joined by numerous muckraking journalists, voluntary associations, and religious groups with similar backgrounds. From 1905 onwards, they pressured their city governments to investigate not just the age-old vice of prostitution but the fall of "respectable" women whose behavior, dress styles, and participation in popular entertainment activities had previously been the mark of "loose" women. In response, the mayors of both cities set up vice commissions, led by social workers who were deeply involved in the major political issues of the day.[9]

The intertwining of vice control and politics calls attention to one of the least understood aspects of Progressive reform. All these reformers might be termed "high" Progressives, those men and women aligned to rising business, professional, and political groups. Generally, they appear to be primarily interested in public welfare and industrial regulation as a means to order the new corporate system through the creation of a powerful state. Yet their equally strong concern with vice crusading suggests that the crisis of the age was not just a search for order or a question of a decline in status; there was also a great sense of family disruption. When these people saw the mingling of classes in public amusements and the new position of women, they equated this domestic breakdown with the other great danger of the corporate order. Not only did modern industrialism unleash conflict and exploitation, but the breakdown in class divisions within amusements and the great increase in consumption of goods and services that followed seemed to threaten the old democratic culture. In response, Progressives tried to unify all groups around vice and civic reform, in order to restore the good family as the controlling force over society. More than searching for order, these people tried to recreate the sexual order of the past, and make it relevant to the modern era.

Precisely what emotions underlay this outpouring of elite concern can be ascertained by looking at two of the most active progressives. Frederic Howe was a model leader. Like other such crusaders, Howe identified with the New England reform tradition. Like Canby, Howe grew up in a small Northern town where church, family, and society were bound together in ethnic unity. But at The Johns Hopkins University, he learned from his instructors Woodrow Wilson and Richard Ely that this value system was challenged by "economic feudalism." This was manifest in his own life when he became a lawyer for a large firm that thwarted his ambitions for independence. His sense of self was also challenged by the woman he married. He expected his wife to stay in the home and assist him in the climb to success; but she shattered that vision by wanting "economic independence." Howe confessed that even though he spoke for women's rights, he did not like it; for a man who allowed his wife to work was deemed a "failure."

Howe's anxiety over the industrial system and women's status translated into his career. He confessed that as a social worker, mu-

nicipal reformer, and Wilson administrator he and other liberals
were dedicated to imposing Victorian values onto the complexities
of modern life. One of his first jobs as a vice crusader was as inves-
tigator for the Reverend Charles Parkhurst of New York City.
Parkhurst's main targets were the "libidinous harpies" of Tammany
Hall who protected saloons and amusements where respectable
women might lose their chastity. Howe then became assistant to
the reformist mayor of Cleveland, and during the Red Scare of
1919 was head immigration officer at Ellis Island in charge of exporting radical aliens, many of whom were falsely arrested for
prostitution. Howe realized that these foreigners never actually
engaged in the selling of sex. But he nevertheless associated them
with disorder, and considered them politically dangerous.[10] This
same assumption infused his other important role as a reformer:
Howe became president of the first national motion picture censorship board.

The women who mobilized support for this board and staffed its
agencies shared many of Howe's anxieties. Unlike women who
were moving into the work force as well as new realms of style and
leisure, these women justified their public activity in terms of nineteenth-century moral guardianship. Finding their old guardian
roles undercut in the sharply segregated metropolis, they turned
their voluntaristic impulses to an even wider sphere. Their efforts
went in two directions. One was to push for national legislation on
female suffrage and prohibition. Another was to zero in on the
poverty-stricken areas of the cities. The major innovation along
these lines was the settlement house. As one social worker phrased
it, women were "no longer willing to be put in niches and worshipped." In New York, Pittsburgh, and Chicago, settlement
houses drew on the energies of graduates from Eastern women's
colleges who devoted a brief period of time before marriage to the
needs of the poor.[11]

Jane Addams, the founder of Chicago's Hull House, embodied
these drives for an entire generation. In the popular press of the
day, she was hailed as a saint. But her path to glory was strewn
with obstacles. Addams was born in a small Illinois town where
her father was a bank president and noted Republican reformer.
Educated at a missionary school where her father was the primary
trustee, she matured into the affluent, genteel world of the Victo-

rian elite. But after her father's death, she was overcome by a sense
of uselessness. With no poor needing help in her immediate neighborhood, she was "filled with shame" that "with all my leisure I do
nothing at all." So rather than becoming an "invalid once again,"
she called upon women of her generation to extend their domestic
role to the impoverished sections of the industrial cities.[12] Many
criticized her for defying women's proper sphere. Yet throughout
her life she maintained that "Christ's message" could be carried into
the poor areas. Answering her critics, she argued that "domesticity,
like every other element of human life, is susceptible to progress
and from epoch to epoch its tendencies and aspirations are enlarged, though its duties can never be cancelled."[13]

Forging into new areas of endeavor, however, could lead to a
serious loss in status if the women did not maintain the code of purity intact. Such fear made Jane Addams and her fellow social
workers all the more vigilant in upholding the cult of the home.
Hull House embodied thus the best and the worst in Victorian asceticism. Social workers were able to secure the support of liberal
businessmen by arguing that women could represent the benefits of
the small town in the city. Without arousing class antagonisms, settlement work would provide the worthy poor with ethical and
practical skills which would help them overcome a harsh industrial
environment that threatened the good, just community.[14] In this
Americanization process, Addams did not think that immigrants
were racially inferior or incapable of becoming citizens. But she,
like other social workers, felt that their cultural baggage weighed
them down and prevented them from adequately coping with the
industrial system. Over and over the cry arose that the immigrant
family was falling apart. Reformers saw several overlapping sources
at work. Corrupt machine politicians allowed urban neighborhoods
to decline; greedy businessmen exploited foreign labor; and the immigrants' pre-industrial customs inhibited conformity to American
mores. Although some of their perceptions were accurate, recent
historians have shown that the immigrants' family structure remained very much intact. But it was not intact as the social workers wanted it to be. They felt that only a home modeled on Victorian values could reinvigorate the community with spiritual bonds.
Consequently, while Hull House answered welfare needs, it also

offered classes in self-government, "modeled along the lines of a New England town meeting." As Jane Addams recalled,

> We believed that widespread discussion might gradually rid the country of the compulsions, the inhibitions, the traditions and the dogmatisms which the newly arrived suffered. The method was not without success . . . thousands became the typical bourgeois citizen.[15]

It followed that the amusements proliferating in working-class neighborhoods also threatened this effort. Social workers were alarmed at the spread of Raines Hotels, saloons, and dance halls. Yet even more dangerous was that these immigrant entertainments seemed to be moving out of the vice zones and attracting "respectable" women. Jane Addams and her colleague Louise de Koven Bowen echoed other observers when they saw that working women of all classes were drawn to arenas which had previously been the preserve of prostitutes. When coupled with the new freedom in women's dress and the advent of new dances that emphasized sensuality, it seemed that women's morals were degenerating. Addams outlined this uneasiness in two books, *Youth and the City Streets* and *A New Conscience and an Ancient Evil*. As she explained,

> We cannot expect the fathers and mothers who have come to the city from the farms or have immigrated from foreign lands to rectify these dangers, we cannot expect that youth themselves will understand this emotional force which seizes them, and when it does not find the traditional line of domesticity, serves as a cancer in the very tissues of society and as a disrupter of the securest social bonds.[16]

This great fear lay behind the white slavery campaigns from 1905 onwards. Virtually all social welfare progressives were obsessed with this anxiety. Unwilling to recognize that the roles of women had changed, Victorians assumed that "tango pirates," "white slavers," or gigolos engaged women in sexual behavior that they otherwise would not want. These evil men were depicted as Simon Legrees who were usually foreign or Jewish, vain, afraid of work, and lascivious.[17] Yet beneath these stereotypes was the fear that Victorian controls were no longer working for the "respectable" classes. As *Current Opinion* phrased it, "Sex O' Clock" had struck in America. No longer were genteel women able to overcome that "dangerous period of puberty when nature goes through a sex awakening with all its morbid psychology and impulses." If women lost their "hereditary instinct of femininity," they might allow sexuality to invade the home and destroy the will power of men as well. Yet just as often the editors were quick to point out,

> The laxity in sex matters cannot be due to the broadening of women's views. The women who have entered the life of civic and social enlargement are not the parasite women, the indulged women, the women who don't think. I don't believe in the theory that women have the same passions as men. I too have been to Cyprus and the woman of passion is a pretense. The idea that women of any great number would resort to promiscuity is absurd. Not intelligence, but ignorance recruits the ranks of the social evil.[18]

To explain these developments, reformers analyzed the larger historical forces at work in familial terms. This was natural for people like Jane Addams and Frederic Howe, who felt the onslaught of modern life disrupting their early values. In their minds, the industrial order had run wild, taking victims in its path. Prostitutes were no longer seen as inherently depraved, but as victims of an urban life which had destroyed domestic bonds and unleashed chaos, lust, and exploitation. Greedy businessmen took advantage of the factory system to exploit the labor of small-town women and immigrants, who worked long hours for low pay. When they left the job, they encountered the industrial elite who flaunted extravagant consumption before "all eyes" in the city, creating false examples. Unable to afford the luxuries of the rich, they turned to unregulated and degrading amusements. Soon they encountered "white slavers" who took advantage of the fact that the city had removed young people from familial controls.[19] With all the allures of the city, the white slaver could seduce women away from the old code of chastity. In the words of one reformer:

> Girls from good homes all in a mad pursuit of pleasure having their moral sense blunted, reaching headlong into danger, all because the people are willing to let any kind of amusement exist. . . . By their very indifference to the public welfare they are helping along the great crime which is besetting the American people today, the social evil.[20]

Beyond the awareness of an exploitative environment, reformers had a particularly keen insight. Even if the material needs of the population could be satisfied, they realized that the corporation undercut the old work ethic. As John Collier, head of a major settlement house in New York, explained, modern man had lost "all identity with his product." Formerly, a man took pride in craftsmanship and independent production; but he was now thwarted by ✓ large organizations. A Protestant in particular might find that he could no longer model himself on a symbolic father such as a self-made industrial titan. Encountering routine on the job, the modern employee tried to find freedom and independence away from work. One noticeable development was that he now used his increased earning power for urban entertainment. Collier realized that "leisure has come to millions in the past few years. It has come with shorter hours of labor and surplus wealth."[21]

Given that modern industry disrupted the family with the dual forces of exploitation and mass production, the values of the good home had to permeate the entire city. Without rejecting the ethics of business, reformers argued that the citizenry might be inspired to save the one interest that everyone had in common. By creating a state which would serve as a good parent, government would be called in to humanize society. In this way, the crisscrossing threads of Progressivism might be woven into one tapestry. The state would rescue the family through social welfare legislation that regulated unfair business practices. Within the factory, industrial reforms such as minimum wages, shorter hours, and improved working conditions would allow a worker to be a better provider. At the same time, protective legislation for women and children promised to minimize the ill effects of industry upon the home.[22]

Moral crusades complemented these efforts. Corrupt business practices could exploit people off the job as well. Therefore, the state would again serve familial functions. Since "amusements of one's leisure have more to do with character building than any other influence," wrote the Chicago Vice Commission, the soil that nourished the designs of white slavers had to be purified. Part of the rationale for movements such as eugenics, prohibition, and raising the age of consent flowed from this logic. Some of these efforts resulted in laws which gave the police power to rid the cities of prostitutes and saloons. Likewise, compulsory education and child labor laws would help keep youths off the streets, preventing their contamination by vice. One way to further these efforts was to give women the vote, for only they were capable of conveying domestic virtue to public life.[23]

Ironically, however, reformers constantly maintained that they were not being "puritanical." They favored uplifting amusements rather than abolishing them. Realizing the need for healthy forms of recreation to compensate for alienating work, they hoped to bring people together in these arenas of enjoyment without economic barriers or class conflict. In order to reinvigorate the elements of Victorian culture, they called for a "redemption of play." As the head of the Playground Association wrote, "The boys' life we are sacrificing to our industrial civilization is our own. If we could provide a generation of boys who fit into the straight jacket of modern life, we should find that we ourselves, our lives, would be maimed and disappointed in the result." Consequently, reformers looked to the state to create municipally supervised parks and amusements. "This is clean up, not close up," commented the Committee of Fourteen, "hundreds of places formerly notorious for evil have been forced by the Committee to reform on penalty of being closed outright."[24]

The result yielded one of the most important innovations of the era. Long before the twenties, reformers created legitimate institutions where all classes could mix and spend the money and free time that the industrial order produced. Perhaps one of the reasons this development has eluded historians is that it was not done to build a stage for moral experimentation. Rather, urban Progressives were uneasy about affluence, and worker alienation. They hoped to use this reoriented leisure realm as a place to restore American ideals in a pure form. When trying to convince the population of the need for these measures, reformers turned to the movies. In fact, film's very power for evil might be used for good. Because films were mass produced, they ran rampant all over the cities. But for the same reasons, they could cut across the population and serve positive goals, provided they could be centrally regulated, before being sent out to the thousands of theaters around the country. Unlike other urban entertainments, movies could be censored before they were exhibited. Here was the possibility of spreading the ideology of reform and penetrating immigrant life in ways that the settlement house or conventional politics never could. Jane Addams saw that at Chicago's 500 nickelodeons workers identified with screen heroes who showed that "man could be master of his fate." She believed that movies were "making over the minds of our urban population," and hailed the new medium, for "the good in it is too splendid at rock bottom to allow the little evil to control and destroy it." Rightly developed as a municipal institution, it could be a benefit and not a menace.

Furthermore, the power of the movie medium could bring about a secular conversion among the masses. One reformer's report claimed that film was "five times more powerful than any other form of communication." Shown in a darkened room, its screen images penetrated the subconscious with its silent message. In a city population where many people still spoke their native tongues at home, or had trouble with English, it could spread American values through the universal language of pictures. "The popularity of this cheap form of entertainment," wrote a reporter for *Harper's,* "is not to be wondered at . . . the newly arrived immigrant from Transylvania can get as much enjoyment out of them as the native. The imagination is tapped without circumlocution. The child whose intelligence is unformed and the doddering old man seem to be on an equal footing in these stuffy, box-like theaters." Provided film could teach Anglo-Saxon ideals to all peoples, it might draw the masses away from saloons and vice, creating a model citizenry. Then the movies could function, as one reformer phrased it, like a "grand social worker," allowing the viewer to go home and "sleep the sleep of the just."[25]

Paradoxically, the effort to gain support from groups farther down the social scale began when Mayor McClellan closed the movies of New York on Christmas Day, 1908, as part of a large campaign to eradicate the worst features of urban amusements. In the aftermath of this dramatic event, several social forces began to coalesce around the ideal of uplifting the movies. One of the most important thrusts came from the film producers themselves. Put on the defensive by bad publicity and the closing of their films, theater managers gained a court action to open their movies again. The crusade had taught them that the suggestion of immorality was bad for business. But avoiding the stigma turned out to be more difficult. They lobbied forcefully against bills calling for national censorship that had reached Congress. Still they wanted adequate guidelines. As one business paper phrased it in 1908, "Many

Picture Men Are All Out at Sea" on what is an "objectionable
film." To avoid "all the difficulties with the police," the movie industry of New York began to cooperate with reformers. The result
was the first national censorship board for the movies, based on the
voluntaristic tradition, and dedicated to protecting free speech.[26]

The National Board of Review, as this agency became known,
operated in conjunction with one of New York's most famous settlement houses, the People's Institute, located in the Jewish and
Italian sections of lower Manhattan. The Institute's founder,
Charles Sprague Smith, had resigned a Columbia professorship to
work to reestablish a relationship between the elite and the poor
immigrants which had been disrupted by the modern city. Gathering together a number of social workers, he equated his efforts with
America's "divine cosmic mission to avert class conflict and socialism." He called for an "informed public opinion above dogma and
party," appealing to the "patriotic rich" to "help people most effectively by teaching them how to help themselves, not only physically and mentally but morally and emotionally." After the turn of
the century, Smith and the Institute had joined with the Committee of Fourteen in a crusade to reform the Raines Hotels, the low-
priced theaters, and the movies. Since this was "clean up, not close
up," they wanted to establish "high class" cabarets in exclusive hotels, and censor the movies, in order to provide appropriate recreation for both segments of the population.[27]

So in the great campaign against the movies in 1908, Smith
spoke for regulation and gained the support of the producers, who
saw the Institute as an important ally in their effort to weed out
"objectionable" films. Adding legitimacy to the voluntary Board
was the list of local notables on the executive committee. Nearly all
of them were wealthy Protestants, with a few German Jews. Andrew Carnegie, Samuel Gompers, Shailer Mathews, and presidents
of major universities sat on the main board, along with representatives from the Federal Council of Churches, the YMCA, the
New York School Board, the Society for the Prevention of Crime
headed by the most powerful vice crusader in the city, the Reverend Charles Parkhurst, and the moralistic Postal Inspector, Anthony Comstock. While this all-male panel presided, the actual
viewing was done by 113 female volunteers from these agencies. In
accordance with Victorian assumptions, men had the ultimate au-

thority, but women were the moral guardians who enforced the code. The Board's members presumably subsumed their own personal judgments under the mantle of "public opinion." Since they were not acting as agents of the state, they were not infringing on free speech. Yet one observer revealed the power behind this voluntarism: the censors "must be considered as having the social standards in accord with those of the general public, since the membership is representative of the upper and middle stratas of the population."[28] Under this criteria, the Board approved approximately 600 films a month. During October 1914, for example, its members reviewed 571 films, eliminated 75 scenes, 10 reels, and 3 entire movies.[29]

Producers found in the Board a prestigious group to help them define a legitimate film. However, for an audience still largely foreign born, the standards of censorship rested on solid assumptions of Anglo-Saxon America. The democratic family provided the model for community, class, factory, and nation. According to the contemporary social gospel, disruption came not just from class conflict or economic exploitation, but from individual greed, passion, and corruption. The Board condemned "lechery and the decadence of pagan culture" in order to "arouse fear in the mind of the spectator who contemplated sexual misconduct." In typical Progressive fashion, the censors advocated a strong state to expurgate dangerous conduct emanating from above and below.[30] This was the view of the "great civic majority . . . the eight-tenths lying above the depraved and submerged tenth, and beneath the few who belong to the moneyed aristocracy."

Interestingly enough, the Board's standards were not only accepted by the producers, but also by the police and city government. In the past, the immigrant voters had elected local representatives who were highly skilled in ignoring Protestant reforms. One such leader was William Plunkitt, who in 1904 made no bones about his hostility to civic morality. As an Irish ward healer for the Tammany Democrats, Plunkitt's personal inclinations merged with his political self-interest to protect his Catholic and Jewish constituents. In the face of temperance crusades and Sunday closing laws, Plunkitt helped protect the saloons, which served as gathering places for the Democratic political machines and the cultural festivals in his neighborhood. When elected to office, men like

Plunkitt fought the upstate "hayseeds" and made sure that moral legislation would not be enforced. If this meant a little "honest graft" for himself and the police, so much the better. For there was no love lost between the urban machine and the Albany law-makers: "The Republican legislature and the Governor run the whole darn shootin' match. . . . If they don't like taking a glass of beer on Sunday, we must abstain. If they haven't any amusements in their backwoods, we mustn't have any. We've got to regulate our lives to suit them, and pay their taxes to boot."[31]

Yet the world of Plunkitt was shaken when Tammany inadver-tently helped elect a reformist Democratic mayor, William Gaynor. Gaynor was the son of an Irish Catholic father and an En-glish mother. In his early years he had considered joining the priesthood, but instead turned to law and politics. As a Brooklyn judge in 1893, he attacked civic corruption, and like so many Dem-ocrats, resisted Charles Parkhurst's moral crusades, for he felt that saloons and amusements were harmless male diversions. In fact, he became famous for rescinding McClellan's order closing the movies in 1908. Shortly thereafter, he gained the support of Tammany and ran as an independent for mayor. Once in office, Gaynor surprised his machine backers. He tried to reform the police and streetcar monopolists. Worse still, he began to change his attitude toward the new amusements of the city. Perhaps because as a presidential hopeful in 1912 he needed the support of reformers, or perhaps because his two daughters had eloped with men they met at cabarets, Gaynor launched a crusade to control the "lascivious orgies going on in these so-called 'respectable places.' " He now made certain that the police enforced licensing provisions and Sun-day closing laws. He also initiated a series of city ordinances to control amusements. In this way, he forged an alliance between strange bedfellows: a Democratic mayor and the city's re-formers.[32]

One of the most important of Gaynor's laws was the Motion Pic-ture Ordinance of 1912, which created stricter licensing require-ments and gave the police additional manpower to enforce them through periodic inspections. The old licensing fee went up from $25 to $500, in an effort to bring a "better" class of businessmen into the movies. The law also had a broadly defined "safety" provi-sion for theaters. A building could not be made of wood; it needed clearly marked fire exits and adequate ventilation; carpets and floors had to be cleaned daily. While these were indeed important standards, other requirements focused on the "moral tone" of the theater. To lessen the danger of promiscuity in the darkened room, children under sixteen had to be chaperoned, and immoral behavior in the theater or on the screen was illegal. Some managers ran ads telling female viewers to report to the management if any strangers bothered them. All in all, a theater owner had to create an environment which was morally and physically clean—and therefore inhospitable to "white slavers"—or risk having his license ✓ revoked.[33]

When the city government had solidified this pattern of informal controls, it gave the National Board of Review a prestige which made its seal of approval acceptable to most of the nation. All parts of a reformist consensus seemed to be coordinated: citizen complaints about the movies could now be directed to New York's license bureaus or vice squads. Obviously, those most likely to register complaints were members of the National Board of Review or the Committee of Fourteen; and any theater that did not meet their criteria might be closed. "No immoral films are allowed in the city," explained Mayor Gaynor, "for the evil doer would soon find himself in the hands of the police." Because New York was the largest and most important city in the nation, and the Board included some of its most prestigious leaders, a film which passed its stringent review would probably be acceptable in most places. In fact, the executive committee was officially aligned with police and censorship boards across the country. Thus a film which carried the Board's seal of approval prominently displayed on the credits would be passed without another viewing. The Board's president, Frederic Howe, explained why it would be suicidal for a film maker to resist these "voluntary" controls:

> If a producer refused to abide by the action of the Board, pressure is brought to bear on him by the rejection of his output by the local agencies throughout the country, which if continued long enough will destroy his concern, his standing, or seriously cripple his business.[34]

Ultimately, the power of the National Board of Review, aligned with numerous local censors, gained the support of the judicial system. There were recalcitrant film makers who argued that a "single standard" should not apply to all age groups, since in effect it made the same restrictions apply for minors and adults. Those questioning the system could have pointed to other countries. The French had no controls; and the German state used a graded rating system, whereby some films were acceptable for children and adolescents, while others were restricted to adults. Yet ironically in America, where the state avoided formal censorship, the moral standards were much more rigid. In explaining why the courts whole-heartedly backed the Board, Daniel B. Trudge of the Chicago Juvenile Court defended the single standard:

> If it is fair to legislate for the child on the theory that the child is not fully developed mentally, there are many grown people in our community who occupy the same relation in reference to the community. For we are not all of the same intelligence and there is a group of citizens who you might just as well classify with the child and you must legislate for that group of citizens, and at the same time those who are developed beyond that grade mentally would be satisfied to accept that rule, I should say.[35]

Beneath this desire for a single standard at the movies a deeper assumption lay at the heart of Progressive reform. Articulating this philosophy, two noted sociologists, Simon Patten and Edward Ross, wrote extensively about the advent of modern society. Reflecting their small-town Protestant backgrounds, they expressed apprehension over labor-management conflict and over unregulated immigration which allowed foreigners with "lower standards" of family life into the country. These forces were particularly dangerous in the cities, where the internal controls of Protestant Americans met their most severe challenge. The combination of routinized work and affluence that released people from the struggle for survival opened the possibility that the society might be unable to overcome these threats. Yet Patten perceived that mass consumption, especially the movies, could be utilized to regenerate "passionate citizenship," for "amusements and sports might be the only way to elevate men overworked and degenerated by overcrowding." Ross seconded this view. As he explained to a group of film exhibitors,

> Popular art does not precipitate us into the class struggle. The conflict is not so much between the warring classes as it is the two sides of human nature—appetite and will, impulse and reason, inclination and

idea. Here if anywhere is the place for ethical considerations. Leisure is a conscious matter. A youth submits to work, but chooses recreation in freedom. To acquaint young people with the good or ill effects of different varieties of recreation on the higher self is the surest way to wean him from what is frivolous and debasing.[36]

When all of these expectations came to focus on the motion picture industry between 1905 and 1908, they added up to a major transformation. In a city environment where the idyllic vision of family life seemed to be threatened on so many fronts, reformers initially saw the amusements of the "lower orders" as the most visible form of decay. Yet in looking for a tool to restore progress, they looked outside institutions of power toward the potential of leisure. As an amusement which could dramatize the reality of modern life, the movies became a prime conveyor of reformist goals. This centrally controlled medium might arouse the various groups and classes in the city to transcend their selfish interests in favor of a higher moral law. In this, they had set the stage for sanctioning mass consumption and leisure for the middle classes. Rather than condoning new values, movies would serve to counter the forces that were undercutting the Victorian world. Summing up this view was an article in *The Outlook* which claimed that the "very potency of the motion picture for degrading taste and morals is the measure of its power for enlightenment and education."[37]

Ultimately the effort to make mass culture an extension of Victorianism rested on the larger political crusade's success. Urban Progressives hoped that modern amusements would no longer solely tap the desire for a release from work or sexual experimentation. Rather, they hoped that a reoriented, classless realm of freedom might become a modern utopian ideal against which society might be judged. From that the population would spread familial norms into the state, the economy and social order, mastering thereby the forces that threatened to entrap the individual. Movies in particular would dramatize the dangers in powerful, new ways, and show the way to redemption through reform actions. Once self-government and control had been restored to the wider society, then leisure would exist in harmony, instead of disjunction, with the highest values of history. In this unified view of leisure and politics, the first great hurdle would be to convince the film makers and their audiences of 1908 that such a mission was in their interests as well.

# Chapter Four

# APOCALYPTIC CINEMA:
# D. W. GRIFFITH
# AND THE AESTHETICS OF REFORM

> Do you know that we are playing to the world? What we film
> tomorrow will strike the hearts of the world. And they will
> know what we are saying. We've gone beyond Babel, beyond
> words. We've found a universal language—a power that can
> make men brothers and end wars forever. Remember that,
> remember that when you go before the camera.
>
> DAVID WARK GRIFFITH, 1914[1]

Six years after McClellan closed the movies, the film industry
achieved something that would have been impossible earlier: the
approval of the most powerful vice crusader in the city, the Reverend Charles Parkhurst. As the head of the Madison Avenue Pres-
byterian Church, Parkhurst had sermonized against the decline of a
Calvinist tradition. Modern forms of work, he argued, no longer
built character. As a result of routinized labor and increased luxury, the masculine conscience, which should work like a "clock,"
was broken. Even worse, his female peers had become "freaks" by
indulging in urban amusements. Initially, Parkhurst's politics had
been devoted to defeating Tammany Democrats who allowed
unregulated entertainments to exist. In fact, he was McClellan's
right-hand man in closing the nickelodeons on Christmas day,
1908. Yet now he was part of the National Board of Review and
reflected with satisfaction that all his crusading had reaped rewards. Movies offered an audience of respectable people healthy
recreation. More importantly, they served as a guide to solving
contemporary social problems. Turning movie reviewer, the Reverend Charles Parkhurt even began praising the work of David
Wark Griffith, the most popular film maker of the day. Indeed,

Parkhurst saw that "a boy can learn more pure history and get more atmosphere of the period by sitting down three hours before the films which Mr. Griffith has produced with such artistic skill than by weeks and months of study in the classroom."[2]

Praise for David Wark Griffith has not been uncommon, in his day or ours. Generations of film critics have applauded the countless innovations he pioneered between 1908 and 1915. Yet few have realized that his mastery of the new art was only one reason for his enormous success. His aesthetics were used to dramatize the social and cultural tensions of the era, giving them an explicitly Protestant tone. Reporters referred to him as the "messianic savior of the movie art, a prophet who made shadow sermons more powerful than the pulpit." While creating a style that evoked such metaphors, his films dramatized every major concern of the day: labor-management conflict, white slavery, eugenics, prohibition, women's emancipation, and civic corruption. In all his cinematic dramas, he affirmed a cultural tradition that placed familial values at the heart of political life. Griffith's aims were no mystery. As he wrote,

> Are we not making the world safe for democracy, American democracy, through motion pictures? The increase of knowledge, the shattering of old superstitions, the sense of beauty have all gone forward with the progress of the screen. Our heroes are always democratic. The ordinary virtues of American life triumph. No Toryism. No Socialism.[3]

So closely was this philosophy in tune with national issues that he maintained a lively correspondence with Woodrow Wilson, William Jennings Bryan, and Josephus Daniels, all of whom considered themselves his "great admirers." In testimony to his achievements, his films twice received special showings at the White House.

The merging of politics, vice crusading, and films represented in Griffith's career offers a chance to probe one of the great historical dilemmas of the era. Over the last two decades, scholars have described the Progressive movement as so divided that its central purpose appears unclear. Some claim that the reformers came from many of the same groups that dominated the vice crusading efforts and the censorship boards: the businessmen, professionals, and

managers who composed the Republican party and wanted to order
rather than destroy the corporate system. Others point to those
who composed the early motion picture audience and producers:
small propertied men and upwardly mobile workers, usually Democrats, who wanted to resist the new economy in the name of open
opportunity. (See Appendix I.) While historians have correctly observed that the material interests of these two groups were often at
odds, the way in which they interacted in the early motion picture
industry of 1908 to 1914 suggests that they could unite in a common cultural crusade. At a time when the corporate order seemed
to be trapping the individualistic spirit and altering traditional sex
roles, this sense of crisis reached far down the social order, binding
together people of diverse interests. By looking at D. W. Griffith's
work against this backdrop, we might be able to answer a number
of questions: How could this reformist crusade take on aesthetic
dimensions? Could the rescue of Victorianism unite all groups?
Could the quest for moral order take precedence over the need for
economic transformation?

   Griffith's art does suggest that the movies were beginning to portray the concerns of anxious Victorians. Yet this did not occur in a
vacuum. In fact, few would have believed in 1908 that films could
project the ideals of vice crusaders and still remain popular. None
of the early film makers welcomed controls over their creations. Although the major companies were headed by producers who shared
a common American Protestant tradition with the reformers, they
feared that the anti-amusement forces would destroy their businesses. Initially, these film makers were not interested in moral
crusading. They came from careers in optics, iron making, or elec-
tronics, hoping to make money on movies. By making their own
improvements on the camera, they skirted Edison's patent rights.
They then exploited the immigrant markets as a realm of vice—and
were careful to keep their questionable product away from their
own families. This proved to be quite lucrative. One early film
maker acquired a box at the Metropolitan Opera House; another
bought an estate on Long Island next to Theodore Roosevelt's.
When Edison tried to sue these men for violation of his patent,
they militantly resisted, and battled his lawyers from 1900 to 1907.
By this time they were in no mood for elite reformers moving in
and closing down their prosperous establishments.[4] (See Table 1.)

   Yet one side of vice crusading might work in their interests: the effort to utilize film as a positive social force. After gaining judicial support for reopening the theaters McClellan had closed, these early producers joined with Charles Sprague Smith in creating the National Board of Review. Cooperation promised to provide reasonable guidelines that would define an acceptable film. Not only would this serve their business interests, but it would also protect their own wives and daughters who enjoyed the movies as much as anyone else. As film maker George Kline expressed it, films made for "continentals and their colonies" were not suitable for his own Protestant family.[5] Yet now that his daughter went to the movies, he too wanted better films. Furthermore, the early producers saw that censorship might help them monopolize the market. In 1908, they joined with their former foe, Thomas Edison, and formed a patent trust. By consolidating their companies, they hoped to limit the entry of others into the market. Jeremiah Kennedy, head of this trust, noted that with the vice crusades, this "whole mess might turn out working for us." If they could control the censorship board, it would be difficult for competitors to gain the seal of approval which would guarantee a wide distribution. Accordingly, these eight companies paid the entire operating costs of the National Board of Review. At $3.25 a reel, this came to $38,000 a year.[6]

Yet these plans proved naive. Because markets were expanding rapidly, a number of "independents" entered the field with ease. In 1908, the eight patent members were the only ones releasing films; but by 1914 over forty new producers were also making movies. Like the original trust members, they too purchased their cameras from abroad and made their own innovations. In response, the patent trust itself tried to stamp out these new producers through legal action and economic pressure. Yet the "trust" was not an integrated corporation like those emerging in steel, railroads, or retail chains. As producers only, they had virtually no control over supply, for the players could. work for anyone. Most importantly, films were still sold on an open market to thousands of independent theater owners all over the country. Consequently, as corporations spread in other industries, film making remained an economic "frontier." As *Munsey's* magazine noted,

> With the possible exception of the automobile, no other product of human invention has advanced with such amazing swiftness from a

toy to a necessity. . . . It has created a whole new line of millionaires. It has given American enterprise a fresh distinction, and has
added a picturesque array to the ever-fascinating drama of the self-
made.[7]

The independents were also aware of the potential for tapping
markets beyond the immigrant neighborhoods. They saw that censorship would legitimize their product for a national market, bringing the lower and lower-middle classes into the audience. Previously, local censors had banned films, or movies had met
resistance in the cities' better neighborhoods. But with the seal of
approval and licensed theaters, motion pictures became acceptable
to the people who would have shunned them earlier. After 1908,
theaters began to spread into the affluent neighborhoods of Boston,
New York, Chicago, and Philadelphia. This rapid proliferation
was definitely aimed upward, for few new movie houses opened in
the poor sections of these cities.[8]

As movies began to move up the class order, producers had to
create a product acceptable for an "American audience." In helping
to develop appropriate themes, critics in the new trade journals offered abundant advice. They made a direct assault on the importation of hundreds of foreign films that were flooding the market. As
one wrote, "We heartily fear that the increased importation of
foreign films is luring the director away from the path of cinematic
righteousness. . . . Many European features depict sexual problems with a candor and a crudeness intolerable outside a clinic or
psychiatric hospital." They also despised the short films made by
the domestic producers for the immigrant audience. After viewing
forty films released in June 1908, one critic asked, "What is an
American subject?" Of the twenty that were made domestically,
only ten seemed to be acceptable entertainment. The rest "might
have been made in Europe." "After ten years of plugging away, the
American subject does not seem to have secured a predominant
part in the films of the United States." When producers protested
that this was the only way to make money, another critic replied,

The man, whether he be playwright or producer, who says that our
people want to see pictures with vitiating things is ignorant of what is
going on around him. The whole country is aroused on the question
of race betterment. . . . We do not desire to stimulate what is low in

our children, but to train them to exercise self-control, to let their minds dominate their animal natures. We hope to make them better than we are. Moving pictures are now a factor in that evolution.[9]

Ultimately, all the hopes for a higher quality film came to focus on a longer and more elaborate product, the "photoplay." Unlike the earlier one-reel "shorts" which merely titillated the senses, the photoplay carried a moral lesson. In this, critics saw that film might become an adjunct to libraries, schools, and museums. They argued that a wealthier clientele could be attracted, and higher prices charged, provided these feature films told a complete story, with a beginning, middle, and end. All dramas should portray cause and effect, which showed the ethical order lying at the core of the universe. Subject matter should be drawn from "high" art: formal literature and history rather than cheap melodrama or vaudeville. After all, wrote one critic along these lines, the word "*classic* has some meaning because it appeals to the best people in the most enlightened times. The merits of a classic are known to few men. It is the business of the motion picture to make them known to all." Happy endings would show heroes defeating "grafting politicians and other birds of prey," and applaud the "nobility of splendid efforts." Tragic endings were acceptable as long as they portrayed the "disease of bad habits that would befall the dependent and resourceless manhunters of civilized society, the women who rely on sex attraction rather than sex qualification."[10]

As these photoplays began to gain popularity, the industry seemed to be taking on a new face. Foreign films and ribald shorts remained, but the demand for refined entertainment brought more long features into the market. Compared with 1908 when over half the films came from abroad, by 1913 the efforts of the National Board and the American producers brought the percentage of imports down to ten percent.[11] Over the same period of time, features which had not existed in the earlier years came to comprise almost half the films produced, with most being made by the independents.[12] Exemplifying the new trend was Harry Aitken's Triangle Company. Aitken, a Midwestern Protestant, advertised himself as a Jacksonian man who managed his own firm, and was one of the first to secure the financial backing of Wall Street investors.[13] Following his strict Victorian values, one edition of his trade journal in 1915 called the motion pictures the "world's pulpit." A cartoon portrayed Uncle Sam pointing to a movie theater and saying to "Miss Liberty," "Now, there is a safe and sane amusement."

Expansion, moreover, served to validate reformist hopes. More engrossing photoplays, their Americanization, and national censorship combined to create the beginnings of a truly mass amusement. It will be recalled that before 1908 a movie house could not seat more than 300 people and attracted primarily the lower orders. Yet four years after the vice crusades, the Russell Sage Foundation sponsored a study by the People's Institute of New York City's four hundred movie houses, and found that large, sumptuous theaters seating over 1,000 had penetrated the lower-middle-class neighborhoods. Laborers still comprised 70 percent of the 1912 audience; but 20 percent were now clerical workers and 5 percent were respectable bourgeois men and women. Without losing the original audience of immigrants, then, the Protestant film makers and censors of comfortable Republican backgrounds had created a medium that cut across class, sex, and party lines. In evaluating the type of entertainment appearing at the city's burlesque, cheap melodrama, and expensive Broadway plays, the investigators also concluded that the movies were far and away "the most positive form of entertainment in the entire city."[14] (See Table II.)

At the same time, the most innovative film makers made the medium the handmaiden of Progressivism. The career of the era's greatest director, David Wark Griffith, illustrates the triumphs as well as the ultimate limitations of this reform spirit. Griffith had come to the industry at precisely that moment in 1908 when the movies were on the verge of being reformed. Working for Biograph company, he began filming classics such as Browning's *Pippa Passes*. Critics pointed to him as a model in the vanguard of film making, and he sparked the New York *Times* to comment, "Since the public has expressed its will through the People's Institute, the public has received a reformed motion picture play." From this auspicious beginning, Griffith made over 300 films for Biograph. Despite the fact that this company was dedicated to uplifting movies, Griffith soon broke from this trust member to join the independent firm of Harry Aitkin. There Griffith gained control over his product; Aitkin merely handled distribution. Griffith's two masterpieces, *The Birth of a Nation* and *Intolerance*, resulted from this collaboration.

Exploring the film art as it had never been utilized before, and breaking into the widest markets yet, *The Birth of a Nation* (1915) became the most widely acclaimed and financially successful film of the entire silent era. This film alone grossed over $13 million, more than any other film before 1934. At the height of Griffith's career, he inspired one critic to write,

> The motion picture is a tremendous uplifting force whose power is not yet measured. Shall we be challenged when we assert that it is the language of democracy which reaches all strata of the population and welds them together? Can it not be made to bring all degrees of people into a coordinated organism, working in harmony for the greater things of the world?[15]

David Wark Griffith could make such an impact not because he was coldly calculating the viewers' tastes but because he saw himself as "above politics" and portraying feelings "bred in the bone." In that statement lies the marrow, for like millions of Americans drawn into the teaming industrial cities at the turn of the century, his roots were deep in small-town rural life. Born in La Grange, Kentucky, he grew up hearing the tales of his father's Civil War exploits as a Confederate soldier. The elder Griffith was appropriately named after the Biblical Jacob, and had moved west from meager origins in Virginia. Embodying the tradition of the self-made man, Jacob acquired a small slave plantation in La Grange, a racially divided community. Soon he served in the state legislature as a Jacksonian partisan. But when the Civil War came to this border state, he resigned to fight as a cavalry captain for the Confederacy. After the defeat in 1865, he returned to rebuild the plantation which "told the world you meant something," and help his fellow whites restore home rule to Dixie. Returning to the legislature as a Democrat, he spent the rest of his days as a struggling farmer, preaching the values of individualism.[16]

In passing on this code to his sons, Jacob enforced strict self-denial. David remembered that Jacob "fought the Indians and any-one who came around," and left a profound impression as to the uses of aggression. One memory that continually reappears in his memoirs was of his "first friend," a yellow dog who "pursued the ladies." But for that indiscretion the friend died at his father's hands. "I didn't like to see it," he wrote, "but I couldn't get out of

the report of the gun." A similar precept "ingrained on my memory" was when his brother "wanted to look good for the girls of
Louisville" and had an ex-slave cut his hair in the latest style. Jacob
saw the result and quickly strapped on his sword, pulled it from
the scabbard, and chased the "old uncle around the estate," claim-
ing that the Negro had "ruined my boy." While David recalled that
the "nigger liked it," he also learned that the life of a dandy or ladies' man was forbidden. In contrast, his father was a model self-
made man. To the young Griffith, Jacob's sword was the "law,"
for it represented "reason, man's sacrifice for an ideal, for love, a
whole world that enters the chaos, reduces it, organizes it." As testimony to his respect for this unifying yet awesome code, he later
wrote that "the only person I ever really loved was my father."[17]

Evangelical religion, an influence mainly of Griffith's mother,
infused his father's code with significance. In La Grange, all the
Griffiths lie buried at the base of a white Methodist church, Mount
Tabor, where David went to Sunday school, helped support the
minister, and attended with his mother. Mrs. Griffith was the
former Mary Oglesby, daughter of a well-to-do Kentucky farmer,
and in her son's words "very religious." The Methodist sect itself
had been brought to America as part of the great revivals that
spread over the South in the eighteenth and nineteenth centuries.
Inspired by a powerful sermon style, Methodist rhetoric appealed
to all classes, but in particular to the yeomen farmers, artisans, and
small property owners of the rural towns. Never noted for its origi-
nality of thought, or rebellion from authority, the Church emphasized a life of self-denial and sinlessness, which would transform
not only the believer, but the entire world as well. In keeping with
its doctrines, Mrs. Griffith warned against the dangers of drink and
dissipation. After one such exhortation, David went for a walk in
the forest and saw Christ appearing in the trees, repeating his
mother's admonitions.

Above all, this religious spirit came to rest on women and the
family, which represented the highest values of civilization. In the
South after 1850, the need to create harmony among all whites
against invasions from the North and from black rebellion demanded unity around a common symbol. As yeomen farmers, the
Griffiths saw themselves tied to the upper orders through a rever-

ence for pure womanhood. Among the elite, recalled David, "even
a wink or a bashful nod towards a young lady would get one a good
piece of hot lead or a kick in the pants." The young Griffith made
sure his "conscience was on guard." He recalled a spelling bee at
school which he lost to his girlfriend. Looking at her when called
upon to spell the word "desire," he faltered. Another time, he tried
to kiss a young lady, but her father turned a hose on "me, a poor
country jake." In the broader community, this code ensured that
"the line between nice girls and the other kind was drawn as
strictly as possible." Yet the men had passions that needed some
form of outlet. Thus extra- or pre-marital sex was tacitly sanctioned, as long as it was removed from their own women. In river
boats or shanty towns, men could find prostitutes, and thereby
unleash their lusts far from Victorian homes. As Griffith recalled,
"Men were expected to remain true to their wives only after a fashion. They claimed their wives considered it beneath them to be
jealous of that sort of thing. If they had an affair with a woman of
their own class, there was the devil to pay, but the other sort of
thing was just a part of life. I know only what the men claimed,
how the women felt, I am unable to say."[18]

The coordinates of Griffith's culture, however, began to crumble
at the turn of the century. The first visible wave of disruption came
from the economy. When David was still a young man, creditors
confiscated the ancestral estate after his father's death. Moving to
Louisville, Griffith quit school and secured a job as a clerk and factory laborer. By 1896 he was thoroughly bored with this work;
despite his mother's warning he followed the "siren" call and joined
a traveling theatrical company. But in the depression of the 1890s,
when the nation faced agrarian and labor unrest, he found himself
jobless in California, and became a farm laborer for large growers.
Griffith, then, had knocked around in the Jacksonian style; he was
a worker before he was a film maker. Yet these experiences also left
him embittered against the new order. He gloried in a past when
self-sufficiency was the rule. Later he would write against the tyranny of monopolists who bred labor unrest by thwarting mobility.
Things were different in the old days, Griffith argued, when "Bolshevism had small chance of gaining a foothold in America because
the worker knew the rich had begun at the bottom and worked

their way up. He knew that the rich had begun as he had. As long as the Rockefellers, Schwabs, and Vanderbilts had begun at the bottom, the laboring man could believe he had some chance."[19]

The second source of disruption came from changing sexual roles. They, too, originated in the modern economy and threatened the striving will. Griffith felt this acutely in his own life. Leaving California, he went to New York City where women not only worked but exhibited new sexual behavior. Among the rich along Fifth Avenue in particular, "alluring femininity" could be found "swishing up and down the streets in their carefully gotten-up rigs." Even more alarming, decent girls were in the "hot spots," because there were "no respectable clubs or places of that kind where the two sexes can meet." In Kentucky, "women who smoked and drank and went to bars were not nice girls and that's that." But in the fast Northern cities, "new women" might weaken the will of Victorian men. This invasion of sensuality into the urban scene was not lost upon Griffith, who wrote,

> New York never seemed like a melting pot to me, it seemed like a boiling pot . . . the flesh of these women was of every color known. They chanted in many languages after the style of the sirens against which Ulysses tied himself to the mast. That was one man who had the right idea. I regretted that I didn't rope myself in on a few occasions. These women chanted in many accents, but they only sang for money. I learned early in life that for all the scheming, busy humanity, money was the king, the devil king.[20]

When Griffith failed to make it in theater, his downward spiral continued. Out of desperation, he sought an acting job in the still unrespectable movies. When he began directing films, he was so ashamed of his work that he did not put his full name on the screen. He also masked his marriage to a motion picture actress, Linda Arvidson, since his mother would have disapproved. Griffith tried to minimize his shame by hiding the fact that he had a working wife. Not even his crew knew. When he was finally able to redeem his self-respect by supporting his spouse, he asked her to stop "working in the street." But Linda Arvidson sought a career for more than money, and when she refused, they separated. The pair remained legally married for the next twenty years, perhaps because divorce was even more unthinkable.[21]

The vice crusades, however, served to turn Griffith's inner turmoil toward regenerating the values of his youth. "Reform was sweeping the country," he recalled of these years, "newspapers were laying down a barrage against gambling, rum and light ladies, particularly light ladies. There were complaints against everything, so I decided to reform the motion picture industry." Though he exaggerated his own role in history, he did see the reformation of amusements as a means not only for the growth of the film audience but for his own improvement. He now put an American Eagle over every caption, placed his full name on the screen, and grounded his new trade firmly on the foundation of his family tradition. Since the movie industry was a marginal realm of the economy, with no unions, corporations, or limitations on production, Griffith saw it as a place where he could revive the frontier spirit of his father. When in 1913 Biograph would not let him make bigger photoplays, he left the "bosses." As an independent, with "no one interfering with my daily commitments," Griffith regarded himself as a typical American working "incessantly" and having "little time for sex." [22]

Throughout these early years, Griffith saw himself infusing Anglo-Saxon culture with a new passion as well. To accomplish this task, his work operated on two very important levels. First, he filmed within an established tradition of western art. Griffith did not share the concerns of a European or American avant-garde in drama or painting. Rather than rebelling against the values, perceptions, and roles of the bourgeoisie, Griffith saw it as his duty to reinvigorate middle-class mores by spreading the message of high culture to the masses. In order to show how beauty was the handmaiden of truth, he drew themes from the drama and literature of Anglo-Saxon culture, and the formal subject matter of nineteenth-century novels. Each was clearly presented, with balanced composition that would be understandable to all, so that the audience would learn how the world operated. To heighten the realism, Griffith would draw on the research of scholars, archaeologists, and academic painters for precision and accuracy. Behind this democratizing drive was an effort to depict the truth about the world, and the morals that operated within it.

Yet at the same time these forms gained a new dynamism. In fact, it was Griffith's immersion in the practical, empirical side of life that led to his break from formal ways of viewing the world. Previous directors in Europe and the United States had heightened film drama through a variety of means: close-ups, which showed details of the face with a new intimacy; parallel editing, which moved the scene back and forth across time and space at will and broke from stage traditions; artificial lighting and a mobile camera which were used to help dramatize the story. And movie making had taken place in natural surroundings such as city streets, wilderness, and real work places. Griffith developed none of these techniques. Each had been utilized before him. Yet he was the first to bring them together in a consistent approach to film, one that made the action on the screen move in entirely new ways. Fortunately, he articulated his motives behind these forms. Ironically, they flowed not from a vision of the future but from a desire to give emotion to the folk culture of American Victorianism. Film was to be a great revival instrument for a threatened culture, inspiring viewers with a new instinctual strength.

Crucial to this endeavor was the film medium itself. Griffith believed that an image projected on a screen could become a tool for completing the great goal of history: lifting mankind from animality. The camera was a God-given means for communicating. Regardless of language, background, or class, everyone could comprehend the universal language of silent pictures. Film not only transcended ethnic or language divisions, but also was superior to books, paintings, or the stage. A viewer watching a motion picture saw a production that had been perfected, duplicated, and sent out to the country. When the patrons entered a darkened theater, they saw a standardized creation. They did not look at a unique performance, for it had been completed in advance. Nor did the spectator choose what to look at on the screen. That had been decided by the director. Audiences then could relax much of their active rational minds, and let the images penetrate deep into their subconscious. Mesmerized in the darkness and absorbed into the crowd, viewers shed the concerns of social life, and even relinquished their individuality, giving themselves up to the magnified, larger-than-life images that raced across the screen.

At the same time, film transported the viewer to a more spiritual realm of existence, a sphere of the sublime. This was possible, according to Griffith, because the crowd watching a film did not receive its message in traditional ways. Screen images were not transmitted through the ears, like music, or the hands. Instead the medium communicated through the eyes, which he considered non-sensory organs, removed from material reality and closer to the purity of ideas. In other words, the human being was seen as divided into mind and body. Other organs were part of the body, but the eyes were closer to the soul. Silent film worked solely through vision; and like the "hand of God," Griffith saw it lifting people from their "commonplace existence" into a sphere of "poetic simulations." Such a power allowed the director to work like those revivalist preachers he must have heard as a child. Using images of sin and salvation, he might provide an experience that could convert the soul from evil to good. In fact, Griffith saw himself as a secular preacher, spreading the Word far beyond that Methodist church in La Grange. As his favorite actress recalled,

> Griffith told us that we were something new in the world, a great power that had been predicted in the Bible as the universal language. And it was going to end wars and bring about the millennium. Films were going to bring understanding among men—and bring peace to the world. Well those are strong words to teach young people. Therefore we weren't important. It was only the films and sense of family in Mr. Griffith's company.[23]

Idealistic as this vision was, it represented an acute sense of cinematic realism. More than any previous film maker, Griffith used the potential of the camera to photograph real people in real settings, avoiding artificial sets. The camera, he argued, was a "cold blooded, truth telling, grim device that registers every gesture . . . every glimmer of emotion." A director should show ordinary people, so that the spirit would be seen as emanating from the democracy. Griffith never used the camera to alter the clarity, balance, and perspective of the world. But he did use realism in the same way as one of his favorite authors, Charles Dickens, to show the way the world ran and inspire the viewers to change it. Through the action of heroes and heroines, the audience learned to identify with their goodness, and with hope follow their example. Explaining these aspirations, Griffith wrote that the motion picture would "keep boys and girls along the right lines of conduct. No one need fear it will deviate from the Puritan plane."[24]

Above all, the main players represented the true dynamics of history and progress. In a democratic society high ideals were found not only in the realm of nobles or the wealthy, but also in the daily lives of everyone. Griffith learned early that the movement of the camera could heighten this message. For one thing, the director could discard artificial sets and film characters in favor of real surroundings, capturing spontaneity. Without contrived poses and backdrops, film making reflected natural life rather than stilted artificiality. In this way, film exposed the viewer to whole realms of experience outside his day-to-day world. Yet to evoke idealism from this extended reality, the director used his tools to manipulate the medium and show God's will surfacing in the chaos of material life. No doubt one of the most noted ways of illustrating this was through the "iris." It is not known whether or not Griffith invented the technique, but the way he used it was unique. On a darkened screen, a small dot would appear. Slowly it opened and a beam of light revealed the action. As the drama unfolded, it was as if the viewer used a spiritual eye to penetrate the truth of life.

Once the iris opened, special lighting would show a world where the demarcations of good and evil were clear. Often heroes and heroines were bathed in light, while villains appeared dark and sinister in the shadows. The audience would have no doubt as to who was among the elect, and who among the damned. Griffith instructed his central characters that they, in turn, must radiate the "light within that puts the characterization across." This was clearly a Protestant concept of redemption, and Griffith was well aware of it. He saw his leading players projecting a "divine fluid" which had given men such as Napoleon and Washington their power to transform the world. Faith in these "images of pure and simple beauty," explained Griffith, "allowed us to believe it was done by God himself." Because these characters were to represent universal ideals, Griffith did not believe in the star system. In his company, actors and actresses must "subsume their personalities in the larger endeavor, and forego billing on the screen," for only in that way would they radiate the spirit of a higher destiny.[25]

Griffith fused this idealism to youth, and heightened the innocence of his characters. The universal and nameless "boy" and "girl" in his films were incorruptible in the face of economic or political evil. In this he was also in tune with his times. Before the twentieth century, no particular age group was seen as the unique bearer of progress. Youth appealed to the mass audience as an alternative to the "old world," as Griffith phrased it, and also because it was a stage of life that cut across all groups in the society. His stars came "all the way from cooking spaghetti and washing dishes to find themselves famed around the world." Yet most importantly, youth could be seen as a force outside evil at a time when organized work and new morals seemed to question the old striving independence. Adolescence offered a hiatus before the burdens of economic responsibility and sexual maturity. Youthful heroes and heroines might mingle in dance halls or new entertainments; but at the same time they stayed true to the parental tradition. In this way, they might represent the best potential of the modern age. As Griffith explained,

> It was all nonsense about youth going away from the old morals. Never since the beginning of time have there been so many girls and boys who were clean, so young, their minds are beautiful, they are sweet. Why? To win the dearest thing in the world, love from mankind. That is the motive that separates our civilization from dirty savages.[26]

The prime vessels containing this youthful ideal were females. Women were saints on earth, a vision of Eden before the fall. Griffith believed that no film could be a success without that "pleasing presentation for which all men yearn." We are not likely to understand the tremendous artistry Griffith poured into this vision if we forget the sources of Griffith's emotional stance toward women. He idealized his family, especially his mother; and this admiration infused his attitude toward the female characters in his photoplays. Although he never found a woman "to duplicate the memories of perfection we all have within us," there was one woman whom mankind might love without thoughts of sensuality. "We all know that the beauty of our mothers is no myth." In seeking to revive that memory on the screen, heroines were less objects of passion than reminders of all the spiritual values embodied in the family. No wonder the player who portrayed this type in numerous Griffith films, Lillian Gish, confessed that her mentor was an essentially lonely man who loved his screen images but feared real women. Consequently, his female players were not the "buxom, voluptuous form popular with the Oriental mind," but the frail, innocent girl who was the "very essence of virginity."[27]

It was not just Griffith's camera but the entire environment of film making that infused his heroines with the proper purity. He started by making his studio a Victorian home writ large. Running it like a "stern father," he never allowed his players long hours or even the "taint of scandal." He dismissed potential female players who did not look "clean," or those who had blemishes on their faces, since these skin defects indicated jealousy, greed, or sexual vice. Heroines were usually chaperoned on the set, forbidden to have men in their dressing rooms, and prevented from actually kissing during love scenes. When a passionate embrace did appear in a Griffith film, he suggested that a caption explain that the girl's mother was present. His favorite actress, the thin and frail Lillian Gish, was perfectly cast for this female ideal. As a girl in the Midwest, she lived in a convent and hoped to become a nun. When working for Griffith, she and her sister Dorothy remained constantly supervised by their mother. She recalled that her director had a "mania" for cleanliness and a body free of germs, and lectured to his cast that "women aren't meant for promiscuity. If you're going to be promiscuous, you will end up with some disease."[28]

Griffith used film to make his ideal of saintly womanhood come alive. Whatever taints of the earthly that remained after Griffith's vigorous efforts and exhortations had to be eradicated by the camera itself. First came "exercise, cosmetics, self-denial" and the "right kind of thinking." Then women faced screen tests which magnified the actress's face "twenty times" until he found the look of "perfect health." Through a series of cinematic techniques, this heroine finally became a heavenly vision on the screen. One of the most famous Griffith innovations was "hazy photography," caused by a white sheet beneath the player's feet. A powerful bright light from above would illuminate the body. "We must erase imperfections," he recalled, "and it was in doing this that I invented the hazy photography . . . the camera is a great beauty doctor." With all human imperfections removed, Griffith would then film a scene over and over until he achieved just the right effect. The resulting close-up became one of his most famous technical triumphs. Griffith explained that the goal was

a face where the skin radiated a smooth soft outline. So with the eyes.
. . . Every other physical characteristic is of insignificance compared
with the eyes. If they are the window to your soul, your soul must
have a window it could see through. The farther the motion picture
art progresses, the more important does this become.[29]

At the heart of Griffith's drama was the struggle of mankind to
protect this female ideal. He highlighted this tension through a
series of masterful editing techniques. In making over three
hundred films, he learned that the way in which strips of celluloid
were arranged could determine the emotional rhythms of the audience. By alternating between characters lighted "like archangels or
devils," the director would personalize the good and evil at work in
the world. Building his story around these contrasts, he might
arouse the audience to identify with righteousness. Then the director showed the heroine suddenly threatened by men who embodied
greed, lust, or tyranny. The climax of his films was the rescue.
Cutting back and forth from evil pursuer to endangered innocence,
the director built a crescendo of fear and hope as the hero rushes to
save her. In one great finale, virtue and sin would struggle in the
"battle of human ethics common to all consciousness." As the hero
triumphs, the audience sees the "consummation of all romantic and
adventurous dreams." To reach this emotional explosion, Griffith
explained,

the pace must be quickened from beginning to end. That is not however a steady ascent. The action must quicken to a height in a minor
climax which should be faster than the first, and retard again and
build to the third which should be faster than the second, and on to
the final climax where the pace should be the fastest. Through all the
big moments of the story, the pace should build like an excited
pulse.[30]

Ultimately, Griffith saw the struggle between virtue and vice infusing the major political and moral reforms of the day. He did not
see his techniques as serving the designs of a master mover manipulating the minds of the lowly. Rather, he identified deeply with his
audience, believing that in expressing his own feelings, he expressed theirs as well. Unlike the Republican reformers who had
censored the movies, early viewers were workers and small property
owners who generally belonged to the Democratic party so dear to

Griffith. The director, too, was only one step removed from the experiences of his patrons. He had been a former worker, and an independent businessman, sharing with the movie goers a hostility to monopolists who thwarted economic autonomy. Although his films were not explicitly political, they did express a broad cultural outlook which appealed to the "producers" of all classes and backgrounds. As Griffith explained, "No matter how contorted, one way or another, the soul may be, the man is still a man, and with recognizable traits common to all men . . . tramps, artists, iron workers, writers, all of us are alike in our souls." [31]

Transcending any artificial barriers was the ability of all peoples to realize the morals embodied in the Victorian home. Griffith used his aesthetics to carry this faith in his films. They were of two general types: lessons and warnings. Either heroes triumphed, or they were destroyed by their failure to live up to the ideal. A typical warning film was *The Avenging Conscience* (1914). It opens on a father insisting that his son prepare himself for a "great career." Yet the boy likes a girl the father calls "common," and finds himself attracted to the amusements of Italian immigrants, who are portrayed as having less restrained sexual habits. The patriarch forbids such behavior. In his rage, the boy contemplates patricide. Despite an apparition of Christ warning of damnation, the youth kills his father. The act is seen by an Italian who blackmails the boy and turns him over to the police. In prison he goes insane, and his girlfriend commits suicide. Yet the film has a happy ending: it is all only a dream. [32]

Nevertheless, the warning is clear: men cannot deviate from the work ethic, or indulge in what are perceived as immigrant vices, lest they forsake the goals of progress passed on by the fathers. From this parental code came the deeds of his heroes who carried out a specific historical mission—that of the Anglo-Saxon peoples. This was demonstrated in a classic lesson film, *Man's Genesis* (1912). Dramatizing the eternal struggles that face the human being, Griffith took his audience to the beginning of time. Amid a desolate landscape, a caveman, "Weak Hands," loves a pure girl, "Lily White." But their spiritual union is endangered by an older, lusty villain, "Brute Force." In response, the youth invents mankind's first tool, a club, with which he conquers the villain. He then marries his sweetheart, and they create a community grounded in familial harmony. The hero is the leader of a classless tribe where love transcends all selfish interests. But the "producers" must strive continually, for Brute Force returns with a mob armed with stolen clubs. To put down this threat to their women, Weak Hands invents an even better weapon, a bow and arrow. Victory once again restores the peaceful community. In the triumph of reason over animality, success is not achieved for money or pleasure, but to elevate society above lust and tyranny.[33]

Following creation, this battle informed the dynamics of world history as well. In his films of the French and American Revolutions, westward expansion, and Biblical epics, "Brute Force" is incarnated in aristocrats, monopolists, or the unruly mob. The struggle is carried into the present, in films of industrial conflict. *A Corner on Wheat* (1909) shows a grain speculator hoarding wheat to increase the price while workers, farmers, and small shopkeepers starve. *The Song of the Shirt* (1908) shows a poor girl suffering at a sewing machine in a sweatshop, while her boss takes the fruits of her labor to live a decadent life. These films condemned the immoral rich; but others condemned the unruly poor. *The Voice of the Violin* (1909) portrays a rich man forbidding his daughter to marry a poor boy. But when the boy turns to a "revolutionary group imbued with the false principles of Karl Marx, the promoter of the communist principles of socialism which in time and under the control of intemperate minds becomes absolute anarchy," he learns that his comrades want to rape his sweetheart and burn her father's factory. In response, he turns against these evil doers, and for his efforts wins the hand of the girl he loves.[34]

At the same time, the dominant motif for films set in the modern era echoed the beliefs of the vice crusaders: women were in danger and had to be protected. In Griffith's films, heroines moved around the city unchaperoned, working in new tasks as clerks, telephone operators, and laborers. This did not mean they had "fallen." Rather, as heroes guarded them in the public realm, these men were even more inspired to conquer the forces of vice. A film such as *Home Sweet Home* (1914) shows a hero drinking and going to dance halls. When he falls to Hell, his sweetheart becomes an angel with wings and flies into Hades to rescue him, and carries him up to Heaven. On earth, such heroines would not be tempted by saloons, foreigners, or men who offer them empires. Rather than

submit, women are willing to die. In several climactic Griffith scenes, heroes, believing that villains are about to overtake them, hold guns to the heads of their pure women—final efforts to protect them from a fate literally worse than death. Final shots of rescue are filled with religious images, such as Christ hovering above the characters.[35]

By 1913, Griffith's art and popularity signaled that the hopes of reformers were at high tide. Instead of movies and mass culture eroding Victorianism, the most advanced film maker of the day had reoriented the industry toward social reform. His films depicted historical events and current life, exposing viewers to an expanded realm of experience. At the same time, Anglo-Saxon culture was portrayed as eternal truth. With its values spreading to a growing audience, motion pictures could inspire the population to unite in a crusade against evil. Women might occupy new positions outside the home without losing their virtue; challenges of modern life would spur them on to uphold motherhood and virginity, and inspire men to protect women and liberate themselves from lusty monopolists, vice lords, and corrupt politicians. Griffith gave this historical dynamic power and passion through innovative techniques, and made it seem as though all parties and groups could unite to transform modern society, without a great social upheaval. It appeared that reformers of all persuasions could still come together around this battle for a classless and blessed order.

Ironically, the first crack in this consensus came as the result of Griffith's greatest success, the making of his masterpiece and the most popular film of the era, *The Birth of a Nation* (1915). This epic film began when Griffith left Biograph, and Aitken brought him *The Clansman* (1905), a novel which had been made into a hit Broadway play in 1908. The story was written by Thomas Dixon, a former Democratic politician who became a Baptist minister and then quit the clergy for the "wider pulpit" of popular art. *The Clansman*, however, was hardly an original conception. It merely put into story form the Democratic party ideology of the Civil War era. The plot condemns the Radical Republicans who during Reconstruction imposed a corrupt regime on Dixie. Using the freed slaves' voting power, they disenfranchised the white citizens and unleashed a reign of terror.[36] While none of these events actually took place, they did express Southerners' fears of what would hap-

pen when the corrupt industrial North aligned with Southern
blacks.[37] In fact, Griffith's own family included politicians who
believed this and doubtless used the same rhetoric to mobilize the
South against Northern tyranny in the 1870s. As Griffith meticu-
lously recreated the atmosphere of the Civil War years, he wrote,

> Stronger and stronger came to me the traditions I had learned as a
> child, all that my father had told me. That sword I told you about be-
> came a flashing vision. Gradually came back to my memory the
> stories one Thurston Griffith had told me of the Ku Klux Klan and
> the regional impulse that comes to men from the earth where they had
> their beings stirred. It had all the decisive emotionalism of the highest
> patriotic sentiment.[38]

The film began its official run at the Liberty Theater in New
York, and quickly became an enormous financial and critical success. Every crisis of the film revolved around threats to the family.
In the opening scenes, Griffith portrays the ideal domestic life on
the Cameron plantation. Shot in a soft haze, these scenes show a
perfect laissez-faire world. As harmony envelops parents, children,
and slaves, neither the state nor hierarchical religions are needed.
The Civil War comes, disrupting this ordered paradise. During
Reconstruction, a Northern white Radical, Senator Stoneham,
lives with his mulatto mistress, and she spurs him to unleash his
lust for gain on the defeated South. He gives the vote to former
slaves, who use their power against the good white people of the
South. Stripped of their property and political rights, the whites
watch helplessly as rowdy blacks pass intermarriage laws. When
this culminates in the attempted rape of the Cameron women, the
brothers form the Ku Klux Klan, uniting Southerners of all classes.
As they ride to the rescue of their "Aryan birthright," the screen
comes alive with Griffith's perfected editing techniques. After the
climactic battle, the South is liberated. And even the Northerners
recognize the folly of miscegenation. Symbolizing the return to
unity, the Cameron son marries Stoneham's daughter. Now the
familial bonds restore order to the stricken land, and Christ rises in
the sky to announce the beginning of the millennium in America.[39]

*The Birth of a Nation* touched a sensitive political nerve.[40] In its
message, the film called for an alliance of the common folk from the
formerly warring sections to overthrow a tyranny based on North-

ern commercial corruption. This was indeed a relevant theme for the
Democratic constituency in 1914. As the film was made, the first
Southern Democratic president since the Civil War, Woodrow
Wilson, had united the various elements of the party—Northern
workers, Southerners, small farmers, and property owners—into a
crusade for a "New Freedom." These were the same groups that
had mobilized against leaders of Radical Reconstruction in 1876. In
contrast to the defeated ex-president, Theodore Roosevelt, Wilson
promised to break up trusts and restore the open economy.[41] True
to this spirit, Griffith filled the film with quotations from Wilson's
historical writings. No doubt this was done to give credence to the
events on the screen. But it was also done to make history relevant
to the present. Here was shown what would happen to whites who
let monopolists strip them of their property and corrupt the political process. As they fell from grace, they would become vulnerable
to tyranny from above and below.[42] Giving power to this metaphor, Thomas Dixon used his friendship with Woodrow Wilson to
have the film shown at the White House. Whether or not the President approved of the film, there was no question in Dixon's mind
that it would make Northerners "Democrats for life." As Dixon
later recalled,

> I told him I had a great motion picture he should see not merely
> because his classmate had written the story, but because this picture
> made clear for the first time that a universal language had been in-
> vented. That in fact was a process of reasoning which could over-
> whelm the will with conviction.[43]

Not everyone shared this acclaim, however. In fact, the film
generated such a fierce controversy that it practically crippled the
National Board of Review, and shattered the consensus of reformers who had hailed movies as a beneficial medium. Although
people like Jane Addams and Frederic Howe shared Griffith's sentiments about the Victorian home, they could not tolerate his racial
attitudes. Unlike Griffith, most of his critics were heirs to an aboli-
tionist tradition. Mounting a fierce protest, they joined with the
National Association for the Advancement of Colored People and
convinced the National Board of Review to cut key racist sections
of the film. But this did not solve the problem. Frederic Howe was
so disturbed by the movie, even after it was censored, that he

resigned as president of the Board.[44] And Griffith attacked his critics, arguing that he was not a racist, and pointing out that loyal black servants were portrayed heroically whereas others had been corrupted by Northern Radicals. He also correctly pointed out that none of his previous works had been anti-Negro, and that his family had always cared for them as "children." Nevertheless, it was clear that Griffith was heir to the white racist beliefs of the South. Although his black characters did not have a monopoly on evil traits—plenty of whites were lustful as well—Negroes were seen as innately dangerous: in spite of their potential for noble deeds, they could never really be trusted. Griffith thus forbid any "black blood" among the players who might have to touch white actresses. Those actors were always whites in blackface. Likewise, when the NAACP condemned the film, Griffith attacked them in the press as a "pro-intermarriage" group, bent on repealing miscegenation laws.[45]

In Griffith's mind, however, the racial controversy was less important than the economic issue. A common loyalty to domestic values could not overcome this gulf either. The fact that the Board that censored *The Birth of a Nation* included Republican reformers was not lost on Griffith or his audience. Sitting conspicuously in judgment were those very rulers who were often condemned in his films: puritanical paternalists of New England, and industrialists who threatened to make whites into propertyless, dependent men, no better than blacks. Now the evils of Reconstruction had invaded the North, and Griffith saw himself as a chief victim, for the censors were "malignant pygmies" who had grown into "black Calibans" and denied him his rights of free speech and property. Before the people knew it, claimed Griffith, they would lay their hands on "Miss Liberty" and thwart his creativity even further:

> You could not even portray the drama of the days of '49 to '70 in the golden west. If you tell the story of this period, you must show the atrocities committed by the Indians against the whites. Some public-seeking fanatic would protest that it was an injustice to the Indians and might raise feelings against them. . . . These people revel in objections.[46]

In order to defeat these forces, Griffith felt he had to inspire the masses once again. Using his most powerful weapon, film, he now poured all the money he had made on *The Birth of a Nation* into making the most elaborate and expensive film of his career. His extravaganza coincided with the 1916 election, and espoused the ideology that would presumably help Woodrow Wilson and the Democrats defeat the Republicans. *Intolerance* (1916) was a new creation, "from my own head," as the director phrased it. This "sun play of the ages" would carry quotes from Wilson, Emerson, and Mill, relating them to a "universal theme running through the various eras of the race's history . . . events are to flash through the mind seeking to parallel the life of different ages and today. Through all the eras, time brings forth the same passions, the same joys and anxieties."[47] To show this, Griffith alternated three ancient tales which depicted the Medici who ruled sixteenth-century France, the Priests of Baal in Babylon, and the Pharisees of Jerusalem in the time of Christ as greedy men who tyrannized the innocent. In France the Medicis unleashed terror against the Huguenot families, in Jerusalem the Pharisees crucify Christ, in Babylon the priests destroy Balthazar's benevolent state. Griffith does not condemn power *per se*, for Balthazar is shown as a good ruler. He did not inherit his kingdom, nor did he maintain it through privilege. Gaining the loyalty of the people solely through his military prowess, he abolished religious establishments and protected economic independence. Eventually his own spiritual family life radiated through the polity, creating unity. But the priests conspired with a foreign prince and destroyed the kingdom.

Although Griffith believed in progress, the portion of *Intolerance* set in the modern era showed that the sins of the past had been reborn with the "autocratic industrial lords" and their social-worker allies. In scenes designed to duplicate the environs of the New York "Four Hundred," Griffith shows a wealthy manufacturer and his reformer wife policing the innocent amusements of the workers. At the same time, the industrialist cuts wages and uses the proceeds to hold an elaborate "charity ball." In protest, the laborers go out on strike. Now the screen fills with labor management battles modeled on the great strike at Lawrence, Massachusetts. Yet since the rich have the support of the government, they used the national guard to quell the outburst. With the poor impoverished and their families destroyed, the heroic "boy" and "girl," unbeknownst to each other, head for new opportunity in the city. But they find the opposite of their dreams. With few jobs available, the "boy" goes to work in a vice den for a "musketeer of the slums," clearly a machine politician. Although he is attracted to "loose women" and the fast life, redemption comes when he meets the "girl." As they fall in love and marry, the hero quits his old job and begins to "go straight," in the path of upward mobility.

Yet the good home is still not free from evil authorities. His old boss corrupts the judiciary and sends him to jail for a crime he did not commit. As the villain then tries to seduce the hero's wife, social workers attempt to take away her child. Finally the "girl" secures a confession from the real criminal, and the stage is set for Griffith's greatest climactic scene. In accelerating parallel shots, the girl chases after the governor's train with the new evidence. Quickly the director interjects scenes depicting the fall of Babylon, the crucifixion of Christ, and the slaughter of the Huguenots. Over and over again, these patterns force the audience to ask, will innocence be crucified again? Is progress doomed to fail? No, for the girl catches the governor, just as the noose is being put around the boy's head. With the governor's swift pardon, the audience learns that in modern America, law is on the side of the good citizen. The state has proved effective in saving the home. Although the industrial system remains intact, the hero is free to transcend it through individual effort and social mobility. And as he had done in *The Birth of a Nation*, Griffith again hails the millennium with a vision of Christ rising in the sky.[48]

In this elaborate, multi-layered film, we can see the full implications of Griffith's art. The hero and heroine were clearly cast as Irish laborers. Yet their universality was not tied to any class or ethnic group. Never were they connected to the Catholic Church or the pre-industrial culture protected by the urban machine. Nor does Griffith's assault on the industrialists contain a criticism of capitalism. His heroes do not advocate class conflict, unions, or labor parties. Rather, they are in rebellion against selfishness in high places. Presumably, if a self-made man like Balthazar rules, the force of his personality would encourage class harmony and open opportunity. In the modern story, the democratic state serves as this just and benevolent ruler, not by overthrowing the factory owners or "moral paternalists," but by saving the virtuous individual. Free labor was not a myth for Griffith, but a living reality. In his commitment to autonomy, during the making of the film he aligned himself with Los Angeles reformers to ban unions from the studios. Symbolic of his entire outlook, when the actor who had played Christ was arrested and deported for sexual misconduct, Griffith struck his name from the credits of *Intolerance*. [49]

The film's reception was a great disappointment, for it was Griffith's first critical and financial failure. This was in part due to the fact that it was four hours long and contained four different stories all mixed together. As one critic remarked, viewing was a "real task and the person who tries to find meaning must feel something like dramatic indigestion after seeing the picture." [50] But it was more than this. The tremendous success of *The Birth of a Nation* brought movies squarely into the middle-class market. It was crucial to draw this affluent audience to recoup the enormous financial investment Griffith had poured into *Intolerance*. These new viewers may have liked the opulence displayed on the screen, the magnificent sets, and the historical themes, but they were not receptive to the antagonism toward the rich that the film portrayed. They did not want to see that the "poor are oppressed, and forced into an environment which ruins their lives, and this merely for the purpose of producing additional funds for the wealthy, which the latter uses to advertise themselves as reformers of the poor, who in actuality they repress." As this Philadelphia critic concluded, the "interest of the community will be served by our friends staying away from the theaters where *Intolerance* is shown." Ironically, Griffith recalled being labeled a "communist" for making the film. [51]

Obviously, Griffith was no communist. In fact, as Heywood Broun of the *New Republic* correctly observed, the film advocated "laissez faire," the "battle cry of a lost cause." [52] Broun suggested that with the failure of *Intolerance* Griffith's career may have been doomed. While that prediction was premature, the events surrounding the making of the film shattered the reformist unity. Never again would Griffith produce a film that advocated the transformation of the industrial system through a mass movement. Nor would the National Board of Review, composed of his former allies, have the same strength to impose its will on mass culture. Several members had resigned in the wake of censoring *The Birth of a Nation*. Now the remaining prominent members of the Board realized they had lost power; few would agree to serve on its execu-

In this shot from Griffith's *Man's Genesis* (1912), "Weak Hands" protects "Lily White" from "Brute Force," beginning the rule of reason, science, and love over base instinct. (Museum of Modern Art/Film Stills Archive)

In *The Avenging Conscience* (1914), Christ appears and warns the boy against murder and the destruction of Victorian familial authority. (Museum of Modern Art/Film Stills Archive)

Here the Confederate attack on the Yankees in *The Birth of a Nation* (*1915*) is given emotional dynamism by the innovative use of the iris, Griffith's "spiritual eye." (Museum of Modern Art/Film Stills Archive)

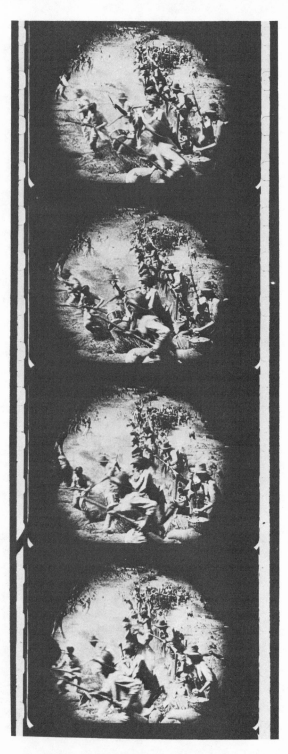

Griffith's masterful editing heightens viewers' emotions in the dramatic climax from *The Birth of a Nation*. Within the iris, the Klan's ride to the rescue appears to lurch off the screen and involve the audience directly. (Museum of Modern Art/Film Stills Archive)

A classic scene of racial violence in *The Birth of a Nation* shows the Klu Klux Klan attacking a black. Such episodes aroused the anger of reformers and critics. (Museum of Modern Art/Film Stills Archive)

Griffith's favorite actress, Lillian Gish, in close-up with a heavenly glow, embodies all the saintly attributes of purity and motherhood, binding together the eras of *Intolerance* (1916). (Museum of Modern Art/Film Stills Archive)

In the modern segment of *Intolerance*, the director scorns the lavish parties given by the rich, who exploit their workers. He modeled this scene on contemporary society balls of New York's Four Hundred. (Museum of Modern Art/Film Stills Archive)

One of the most powerful scenes of labor unrest ever filmed portrays the workers' battle against *Intolerance*. Pinkertons and state militia aligned with capitalist exploiters. (Museum of Modern Art/Film Stills Archive)

The heart of Griffith's inspiration: the Christian Cross rising over the battlefield in this final sequence from *Intolerance* signals the coming of the Millennium and an end to war, prisons, and economic oppression. (Museum of Modern Art/Film Stills Archive)

tive committee. Soon other motion picture producers would find it unnecessary to have films sent to the Board for its seal, for now that the movies had been legitimized, that seal was no longer needed. As the weakening of the Board was reported in the press, the consensus that had existed in the industry prior to 1914 lay in ruins.

Yet the coming of World War I gave rise to a temporary revival. Under the threat of outside attack, reformers called the nation to unite in a crusade which was seen as the peak rather than the end, of Progressivism. The state drafted the movies into the war effort, making the industry at last a full-fledged partner in patriotism. This allowed Griffith to make a flurry of patriotic films that kept him in the limelight for a few more years. *Hearts of the World* (1918), for example, was a successful propaganda film for the Allies, which he personally dedicated to Woodrow Wilson. This film earned him an invitation to London's 10 Downing Street to meet Prime Minister Lloyd George. Later, when Russia was in Communist hands and strikes erupted all over America, Griffith made *Orphans of the Storm* (1921). Using the French Revolution as a metaphor for the modern danger of Bolshevism, this film portrays Reds as lustful and violent, similar to the Huns and blacks of earlier films. This highly political film was shown at Harding's White House. As Griffith said of its message,

> A similar condition exists in Russia today. It is also a great lesson for our own government. Recently here in the United States we find that a small but aggressive minority seems to be able to get almost any kind of laws passed they desire. It is well for us to keep our eyes open, as it is not impossible that we may lose our democratic form of government, just as the people in France did at the time, and come under the tyranny of small but aggressive parties that could hold all government and run things for themselves, while the rest of the people are asleep.[53]

Afterwards, Griffith's worst fears materialized in his own life. But the threat did not come from the political world. Industrialists in the post-War period associated Reds with the labor strikes spreading over the country. As the Wilson administration deported radicals and suppressed labor unrest, motion picture producers broke strikes in their own companies. Griffith supported these measures, but this boost to business expansion also paved the way for consolidation. Gradually, eight large firms began to absorb the smaller companies.⁵⁴ Griffith tried to resist by establishing his own studio in Long Island, and financing his own films. But by the mid-twenties, he too was forced to sell out and come to Los Angeles, a city he hated for its "dissipating" atmosphere. Part of that dislike was due to the fact that Griffith had finally joined what he always fought against, a large firm where access to the top was closed and employees had to punch a time clock. No longer was the great director autonomous, an artist who supervised his labor force, hired and fired players, and wrote many of his own films. His loyal cameraman Billy Bitzer echoing Griffith's sentiments, explained what it was like:

> Neither Griffith nor I could be his own man. Everything was taken over by efficiency. We belonged to the corporation, the very thing we had fought at Biograph, and the reason we had left there. The business office was on top again.⁵⁵

Not too surprisingly, the master's later films reveal a deepening pessimism. Starting with *True Heart Susie* (1919) and *Broken Blossoms* (1919), the "boy" and "girl" become defenseless against brutal men and women, or they succumb to the temptations of urban nightclubs and sexual allure. In *Dream Street* (1921), a seductive jazz musician rips off his mask to reveal himself as the Devil Lucifer. Now that the spirit of reform had waned, Griffith no longer maintained faith that the evil forces could be conquered. Heroes and heroines in these films had to retreat to small town life for salvation. His last film reveals the source of the problem. *The Struggle* (1931) portrays a man trapped on an automobile assembly line, often out of work and destroying himself and his family by drink and decadence. These themes were not popular in the 1920s; and Griffith had lost his talent for making successful films. This was not so much the result of declining abilities as the fact that he had outlived his era. Explaining why studios no longer hired the great director, one critic noted:

> Mr. Griffith you have reached the point where your abilities are at a standstill. . . . You cannot be the evangelist of the screen. You refuse to face the world as it is. . . . I'm not recommending that you acquire a set of puttees or a squad of Jap valets. Yet if I had my own way, I

would imprison you with Cecil B. DeMille and loan you all of his
Hollywood trappings, each and every one of them. Let someone else
take charge of your soul for a while.[56]

Needless to say, Griffith never did. The man who dressed like a
plain businessman and continually poured profits back into his own
works was alienated from the "mad influx of post-War foreign influences." Equally hostile to the political world, he wrote letters to
newspapers and politicians arguing that mobility was thwarted by
the income tax which confiscated the earnings of the "producing
classes," while the rich remained untouched.[57] By the thirties and
forties, he appeared as a lonely wanderer often seen inebriated in
the bars of Hollywood, presenting roses to female acquaintances.[58]
Occasionally, he revived the old spirit. During the thirties, he finally divorced and then married a young Kentucky woman in the
old Mount Tabor Church. He tried his hand at land speculation in
Los Angeles. Then in 1934 he built a large marble monument over
his parents' graves. On the enormous marker, he inscribed a me-
morial to his father's Civil War heroism and his mother's service
while her husband was in battle. In a remarkable statement, the
great director wrote, "I take more pride in this than in anything I
have done or as far as I am concerned, anything anyone else has
done." In essence, Griffith remained loyal to the past. That familial
loyalty generated his earlier creativity; but it ultimately proved to
be his cage. When he, too, was buried in that same Methodist
cemetery, an old colleague remarked,

> You could tell Mr. Griffith by his conversation. Everything he lived
> and breathed was his pictures. He was in touch with his times . . .
> but the box office receipts were indicative of the popularity of his
> films. They were the things people wanted to see at that particular
> time. He realized that, and by the same token that may have been his
> downfall. . . . He pursued that course to where it was no longer pop-
> ular. At that time he was perhaps outmoded.[59]

Griffith, however, was not the only one who was outmoded. By
the 1920s, almost all the early independents and their cinematic
themes had disappeared. Yet from 1908 to 1914, Griffith's artistry
had expressed the aesthetics and social goals of a great movement,
hoping to include elite reformers, an expanding urban audience,
and independent Protestant film makers. Holding these strange

bedfellows together and sparking Griffith's great creativity was a commitment to saving Victorianism in the face of major external threats. In Griffith's hands, this common belief in individualism and family harmony fit his commitment to Wilsonian Progressivism. At the same time, it also legitimized movies, bringing the former pariah institution into the American mainstream. However, because the defense of the old culture, particularly sexual ethics, was so strong, it precluded any questioning of nineteenth-century values. What entrepreneurs like Griffith needed was an alliance with other groups who shared their hostility to big business. But Griffith's art suggests that their antagonism to workers, blacks, or foreigners, who represented group power and sexual chaos, prevented this coalition. Thus Griffith and others who were committed to ascetic individualism watched helplessly as the corporate order emerged in the nation as well as in the motion picture industry. Such was the real tragedy of D. W. Griffith's life. As the world view of the early film makers collapsed, something new was already emerging to take its place.

# Chapter Five

# REVITALIZATION:
# DOUGLAS FAIRBANKS, MARY PICKFORD,
# AND THE NEW PERSONALITY, 1914–1918

> One should always go forward. . . . It isn't good to go back
> to anything, not even to the old home farm, or one's old loves
>                                    MARY PICKFORD, 1928

> Fairbanks stimulates us to fight for our ideals and revive them
> if they are dying.                      GEORGE CREEL, 1914[1]

At the point when Griffith's masterpieces infused Victorianism
with moral passion, there arose from the ranks of his company two
offspring who began to match the promise of the media to something dramatically new: a cultural reorientation. These disciples
went far beyond their master in creating images for the modern
era. Douglas Fairbanks and Mary Pickford became so popular that
from 1914 until America's entry into World War I, they may have
been more widely admired than their political counterparts,
Woodrow Wilson and Theodore Roosevelt. "Doug" and "Mary" had
risen to fame by becoming something truly new: movie stars. Pickford's films gained such acclaim that magazines voted her the "most
popular girl in the world" and "America's Sweetheart." Yet the
"Queen of Our People," as the *New Republic* called her, gained that
love not by radiating pure womanhood, but by doing what seemed
impossible, merging the virgin to the harlot, and moving beyond
the spheres which had divided the sexes in the nineteenth century.
At the same time, her weekly columns in the press and her screen
roles depicted her as the modern working woman who supported
suffrage and was emancipated morally as well. As the perfect parallel male, Fairbanks merged the cowboy to the athletic urbanite at a

time when it appeared that the frontier might be gone. When they married in 1920, the circled closed. On the screen as in reality, their celebrity showed that leisure was not an extension of the past, but something dramatically different.

Where did this come from? What did it mean for the modern urbanite? In the beginning of Pickford's and Fairbanks's careers in 1914, it was by no means obvious that such a reorientation was possible. D. W. Griffith's great film, *The Birth of a Nation*, had not only given the art a tremendous dynamism, but it infused moviegoing with a sense of energy it would never lose. Nevertheless, Griffith's forward-looking techniques were fused to a backward-looking ideal. The great director's work would continue to be popular until the twenties; but in 1914 new producers arose who realized that resistence to the modern age in the name of Victorianism was no longer viable. These film makers had to appeal to the special needs of an audience gathered after 1914. The "new" middle classes had now joined workers and small property owners, and together they confronted large organizations as a fact of life. Neither these viewers nor the film makers could return to the old ways. Still, as people who had inherited the Anglo-Saxon tradition of ascetic individualism, they were sensitive to the reformers' critique of modern life. The central question in their lives was how to find a morality appropriate to the corporate order, one that solved the difficult issues of work, family, and class status that had infused the politics of the era.[2]

Generally we are accustomed to thinking that the vast cultural and economic changes of the era occurred separately, rather than in some dynamic relation. Yet for the movie audience created after 1914, these forces were vitally connected. Clues to this symbiosis can be gleaned from recent studies which show that the "new middle classes" were undergoing a major political reorientation. In contrast to the pre-1914 audience of workers and small property owners, these groups were not concerned with rolling back the clock to an entrepreneurial world. Rather, as employees and managers of large organizations, they followed the new nationalism of Theodore Roosevelt, believing that well-run corporations and professional organizations might serve the public interest.[3] In this, the code of expertise and efficiency superseded earlier values of local control and individualism. Thus they were not so concerned with moral crusading or attacking large business concerns. In fact, although these people were heir to an Anglo-Saxon tradition, they were shedding the asceticism that demanded control over property, production, and oneself. Describing this change, one participant recalled,

> Our fathers' businesses were run by other men, brought from elsewhere. Our first families became absentee landlords of distant corporations rather than magnates of industry whose gates gaped for us, and if this brought economic evils with it, it at least ended the tyranny of business over the mind of youth.[4]

The result brought a transformation in personal and social behavior. Vice crusaders' worries were not totally unfounded. Recent social historians have documented a measurable change, particularly among the urban middle classes. There was not just a shedding of Victorian norms, but an increase in the pursuit of pleasure. Dress reform, "exotic" dances, and the advent of sports were visible to observers; but there is also hard evidence to show a rise of consumer spending and sexual experimentation during the first two decades of the twentieth century.[5] Contemporaries saw this shift manifested most dramatically in the home. The family seemed less concerned with self-denial and more geared toward self-indulgence. In the Victorian era, youth was something to master and shed, along with play, upon reaching maturity. But now adults seemed eager to bring these elements into their lives as well. As Henry Seidel Canby recalled, "Self expression for youth is supposed to have brought about the change in family life that came with the new generation. It was a cause, but an equally powerful one was self-expression for parents who wanted to stay young and live their own lives, while the boys and girls were sent off to camps and schools. Fathers and mothers in the earlier time put fatherhood and motherhood first."[6]

The fact that the economic and cultural changes occurred simultaneously opens the possibility that the moral revolution was helping to ease some of the fears people had about the rise of big business. A previous generation of reformers had tried to master the new economy with the values of Victorians and small entrepreneurs. They saw that an organized work world thwarted the sense of freedom and autonomy found in the open market place; and the hierarchical order also disrupted the sexual and family roles of the past. People then used affluence to enjoy urban amusements formerly considered degraded. Yet to unleash consumption seemed to threaten the code of asceticism needed for success. Abundance might erode the work ethic which rested on incentive. With so much at stake, how was this task with its dangers of class and sexual chaos accomplished? How could a new urban middle-class ideal be attained, one that might solve the problems of alienating work and social conflict? While few businessmen had solutions to these problems, and reformers tried to master them through state action and Victorian policing, those who had inherited the new order were pioneering new realms of democratic freedom in arenas outside conventional life.

Nowhere was this quest more evident than in the motion picture industry. Before 1908, vice crusaders had seen the movies as a dangerous example of mass culture. The movie theater was a place where people broke from the formalities of work and socializing institutions. In reforming amusements from 1908 to 1914, crusaders hoped that movies could help resist the ill effects of modern life. Paradoxically, *The Birth of a Nation* was both the culmination and collapse of this thrust. It clearly identified motion pictures and mass culture with a reinvigorated sense of individualism against the corrupt powers of the day. It also brought more affluent audiences into the movies. Yet the controversy surrounding the film cracked the consensus of film makers and the censorship board.[7] Then, the expensive failure of Griffith's *Intolerance* signalled that the audiences he helped to generate were not drawn to the themes he cherished: attacking big business and restoring the entrepreneurial economy. Other producers now realized that with the Board in disarray and corporations here to stay, it was time to break away from the old Victorian patterns. In that quest, they would use the liberating aesthetics pioneered by the master, but merge them to new social themes.

One clear indicator of that change was the rise of the movie stars. The use of a featured player to attract audiences had been the custom on the Broadway stage, the nineteenth-century touring companies, vaudeville, melodrama and ethnic theaters catering to the workers. Such players radiated a sense of power and personal magnetism that towered over the story. Yet film makers in the period after reform rarely gave players featured billing. This was partially due to their efforts to cut costs; they did not want to spend money on a "name." More importantly, directors like Griffith saw their art as separate from the entertainment popular with the rich and the immigrants. As agents of a higher destiny, his characters subordinated themselves to the larger message of the plot. Consequently, when movie producers after 1914 began to draw featured players from Broadway, vaudeville, and ethnic theaters, it signaled a crack in a long-standing tradition. Audiences might see characters who did not just serve a higher ideal, but were unique and dynamic personalities. As they came into the movies, they carried with them the aura of upper and lower class styles that the bourgeois had previously avoided. Now marquee favorites might offer models for dealing with the questions of cultural mixing and sexual experimentation.[8]

Running parallel to the rise of the star system was an alteration in the themes of film stories. An examination of the plots listed in the major trade journals from 1907 to 1919 reveals a subtle shift. In the period from 1908 to 1912, the newer photoplays made by the independents had Victorian themes made so popular by Griffith. Shortly thereafter, the Anglo-Saxon tradition began to be questioned. More plots revolved around characters who succumbed to sins that previously had been attributed to foreigners, villains, and aristocrats. Usually the hero or heroine overcame dangers such as drink, overspending, and sexual women, suggesting that the conscience of the old culture still prevailed. Starting around 1913, this began to change, first with the comedy genre. Formerly, the viewers had laughed when characters failed to meet Victorian standards; now they laughed at the Victorian standards themselves. Still none of these films mocking formal roles offered a viable alternative. Eventually, around 1914, the full implications of this questioning yielded a completely modern approach to family life, as well as a reformist style different from Victorians or Progressives of Griffith's ilk.[9] (See Table II.)

The coinciding of the star system with the unfolding of new film plots reveals how these changes came about. One important genre that made the star a figure who dealt with the disintegration of Victorianism was that of the cowboy, who since the nineteenth century had embodied the ideal of Protestant manhood. It was only natural that in a period when politicians such as Theodore Roosevelt capitalized on the cowboy imagery, or when writers like Owen Wister revived the Western motif, the movies would turn to the classic formula as well. After the vice crusades, film makers began to make a number of shorts where the ideals of America came alive in the western. During the next five years, the main cowboy figure to gain popularity was Gilbert Anderson, known at the time as "Broncho Billy." Born in Little Rock, Arkansas, around 1880, the son of a small-time clothing merchant, Anderson moved to Chicago in 1900 and began Essanay with William Selig. Like many early film makers, he owned his own company and controlled his own productions. In his more than two hundred short films, he played, wrote, and directed the character of Broncho Billy. As Anderson "pumped them out like popcorn," he lived a highly spartan life, working long hours in his northern California studio. In appropriately titled films such as *Broncho Billy's Bible* (1912), the individualistic hero saved the Anglo-Saxon community and women from the danger of lusty saloon keepers, monopolists, and outlaws. He never succumbed to temptation, nor did his sweethearts deviate from the straight. and narrow. In these stories, Anderson taught young immigrants in his audience "their first values of American manhood . . . shoot straight and build railroads."[10]

Broncho Billy's popularity waned after 1913, perhaps because his films did not reflect the new cultural attitudes. But a fresh cowboy star did. William S. Hart had come into the movies in 1914 from Broadway where he had been a Shakespearean actor. But he found that life among the rich and the city atmosphere were "dragging" him away from the morals he had learned as a youth. Hart was the son of a small propertied entrepreneur who had roamed the West in the late nineteenth century setting up flour mills and looking for economic opportunity. William had seen his father practice a strong work ethic, and challenge with his fists men who flirted with his daughters. When Hart entered the movies, he identified with the ideals of his "brother cowboy," the revivalist Billy Sunday. Writing and directing his products, he carried this Protestant work ethic into films like *The Patriot* (1916), *Hell's Hinges* (1915), *The Disciple* (1915), *The Toll Gate* (1919), or *The Aryan* (1916). In these productions, Hart embodied the "spirit of the men who built the thirteen colonies." Yet his expressive and tormented face became famous for personifying the sense of crisis facing the audience.

Drawing on Griffith's powerful techniques, Hart developed a unique style of his own which fused his camera work to his themes. Wherever his character was found on the frontier, the environment was shown in all its stark reality, a physical presence which almost overwhelmed man. Horizon lines were shot low so that it appeared that the land, the dirt, and the elements threatened the hero. In the midst of this natural world, Hart's characters were portrayed as emissaries of Christ on earth, dramatized by the Lord appearing over his head and titles quoting the Scriptures. At the same time, he finds that as a farmer, minister, or even outlaw, his independence from evil authority is threatened by powerful men who have corrupted the government and the old frontier economy. Hart's plots infuse the old literary western saga with this modern political message. In an even more dramatic break from the past, the hero often falls before the temptations of drink or sensual women, or pure females yield to the lure of foreign sexuality and good times. A classic example is *The Disciple* (1915), where the hero is a Protestant minister, "Shootin' Iron Houston," who uses his guns to tame a lawless frontier and close a local saloon. Yet his wife becomes attracted to the bar keeper, an "oily Mexican" who promises to take her to "places where people know how to live." So she deserts the home, and the minister forsakes his "battle for the Lord," becoming a drunkard. Only when their child becomes sick does the repentant wife return. Now that the hero is redeemed, he musters up his struggling will and continues his work of cleaning up the West.[11]

Hart's films rarely if ever pointed to the social basis of the weakened masculine will, other than to suggest that the old independence was endangered by traditional villains. But increasingly, film makers began to focus upon the forces of modern life that were making men and women restless. Over and over again the underside of progress appears as young men find themselves trapped in modern bureaucracies created by their parents. Sometimes heroes sought liberation by going west, or looked to the city for new opportunities. Other times they violently turned on their oppressors. *The Clerk* (1914), for example, concerns a "problem of our social life, the slave of the office who has no labor union to champion his

cause and faces a lifetime of drudgery." The film opens on a young
man constrained by a drab office, a time clock, and a boring job.
Seeking relief, he turns to romance with a young secretary in the
office. Though they fall in love, the hero eventually loses her to his
boss. In despair he kills his employer and goes to jail.[12]

Pessimism of this sort was rare. A much more common response
to the new order was to show alternatives, particularly freedom
found elsewhere. Initially, this took the form of comedy, which attacked the older approach to work and family life. It is significant
that these subversive ideals first came into view not through serious
drama, for that would have been too frightening, but in comedies.
The first popular figure to reflect this approach was Michael Sin-
nott, later known as Mack Sennett, a former assistant to D. W.
Griffith. Like so many innovators after 1914, he learned his trade
from the father of the movies, but then went on into his own creativity. Sennett began to make a series of extremely successful films
after 1913. On the surface, these were merely slapstick comedies
satirizing human foibles. But at the same time, the attack drew on
immigrant humor, from Sennett's own Irish Catholic background.
Unlike earlier film makers, Sennett came to the movies from an
ethnic, working-class past. After his family had fled the famine in
Ireland and migrated to Canada, he moved to Connecticut at the
turn of the century with his father. There he worked as a factory
laborer and discovered his entertainment talent performing at Irish
wakes. Soon he was on the vaudeville circuit, satirizing the native
bourgeois to the delight of his working-class audience. After mod-
erate success on the stage, he joined Biograph and became an assistant to D. W. Griffith. After learning the directorial trade, "my
natural instinct," he recalled, "to satirize everything Griffith took
seriously became the turning point in my career."[13]

That turning point led to Sennett's own independent firm, Keystone, aligned to Triangle. He brought into Keystone actors and
writers drawn from circuses, prize fights, and vaudeville. Sennett
utilized Griffith's techniques in ways the master abhorred, taking
glee in chaos and tromping on social proprieties. On top of mocking some of the most treasured values of the bourgeois,[14] he was
one of the first to focus on women as having positive, strong sexual
traits. Recalling the police raids on vaudeville and burlesque shows
of his early career, which hit the headlines and sold newspapers

"like hot cakes," he determined to capitalize on that naughtiness. Starting around 1914, beautiful young girls dressed in scanty clothes began to appear in Sennett's films. Soon they became famous as the Sennett Bathing Beauties, who wore swim suits that were shocking at the time. Although he insisted that the girls hide their curvacious busts and hips, and had his own mother chaperone them on the set, his heroes were definitely attracted to their coy sexuality. When censors and police tried to cut his films, Sennett discovered that the ensuing publicity only served to make his light-hearted approach to sex more popular: "The sight of the most cur-vaceous girls I could get caused a riot," he recalled, "women's clubs, reformers, preachers and the police gave us a million bucks worth of publicity. In any other medium but comedy it would have been stopped. But the comedies weren't amorous or sexy. They were just plain slapstick and humor."[15]

Sennett added to this titillation by satirizing the police, not as protectors of property or life, but as enforcers of obsolete Victorian blue laws. His players heightened this farce, for they all looked ri-diculous. Heavenly glows never adorned the visages of Fatty Ar-buckle, Ford Sterling, Charles Chaplin, or Mabel Normand. Nor did suggestive titles like *The Village Scandal* (1916), *He Did and He Didn't* (1916), *Wife and Auto Trouble* (1915), *The Bright Lights* (1916), *Temptation* (1916), or *Fatty and the Broadway Stars* (1916) evoke vi-sions of spirituality. One typical film, in fact, suggests just the op-posite. *A Bedroom Blunder* (1916) opens on a young clerk, Mr. Mur-phy, who slaves at his office, rarely finding any excitement in life. Finally he takes his staid wife to Atlantic City, one of the new amusement beaches. But when she "was careless enough to let him sit by the window," the sorry hero looks out to the strand where beautiful women sunbathe. Among the Sennett Bathing Beauties is Mary, whose flouncy stride makes her "the chief wigglette of Wigglesville." To make matters worse, during the dinner hour when Mrs. Murphy is out, the hotel clerk accidentally puts Mary in Mr. Murphy's room. Soon the police are called in, along with the house detective, to put a stop to what seems to be a bedroom affair. Chaos descends and a chase follows wherein the police, the hapless couple, and Mary are all made to look ludicrous. Finally, after a "frenzy of doubt and disaster," the Murphys are reunited.[16]

In the next few years, a Sennett protégé, Charles Chaplin,

turned this satire into a fine art. His most famous creation, the
little tramp who was down on his luck but ever valiant, became
an astonishing success. Like Sennett, Chaplin's creativity drew
on his background. He grew up in the slums of London, England, in a fatherless home. His mother had been an aspiring
actress who failed. Several of her friends had married aristocrats, and she too tried desperately to maintain an aura of gentility, despite her poverty. She read her children the Bible, and
often visited the luxurious mansions of her friends. As Chaplin
matured in this atmosphere and then went on to the vaudeville
stage, he merged this dual tradition of poverty and artistic
grace in his art. When his company toured the United States,
Mack Sennett discovered him and brought him into the movies.
During the next few years, his tramp character became known
throughout the country.

That character, as Chaplin described him, was "a series of
contradictions." Initially, he embodied the resentments of the
lower orders against the upper classes. This was very popular
among the early film viewers. But the tramp was also a "gentleman," with an aristocratic grace of his own. With this double-
edged sword he thrust at the moral paternalism exercised over
the poor by their "betters," and the jobs the people of the city
had to accept. In *Work* (1915), *Making a Living* (1914), *His New Job*
(1915), and *The Immigrant* (1915), Chaplin ridiculed the state bureaucracy, the police, routinized labor, and the "land of opportunity" facing poor immigrants. He then turned his satire against reformers who infringe upon the ordinary folk in their amusements.
In *Caught in a Cabaret* (1914), *Tango Tangles* (1914), *The Masquerader*
(1914), as well as longer films such as *The Kid* (1920), *A Dog's Life*
(1918), *The Cure* (1917), and *The Pilgrim* (1923), he alternated his attack with a quest for new alternatives.[17] In these films, he portrays
in a positive light the atmosphere of night clubs and the allure of
sensual women.

The "lower orders" were not the only ones drawn to this style.
More "respectable" urbanites also enjoyed these attacks on outworn
propriety. Yet while these tantalizing facets of life intrigued them,
sexuality and indulgence still seemed dangerous. Embodying this
ambivalence was the "vamp" who became very popular for a brief
time between 1914 and 1916. Although there were many imita-

tions, the classic "vamp" was Theda Bara, whose erotic aggressiveness suggested that she, like a vampire bat, could suck the red-blooded energy out of men. Unlike the blond young virgins who came before, Bara was voluptuous and dark. Press releases portrayed this mysterious beauty as the daughter of a French nobleman and an Algerian princess; but in reality she was Theodosia Goodman of Cincinnati, Ohio. Her exotic façade allowed the audience to identify sensual evil with foreigners. Yet it was also clear that she represented the quest for excitement—and the danger of taking it too far—facing bored and anxious urbanites.

*A Fool There Was* (1914), Bara's first and most successful film, showed the vamp as a wealthy woman living on Fifth Avenue surrounded with Asian servants and luxury. On the way to Europe she seduces a wealthy lawyer whom the president has made ambassador to England. Next we see this reformer luxuriating in tropical Africa with the vamp. As blacks fan him with palm leaves, he drinks and dissipates. Newspapers broadcast the scandal, and the man's family weeps with shame. The final scene shows the statesman as a disheveled bum in New York, for the vamp has discarded him. In some films, Bara shows how vice filtered down the class order. She appears as the rebellious wife of a factory owner or plantation manager who mingles with workers and slaves, eventually leading them in revolt against her husband and the established order. Others emphasize the threat to state leadership. Bara portrayed Cleopatra, Salome, and Madame de Pompadour, women whose erotic allure destroyed men who ruled over vast kingdoms. The vamp thus embodied the most ominous warning of the vice crusaders: sex could destroy the social order. Yet at the same time, she tapped some of the restless urges for excitement fueling that perceived threat. As she explained in 1914,

> Women are my greatest fans because they see in my vampire the impersonal vengeance of all their unavenged wrongs . . . they have lacked either the courage or will power to redress their grievances. Even downtrodden wives write me to this effect. And they give me the greatest compliment: "I know I should sympathize with the wife, but I do not." I am in effect a feministe.[18]

Still it was all too clear that even women who did not consider themselves feminists were restless with their old roles. Repeatedly, the fan magazines featured articles on young women, and identified them with "youth" itself. Mass culture, especially movies, appealed to these females because it offered excitement outside the Victorian home or the work world. Typically, writers described the lives of young women who had left the parental domicile to venture forth and find a job in the city. When full-page photographs or cinematic close-ups magnified their faces, "it was as though beauty were weighted in the scales against talent, training, and even genius and out balanced them all in the value of public opinion and rewards." It was not clear if this vampish quality might be used for social good. But there was no doubt that it appealed to post-Victorian males. As one otherwise prudent critic wrote,

> We look to the heroine for what beautifies existence and as interest is stimulated by what is seen, it becomes concentrated on the heroine of the story, for she delights the eyes and stirs the pulse of responsible men with a dazzling array of potent womanly attributes. She wins because she represents the ideal creation of our heartaches and dreams. She goes over. Any man who doesn't think so should send for Doctor Osler.[19]

In searching for some way to graft this quality onto otherwise "good women," film makers in this early transition period from 1912 to 1914 used the device of amnesia. The heroine loses her memory and participates in forbidden activities free from responsibility. *The Devil's Wheel* (1913), for example, opens on a rich girl who is kidnapped by a thief who knocks her over the head and drags her away. She awakens in a dingy cabaret, filled with crooks smoking and drinking, but she has lost her memory. Freed of guilt, the heroine puts on a tight dress and learns to dance the "Apache," a wild, savage dance. Revealing her body and her primitive energy, she wins the adoration of the gang leader. Yet beneath her new persona an "instinct older than memory" surfaces, and she uplifts the villain. Converted from sin, he turns into an upwardly mobile businessman. When they marry, she is restored to her original status, complete with riches, mansion, and respectability.[20]

As producers gradually moved beyond this amnesia formula, they hit upon the idea of the serial queen. In stories that appeared in continuing weekly segments, *The Perils of Pauline* (1912–1914), *The Hazards of Helen* (1912–1915), and *Dolly of the Dailies* (1912–1915) featured the working girl as heroine. These women appeared on and off the screen as healthy, robust, and self-reliant, unlike the "sickly women" of the past. They roamed far and wide un-chaperoned, often leaving their protected "New England" homes for brief periods of freedom in the city. In spite of dangers, this provided opportunities to break into new activities such as horse-back riding, airplane flying, swimming, and exploring all the "wicked places of the world," as the title to one film explained. As Pauline visits an Italian chateau and indulges in real life sports, she does not need amnesia to excuse her attraction to high life. Fan magazines capitalized on this by showing these starlets exploring the estates of the rich. "Our serial queen," wrote one distributor, "meets more celebrities every week than her small-town sisters. Her gowns are perfect visions of delight. The story of her adven-tures in New York is a narrative of all the joys of refined, metro-politan existence."

Nevertheless, the serial queen was still locked into modes of Vic-torian gentility. The clothes she wore never displayed any flesh, no matter how stylish, since temptations "abound for the working girls of New York." Attired in long dresses and blouses which cov-ered her arms, the heroine might enter the dance halls of the city, but she never participated in the fun. There were good reasons for this. The mingling posed even greater threats to their chastity. En-countering one potential seducer, the queen protested, "Mate with you, Umballah, a black? My father would curse me if I did." But the freedom makes her all the more seductive to respectable men who admire her. In spite of her self-reliance, these adventures inevitably get her into trouble; and the loyal suitor never fails to come to the rescue. Thus these women reinforce the vice crusaders' warnings that one must be forever on guard in the city. As the re-formist Mayor Gaynor of New York remarked, "upstate" women coming to work in the city might learn from the serial queens how to "take care of themselves."[21]

For all the resemblance to her Victorian forebears, this modern female opened up an unprecedented possibility for love and mar-riage. Not only does her freedom bring her in contact with a wider range of available males, but the very fact that she attracts them with sexual allure raises the chance for an ensuing union based on something other than gentility. Norma Talmadge was a typical heroine of this genre. In *Social Secretary* (1915), she portrays a working girl who quits a secretarial job because her bosses try to seduce her. So she takes a position with a rich woman, protected by the domestic abode. Yet one night, the employer's son catches a glimpse of her in a revealing nightgown. His attraction leads to their marriage and her leap up the class order. Other films suggested how erotic allure might infuse the marriage itself. One, *Plato's Dilemma* (1914), featured Florence Lawrence as the wife of a young man who thinks that success requires a platonic, spiritual marriage. Yet his playful and seductive spouse finally convinces him that there is more to life than self-denial.[22]

Clearly, these plots and stars suggested that any artist or producer who could go beyond old formulas would gain enormous popularity. For as the vamps' and the serial queens' popularity began to fade, there was little doubt that both sexes were attracted to something other than Victorianism. Precisely at this point of tension between past and present desires, two players emerged, Douglas Fairbanks and Mary Pickford, who offered a transformation of domestic assumptions. Between 1914 and 1918, they became the first major dramatic stars of the films; only Chaplin's popularity and audience appeal equaled theirs. Coming from Broadway, they brought the prestigious aura of the stage into a formerly immigrant entertainment. Each was also part comic who made fun of restraints, while pointing to the future. In the process, they both shed their original names, a symbolic act of separation from the past which would become typical among stars. For these extremely talented figures, cosmopolitan fun and healthy beauty replaced the spiritual symbolism connected to Hart or Griffith characters. Both on and off the screen, their films, success books, columns, and writings showed their fans how to solve the era's major dilemmas.[23]

This was no small task. In endless interviews, Fairbanks related his own struggle against the ropes binding him to the past.[24] As he told it, he was born in Denver, Colorado, in 1883, and grew up in the heart of a culture that glorified the self-made man. His father was Charles Ulman, the scion of a prominent Pennsylvania family who helped found the American Bar Association and served in the Union Army as a Civil War officer. Shortly thereafter, he went west to become a noted industrialist in Denver, where he wrote

speeches for Republican presidential candidate Benjamin Harrison.
Yet for some unknown reason he deserted the family, and his wife
then changed her two sons' names to Fairbanks. Douglas attended
the Colorado School of Mines; but soon he left school for the lure
of the Broadway stage. Quickly he became a star, and married
Beth Sully, the daughter of a Wall Street banker. Fairbanks then
worked in his father-in-law's firm and joined the high society of the
New York rich, participating in the European tours and sports of
those who had the means to spend lavishly.[25]

In 1915, Fairbanks returned to show business, joining Harry
Aitken's company and working with D. W. Griffith. Yet the great
director was soon at odds with the energetic Fairbanks, and the star
soon struck a favorable contract with Famous Players-Lasky. So
popular would he become that by 1920 he could form his own
company with Pickford and Chaplin, United Artists. Throughout
this era, "Doug" made over twenty-eight films in which he usually
had control over his plots, in order to guarantee that the spirit of
the character would reflect his concerns. Typically, the smiling, energetic hero mirrored Fairbanks himself. He has luxury and urban
comfort; but within his mind and soul he still wants to be self-
made. Even though his cheerful persona suggested to audiences a
sense of optimism and a feeling that everything would turn out all
right, the typical Fairbanks film would find the hero loaded with
the worries of modern middle-class existence.

Fairbanks best dramatized the character in *His Majesty the American* (1919). The story charts the life of a young urbanite who does
not know who his father is. Behind the symbolic quest for identity
lies the vision of an expanding frontier where the hero might be a
cowboy. His New York apartment is filled with snowshoes, sad-
dles, and cowboy hats, suggesting that he is ready to master savages and bandits. But he is trapped in an urban civilization where
he is faced with office routine and no challenges. Seeking outlets
for his restless energy, he rescues poor girls from vice dens and
babies from fires. With no thrills left, he goes west. Next we see
him sleeping in a luxury Pullman car. The Indians on the frontier
are all tamed, and he is nothing but a tourist. So he goes to Mexico, hoping to find excitement in the Revolution, but it has been
quelled. Back in the city, there is nothing left to conquer, for

reforms have created order. In desperation, he goes to Europe and finds that his father was not a self-made man, but an aristocrat. Now Fairbanks puts down a rebellion against the nobles at precisely the time when revolutions were spreading across the continent. Here he finds an identity, and marries a princess.[26]

Within this film we see some of the classic dilemmas of the Fairbanks genre. Who am I, what is an American, are questions that reverberate through the film. Usually the hero has a metaphorical name such as Andrew Jackson, Jr., Daniel Boone Brown, or Cassius Lee. He admires the "steel stamina and efficiency" of the symbolic fathers who built and rule the industrial system like Charles Schwab, Andrew Carnegie, and Theodore Roosevelt. Yet at the same time he feels trapped in their creations. Unlike the small producers of a Griffith film, Fairbanks is not outside the corporate system. Rather, he is a manager, clerk, or employee in a large office. His egalitarian spirit is crushed by the capitalists above him whom he admires, but can never equal. These same powerful people have taken his autonomy, and he feels like a helpless cog in the organization. So he dreams nostalgically of a western frontier that is gone. Every now and then a threat to the society erupts, bringing a challenge to the young hero who fears he is not up to the task.[27]

Two central problems face the hero. One is his boredom at work, the other confronts him at leisure. As to the first, through humor, Fairbanks lightened the heaviness of sons trapped in the industrial creations of their fathers. Loyalty to the patriarch, in fact, inhibits rebellion. *Wild and Wooly* (1917) presents a modern urbanite dressed in a suit and tie who dreams of riding a horse across the deserts of Arizona. As the camera pulls backwards from his face, he appears seated in a luxurious New York estate where his father asks the butler to "tell the Comanche Indian we are wanted at the office in ten minutes." At work, Alexis Napoleon Brown punches a time clock and a caption explains that "his boundless energy is trapped at a desk in a button factory." *When Clouds Roll By* (1919) amplified the discontent by showing the hero entering an office where "all time and space is economized." As he falls asleep shuffling papers, his uncle, the boss, pronounces that the boy will add up to "nothing." The youth finds this all too true. He leaves work and confronts the overpowering city, where he loiters around

Fifth Avenue, hoping to rub elbows with the rich. But at the Plaza Hotel, even the waiters echo his uncle and treat him like a "nobody."[28]

Luxury poses the second problem. Initially, as an heir to the Protestant ethic, the hero fears that pleasure will endanger the frontier spirit. A typical Fairbanks film, *The Mollycoddle* (1920), opens on the dissipation of a sheriff's son. His father had won the West, and he became effete and soft on the inherited wealth, gallivanting around Europe. Similarly, the hero of *When Clouds Roll By* works in an office during the day, but at night his nightmares are filled with monsters who feed him by force. In this film, even the inner life is corrupted, for stuffed with rich pastries he is too fat to master his devilish pursuers. Others show the hero trying to re-charge his boring life through cocaine, amusement parks, boxing matches, or the new women drawn to the bohemian life of New York's Greenwich Village. Often, these threatening activities were personified by non-whites. One dream sequence includes men dressed and masked in black toppling Liberty from her pedestal. And in interviews, Fairbanks talked of his fears of Asians and Negroes, whom he constantly wanted to dominate through physical battle. In other words, the softness of modern life might literally drown the hero and make him "no better than a Negro."[29]

Given Fairbanks's loyalty to the parental tradition, the solution came not by transforming work but by changing the nature of leisure. In a vast array of books, articles, films, and interviews, Fairbanks preached an entirely new means for regeneration: sports. As athletics became popular among the urban masses, Fairbanks saw a way to perpetuate the American character. Sport was more than mere play; it offered an arena for restoring the virtues of an expanding West. Competition also served as a great leveler. No longer would the energetic man feel inferior to his social betters; sport provided a place where all men begin as equals and win prizes according to merit. No hierarchy or class order got in the way; indeed, once again it took initiative and will power to succeed. The heroes in Fairbanks's films discover new energy through boxing, tumbling, fencing, or gymnastics. Off the screen he extolled the virtues of training one's body to win the battles of life.

At the same time, athletics gave purpose to old virtues that had appeared obsolete. In the Victorian generation, economic striving necessitated self-denial and yielded a material reward. Games kept alive these parental ethics of temperance and discipline; but now they yielded physical rewards. At the widely advertised Fairbanks gym, always next to his studio, "stout flabby men are made leaner and the thin emaciated ones are made stronger." His success manuals argued that men who work hard at this task find an "antidote to too much civilization," and an alternative to the "sea of sensuousness and sensuality" pervading urban life. In addition, men now had the physical proof of their striving will. Training offered a chance to make a product once again: their bodies.[30]

The rejuvenated sportsman can now use his self-made prowess to conquer savagery, especially those black and Asiatic forces which seemed so dangerous to Fairbanks. No single film dramatized this better than *Mr. Robinson Crusoe* (1932). This classic saga of the Protestant work ethic was a perfect vehicle for Fairbanks, who wrote the scenario, produced it, and starred in it. The story opens on a wealthy man yachting in the South Seas. Sighting a distant island, he bets his friends that despite his softness due to luxury, he can turn the island into a paradise. While his friends watch skeptically, the twentieth-century man swims off. In the next few weeks the athletic hero transforms the wilderness. He builds a modern home complete with consumer appliances, golf course, and tennis courts, where he practices daily. Next he rescues a native girl from cannibals and conquers the savages. Soon the hero civilizes the native girl by teaching her how to play golf and be a good helpmate. Having proved himself equal to the original Robinson Crusoe, the hero wins his bet and returns to New York City. He is now richer and healthier. In the final scene, he sits in coat and tails, applauding the civilized native girl who has become a dancer in the Ziegfeld Follies.[31]

Yet there was much more to Fairbanks's popularity than reviving the traditions of the past. Above all, Fairbanks presented a model for unleashing playful instincts which had been repressed; he was a smiling, comic figure who like his good friend Chaplin ridiculed Victorian restrictions on fun. Sport not only restored the old vigor, it opened the way for the joyous elements of sensuous dancing, boxing matches, and other forbidden amusements to be synthesized into the new personality. The playing field allowed men to break from the overly routinized economy and the stifling family, and revive the chancy, gambling, and instinctual side of life. A community of males gathered together as a team would exude friendly camaraderie and healthy competition. Nothing was more characteristic of Fairbanks than his constant smile, radiating confidence, optimism, and flamboyance. In essence, he was living proof that the spontaneous, joyous side of life would make men happy rather than decadent. As Fairbanks expressed it, "We read so much of work and success that someone needs to preach the glory of play."

Play also provided what seemed impossible for nineteenth-century males: pride in exalting the body. Rather than denying the physical self, Fairbanks delighted in it. Often photographed with a bare torso, he took on part of the primitive being he was always so eager to conquer, showing it to be wholesome and healthy. One of his first films, *The Half Breed* (1914), cast him as a dark-skinned Indian who ran around practically nude, to the dismay of his wife, Beth Sully. Shedding the old formality of work and play, he popularized sports clothes which displayed his bare chest beneath unbuttoned shirts. As fans watched his perfect body on the screen and read his success tracts, they absorbed his religion of health and beauty. Now men could delight in their bodies—something that might make one strong, attractive to women, and above all happy. Fairbanks advocated this physical means to salvation:

> Whenever we find that we are losing our ability to smile, let's have no false illusions. We are neglecting our physical well being. Let us right then and there drop the sombre thoughts and . . . run down the street and if possible into the country.[32]

The potential conflict between expressive play and self-denial dissolved in the youth cult. In the years before 1920, Fairbanks was the crown prince of this phenomenon. Unlike the earlier Griffith brand, Fairbanks broke from the old purity and appeared free of restraint. Or he could mingle as an equal with the rich and poor, just as if they were all school boys again. Dressed in sports clothes—a style he helped pioneer for males—he constantly changed his outfits, shedding the past with each new accoutrement. Yet this rebelliousness also had the advantage of showing that the egalitarian, playful side of mass culture could be made innocent. At a time when expression of eroticism and spontaneity was linked to the vices of the upper and lower orders, youth provided an answer. By incorporating the strength and energy of awakening manhood, Fairbanks could regenerate the serious concerns of life. Booth Tarkington captured this delicate synthesis when he wrote:

> Fairbanks is a faun who has been to Sunday-school. He has a pagan body which yields instantly to any heathen or gypsy impulse . . . but he has a mind reliably furnished with a full set of morals and proprieties: he would be a sympathetic companion for anybody's aunt. Certainly he will never be older—unless quicksilver can get old.[33]

Everything in a Fairbanks production pointed up this quality of a new world. Visually the story has a look of brightness and wholesomeness. While Fairbanks' directors certainly drew on Griffith's technique of editing and general film making, the films do not have the same tone. The master's screen showed dark villains and light virtuous heroines reflecting his belief in the battle between good and evil. In one sense, this was appropriate to Griffith's view of the world as a place of constant struggle against economic scarcity, and the dangers of a harsh environment. By way of contrast, since the Fairbanks character lives in a milieu where the corporation has created abundance, he does not have to "battle" to stay alive. Consequently, the sense of a harsh environment and danger, manifested in shading of black and white, is not as strong as in Griffith's films. Fairbanks's face and body exude goodness, and the lighting is bright and cheerful, with no shadows. His characters never seem to be sad, no matter how bad conditions become. Yet by no means has Fairbanks lost the former sense of energy and dynamism, for he appears to be in constant tension which can explode any minute in great athletic feats. Even though the need for mastering the world is less than before, the hero still wants to overcome all obstacles.

No wonder, then, that Fairbanks was the first player whom we can truly describe as a "movie" hero, for he was in constant motion. Utilizing the techniques pioneered by Griffith, directors accentuated his natural agility through a number of special effects. The stage was set by bouncy titles: *Say! Young Fellow* (1918), *Mr. Fix It* (1918), *The Knickerbocker Buckaroo* (1919), *American Aristocracy* (1916), *Manhattan Madness* (1916), *Reaching for the Moon* (1917), *Reggie Mixes In* (1916), *Wild and Wooly* (1917). Then lighting and camera angles shaved away his forty years, allowing him to appear much younger. Small-scale sets camouflaged his diminutive height. And every photographic device accentuated his musuclar physique. Making the most of the movie medium, viewers really *saw* Fairbanks, literally, in the flesh. Then film editing made his body a vessel of super-human energy. When the hero went into action, he leaped over buildings, ran at triple speed, and mastered all obstacles with remarkable finesse. No wonder he was labeled "Mr. Electricity" or "Mr. Optimist," who beat the clock and moved at "full throttle." [34]

Flowing from the new approach to leisure was a major economic and political reorientation. Probably the best example of this is a classic Fairbanks film, *His Picture in the Papers* (1916). The story opens on a young man who works in his father's office. During lunch hour he pretends to conform to the parental temperance code by carrying a vegetarian lunch bag. Yet it is filled with a martini mixer, and he "indulges" on the job. Off hours he eats "red blooded" steaks in restaurants, and becomes a pugilist in Irish boxing matches. Although his parents disapprove, these shady actions make him attractive to women who are trying to be morally emancipated as well. In addition, these new activities give him the "pep" to rescue a big businessman from criminals. As reporters ask him for the secret to his strength, his answer is "Pringle Products," the cereal his father makes. Soon the goods move off the shelf, advertised as a way to make healthy boxers and robust fun lovers—not dour vegetarians. The boy becomes a success by showing manufacturers how to capitalize on the needs of the new generation. In the process, he has to put pressure on the productive system to provide the goods so that the hero can emulate in small styles formerly reserved for the rich. The message, then, is that the discontent with work and loss of power can be alleviated through consumption. [35]

Now the modern economy can be seen as the agent, rather than the antithesis, of progress. In the first half of the film, Fairbanks showed what a number of contemporaries pointed out. The world of work had become increasingly hierarchical, and a personality geared to conquering a dangerous environment had less to do. So in a predictable, ordered world he turned to mass culture as the arena for challenges. There it was not so much one's productive function that determined status. Rather, one could use money to look and act like the rich, while being drawn to immigrant sports and games. Given the Victorian background, this meant that spending would have to elevate and legitimize what was formerly forbidden. In *His Picture in the Papers* and the advertisements Fairbanks made, we see the new code of success. Men continued to achieve in the world of production; but they now strove equally hard for the money to purchase goods and leisure pursuits to compensate for boredom on the job. The Fairbanks hero was thus expanding the necessities of life. As leisure now supplied a new frontier for male energy, mass-produced but high-class consumer goods became a reward for tolerating the modern economy.

Equally important, this reorientation generated a political culture different from the older film makers, particularly Griffith. By no means was Fairbanks linked to the drive to restore the old entrepreneurial economy. Rather, like his hero Theodore Roosevelt, Fairbanks was much more concerned with accepting the corporations and making them work. True to his upper-middle-class background, rarely was he sympathetic to labor or agrarian unrest. Personifying the upwardly mobile organizational man, the Fairbanks hero utilized leisure to restore his energy, and then used that strength against the lusty enemies of reform: white slavers, vice lords, unpatriotic businessmen, and machine politicians. In films set abroad, this hero becomes the agent of imperialist democracy. In *His Majesty the American* (1919) and *The Americano* (1916), he was a man bored with domestic restraints who found a field for his energy by carrying "capital" and democracy into Europe and Latin America. There he mastered tyrants from above and revolutionaries from below who endangered foreign leaders sympathetic to the expansion of American interests. At the end of one film, he has conquered and gained noble status abroad, and proclaims to a cheering crowd, "I bring a government of the people, by the people, for the people." [36]

In these achievements, the hero also reaped new rewards. One was that he sanctioned elite styles for the middle class; and the other was that he won a different type of woman. In fact, in every one of Fairbanks's films he is looking for a female to complement his own resurrection of play. Each plot revolves around the rescue of heroines and the virtuous home from villains who embody dan-

gerous social forces. Yet at the same time, these females also revealed their bodies, danced to primitive rhythms, and, as Fairbanks
wrote in one of his success books, promised a "new style of love-
making." In *The Nut* (1921), we find the perfect match for the new
hero. The film features a young man living in a New York apartment where machines get him out of bed, dry him after showers,
and brush his teeth. Not surprisingly, work in the office creates
boredom. Seeking excitement, he meets a bohemian woman who is
a social worker in Greenwich Village. Against his everyday routine, she promises to give purpose to his "rudderless life." Her
allure results from the combination of a pure woman caring for
poor children in the slums, and a girl who enjoys the high life.[37]

The wish for this good-bad girl, however, was problematical.
Fairbanks embodied a man of traditional will power, a frontier hero
like Broncho Billy or William S. Hart fit for the modern age. Yet
he also experienced the same ambivalence toward women. Although he was a new man who loved fun and spending, he still
needed to have a woman free of too much sensuality, lest she
disrupt the discipline needed for success. As Fairbanks phrased it
in one book, men had to "nail down loveliness" before the "beauty
rose" became a weed. In other words, exciting heroines still needed
protection, for if they became too vampish, they might destroy the
core of the social order: the home. As the title to one film proclaimed, Fairbanks was a *Matrimaniac* (1916). Yet he wanted a
woman who would take her moral emancipation far beyond that of
the serial queens or other early heroines.[38]

What kind of heroine could walk this thin line between virtue
and vice? The answer for an entire generation came from the future
Mrs. Fairbanks, Mary Pickford. Today's readers might find it difficult to believe not only that Pickford's popularity ran parallel with
Doug's, but that she portrayed a heroine who complimented his
cultural reorientations. Was she not the sweet little girl of Griffith's
films, or the angelic youth of *Pollyanna* (1920) or *Sparrows* (1926)?
True, these films show her persona to be little different from
nineteenth-century stereotypes. Nevertheless, it is well to note that
Pickford did not like her portrayal in *Pollyanna*, and thereafter
deeply regretted conforming to the image of girlhood. One reason
why she disdained that association was that in the period from
1914 to 1918, when rising to unprecedented fame and becoming

the most popular star in all film history, she did not fit that image at all. In fact, during these key years of her career, "Mary" played a female role which made a fundamental break from the past, and embodied many of the aspirations of women in her generation.

Precisely because Pickford attempted the impossible, she became the most popular star of the day. While Fairbanks questioned the male role, Pickford questioned the female role at work and in the family. Over and over again she portrayed women striving to be economically free and morally emancipated. No doubt because these films took place in real life circumstances and seemed so convincing, publishers asked her to write weekly columns for women on how to deal with their own lives. Mary responded by continually backing women's suffrage and echoing the messages offered on the screen. Above all, she was a self-sufficient woman who hired female writers who were much like herself. Together they created the character of a heroine who pioneered new trails for women into the domains of men. Formerly, for example, the ideal of great wealth and upward mobility was reserved for males; but Pickford made the Horatio Alger aspiration viable for women. The press not only praised her work, but paid a great deal of attention to the star's salary—for it was the first time that such a publicly acclaimed "good girl" made so much money in the degraded, at least for women, market place. "Mary Pickford," wrote one typical enthusiast in 1914, "gets more money than the President . . . nine million people would rather see her on the screen than Bryan, Wilson, Roosevelt and Vernon Castle. That is why they will have to pay her $50,000 a year in 1914 and double that in 1915."[39] Indeed, she reached her peak when in 1920 she was the only woman to join Fairbanks, Chaplin, and Griffith to form United Artists, earning the incredible salary of one million dollars a year. Through it all, Pickford realized why she was constantly voted in newspaper polls the "most popular girl in the world":

> I like to see my own sex achieve. My success has been due to the fact that women like the pictures in which I appear. I think I admire most in the world the girls who earn their own living. I am proud to be one of them.[40]

It is no accident that the most noted stars of the era created their unique screen characters largely from their own lives. Like

Chaplin, Fairbanks, and others, Pickford made the most of her origins. Pickford loved to tell the press how she was born Gladys Smith of Toronto, Canada, in 1893. On her father's side she was English Methodist, on her mother's she was Irish Catholic. The father ran a small grocery store, and insisted that the women stay dependent at home. Her mother and grandmother on both sides of the family guarded the domestic realm, forbidding drink or any suggestion of impropriety. Mary's grandmother in particular tried to cleanse prostitutes and convert them from sin. Yet when Mr. Smith died, the mother took the first step away from Victorianism by placing her two girls and a son on the stage, allowing them financial independence. Never did Mrs. Smith remarry; she cut her ties with the past by changing the family name to Pickford, a classier name giving status to their still unrespectable occupation. From the age of about ten onwards, Mary toured the country as a stage performer. But always Mrs. Smith trained Mary to stay clear of actresses who smoked, used bad language, or worked in studios which reeked with the scandal surrounding the Stanford White and Evelyn Nesbit affair. Mary's highest aspiration was to join David Belasco's company on Broadway. Yet reluctantly, out of financial desperation, she joined the recently cleansed movies in 1909.[41]

In this realm of "scandal," Pickford was fortunate enough to join D. W. Griffith's company. But the films she made for the master cast her as a traditional Victorian heroine, giving little indication of her future. *Lena and the Geese* (1911), for example, featured her as a poor peasant girl whose love redeems a young man from his wasted life. When she discovers that she is in fact the long-lost child of a noble family, she accepts her true class status. A slight deviation from this melodramatic formula came in *The New York Hat* (1912). In that production she played an orphan whose guardian forbids her using her inheritance to buy a hat. The local minister, charmed by her vivacity, persuades the oppressive guardian to let her have some fun, and buy the bonnet. Following the success of these minor films, Pickford achieved her heart's desire: Belasco brought her to Broadway. There she starred in *The Good Little Devil* (1913). As the play became a major hit, Pickford's public persona reflected the high life of New York City.

In the following years, as film makers brought established stars from Broadway, Adolph Zukor hired Pickford to star in a photoplay "completely separate," she recalled, "from what I had been doing. . . . They thought I was just another actress, but when I made *Tess of the Storm Country* that was really the beginning of my career." Now audiences saw a heroine who offered more than old femininity. In contrast to her work with Griffith, where she resisted the director's desire to mold her into genteel patterns, Pickford now took on a personality free of abstract ideals of purity. "Little Mary" was above all a person in her own right. No doubt her projection of a unique personality was because she was one of the premier performers of the day. On the screen her character displayed a whole range of emotions, while mixing drama with humor in an utterly convincing blend. Once audiences came to expect the Pickford image as something special, Pickford left standard roles where she had displayed predictable emotions in equally predictable situations. She then became a model of vitality, and a boundless force that could not be confined to one place or social station. As Pickford recalled of her struggle against the old melodramas that forced one into formalized and educational categories, "I always tried to get laughter into my pictures. Make them laugh and make them cry and back to laughter. What do people go to the theater for? An emotional exercise, and no preachments. I don't believe in taking advantage of someone who comes to the theatre by teaching them a lesson. It's not my prerogative to teach anything." [42]

Nevertheless, the quest for personal freedom had deep social implications. In the film that sparked the Pickford image for the next six years, *Tess of the Storm Country* (1914), the heroine is a rebellious, independent, and energetic Cumberland mountain girl whom we first see dancing a jig. She and her hunter father would live contentedly were it not for Mr. Graves, the sheriff, and the local elite. He takes away her father's livelihood by forbidding "poaching in the forest." At the same time, Graves's daughter has an illegitimate child with a lover who dies. To save herself from paternal "wrath," she gives the baby to the heroine, Tess. As Tess raises the infant, the town assumes it is hers. Graves, as the church elder, refuses to baptize the baby, so Tess marches to the altar and sprinkles sacramental water on the child herself. Continuing this rebellion, she leads the farmers and tradesmen in a successful fight against Graves's game laws. Only when the villain learns whose child Tess protects does he soften, allowing his daughter to raise his grandchild and apologizing to Tess. He now repeals the poaching ordinance, and blesses his son's marriage to Tess.[43]

Pickford's spunky heroine who fought economic and domestic tyranny in the countryside was equally effective in the face of urban problems. *The Eternal Grind* (1916) opens on a rural American girl leaving for the city—an experience relevant to much of her audience. Although she is in quest of freedom, she finds that the only employment available for women is routine and menial. So she takes a job as a sewing machine operator and soon becomes a "slave." Lording over the female workers is the boss. He exploits the laboring women and forbids his sons to mingle with them. Yet the dancing and gaiety of the working girls attracts one son who then has an affair with the heroine's best friend. When the girl becomes pregnant, Mary insists that they marry, reinforced by a gun in her hand. But the lad's father forbids it. Meanwhile, the heroine has fallen in love with the other son, a social worker. Together they convince the father to give up his greedy ways, and he finally allows both marriages. Such love also inspires him to install labor-saving devices to improve the conditions for his workers.[44]

Equally important, Pickford broke from the Victorian mode of purity. Half the star's appeal lay in her ability to confront the major social problems of her day, and resolve them on the personal level. But the other half was her vitality. For she expanded the perimeters of respectable female behavior far beyond their nineteenth-century coordinates. Unlike the serial queens who might look but never touch, Pickford rolled up her sleeves and plunged her hands into previously forbidden realms. Some films showed her as an outsider, fighting against the system. But in others, she was caught in it. These films portray her as a genteel girl stifled in a home with a work-obsessed father and a socialite, charity-worker mother.[45] In response to her restlessness, the heroine looks down the class order for excitement. Reflecting the culture's persistent ambivalence, a common device was the kidnap. *Poor Little Peppina* (1916) and *Less Than the Dust* (1916) show her as an American girl snatched from her Victorian home by foreigners. This gives her an excuse for taking on a different personality without guilt. Growing up with gypsies, Italians, Hindus, or Indians, she learns to wear their exotic clothes, assume a swarthy complexion, and participate in public festivals with both men and women. Another formula for breaking down barriers between the sexes was to cast Pickford as a foreigner herself. In *Amarilly of Clothesline Alley* (1918), *Madame Butterfly* (1915), or *Hulda of Holland* (1916), Mary is a real Irish, Japanese, or Dutch girl who mingles in saloons, dances in New York, or embodies exotic qualities of an Asian or European female, complete with bright clothes and a sensual personality.[46]

All of the movement toward a foreign aura found expression in a new visual look as well. Soon producers learned that audiences expected Pickford to do modern things, surrounded by a cinematic vision that fit the role. Not too surprisingly, two co-workers on several films, the director Maurice Tourneur and cameraman Charles Rosher, pioneered a style which carried an impressionistic aura in their compositons, lighting, and use of space. In many ways their innovations carried some of the motifs used by the American realists or "Ash Can" school painters of the day. Like Robert Henri, the innovative painter from Philadelphia, the film maker Tourneur felt the impact of the French impressionists and modern artists. As a Frenchman himself, he had worked with Auguste Rodin before making movies, and his vision of the world broke from the older formalities of artistic expression. He was not given to clear, balanced shots, nor did he define the world with dark and light shadows, as did Griffith. Rather, Tourneur and Rosher photographed Pickford immersed in glittering light that created a sparkling, not clearly demarcated imagery. This vision heightened the sense of atmosphere and mood, and when concentrated on the heroine's effervescent personality, it seemed to say that pure emotion carried as much worth, if not more, than the larger social battle between good and evil. Furthermore, parts of the scenery jutted into the foreground, and objects seemed to reach into the audience, disrupting the former sense of balance. Clearly, here was a new way of seeing the world, fit for a personality who questioned the past.

Soon the audience came to expect the regenerative look, and it complemented the metamorphosis linked to the Pickford personality. In contrast to Victorian heroines who began and ended their films with no change in their characters, Pickford used her assimilation of foreign styles to shed part of the Anglo-Saxon identity that seemed to trap the heroine in the first half of the story. Now she became more sexually attractive to males, and also mingled more widely, bringing her into contact with a wider choice of potential spouses. In this way, her personality promised to chip away at class, ethnic, and sexual divisions of the past. Yet Pickford as a star was able to play a wide variety of roles without ever losing her central identity. This variety showed her audience that synthesizing exotic qualities would add fun to life, as well as male admirers. Among many examples of this chameleon quality is an article in *The Ladies' World* of 1916. Accompanying a feature on Pickford was a two-page picture of the star surrounded by costumes from many of her films. The magazine then invited the fan to make her look Dutch, Irish, Italian, Japanese, Indian or Gypsy, suggesting that the reader could do the same herself.[47]

Implicit in this Pickford reorientation was that primitivism offered a way to strip away formalities, and restore a more natural relationship with men. One of her most popular films, *Hearts Adrift* (1914), presents the ideal environment for unleashing the instinctual life. The story opens on a young woman sailing with her Victorian parents on an ocean liner. Soon it crashes, and she ends up stranded alone on an island. To survive, she becomes self-sufficient, catching fish, building a hut, and making her clothes out of wolf skin. She also displays an earthy quality, showing her bare legs, back, and shoulders. One critic noted that "wild scenery stretched tropically before the eyes and Pickford was definitely part of the primitive naturalism." Into this paradise comes a shipwrecked, genteel man, whom she cares for and nurses back to health. They fall in love and perform a makeshift marriage, and have a child. Yet through it all, the girl stays physically alluring, and lives in a relation of economic equality with the man by continuing to hunt and build. This idyllic life ends when a ship appears, with the man's presumed dead wife. Unwilling to return to civilization, the heroine jumps into a volcano, killing herself and her child.[48]

The tragic ending reveals the enormous difficulties in realizing what was probably a strong desire on the part of post-Victorian women. Equality might be dangerous, both socially and sexually. In order to assuage these fears, Pickford, like Fairbanks, became a prime exponent of the youth cult. Because prolonged schooling was taking more and more adolescents out of the work force, they had the most time to indulge in leisure pursuits. It was only natural that adults would be influenced by this development, but the ensuing emulation of youthful styles went far beyond that. People who had grown up with Victorian values were unwilling to use the quest for sexual mutuality as a means for questioning the economy or the class order. So instead of integrating these forces into a mature identity, they isolate their rebellious impulses into a realm of pre-adult responsibility. Repeatedly, Pickford showed the way by playing sixteen- and eighteen year olds into her own twenties, thirties, and even forties. Over and over again, Pickford was the joyous, spontaneous female who brought into her personality that which Victorians had repressed: the playfulness of childhood and adolescent blossoming. Yet while she revealed more of her body than any star before her, the allure was surrounded by a "radiant image of girlish beauty" which showed that she was "old fashioned but not a prude." In other words, her sexual innocence protected her class status, separating her from "the hectic eroticism of the lower orders and rouged debutantes of the day."

All of this demanded that the enticing body be made pure. This youthful image took a great deal of work to achieve. Unlike a Victorian woman, Pickford constantly had to assure herself and her fans that despite her new behavior, it was still "good." Mary was noted for taking endless hours at the cosmetic table to disguise the fact that she was a mature woman. Yet she did not hide her age; rather, she offered female peers clues on how to look young and virtuous themselves. Popular journals were filled with articles emphasizing her years and detailing her exercise, diet, and beauty treatments. As she told her fans, "We are our own sculptors. Who can deny that passion and unkind thoughts show on the lines and expressions of our faces . . . young people seldom have these vices until they start getting old, so I love to be with them. The impulses of youth are natural and good." Pickford was obsessed with maintaining this look of youth and purity. She never wanted her screen image to suggest that moving about in the rough and tumble world would taint this quality. So the star watched all her film rushes carefully, in order to detect any blemish or frown. As she explained, "No woman can be a success on the screen if she dissipates even one little bit. The slightest excess, the least giving away shows unmistakably in the face and its expression. . . . I cannot remain up at night and have my face clear and shiny." Obviously, it worked. Newspapers of the day printed numerous poems and verses testifying to her beauty. One of the most expressive came from the noted poet Vachel Lindsay in *McClure's:*

> Oh Mary Pickford, Doll Divine,
> Like that special thing Botticelli
> painted in the faces of his heavenly
> creatures. How you made our reverent
> passion rise, our fine desire you won.
> Oh, little girl, never grow up.[49]

Perpetual youth had significant consequences in a time of women's newly found freedom. Despite rebellion, it signalled subordination. This is evident in Pickford's own life. Like the Gishes, Talmadges, and other actresses of the day, Pickford was constantly chaperoned by her mother, who was also her business manager. The maternal presence, on one level, was a publicity device assuring the fans that the star would not forsake "Anglo-Saxon hopes and traditions," embodied appropriately in motherhood. As her moral guardian, Mrs. Pickford would not let her daughter play a "risqué role," or drink and smoke in public. On one occasion the mother actually had a man arrested for making lewd remarks to the star. Nor would "Little Mary" bob her hair, a symbol of emancipation for the twenties women, while her mother was alive. In her autobiography Pickford confessed that her mother was her conscience, inhibiting her sexual freedom. When seventeen years old, she secretly dated her co-star, Owen Moore; but she felt so guilty for defying her mother's "law" that she insisted they marry. This new woman was obviously uncomfortable with sexual experimentation outside of wedlock.[50]

The tension between the Victorian past and moral experimentation also surfaced in her films, providing a clue to one of the social ironies of the time. Historians have been perplexed by the paradox of more middle-class emancipated women entering the economy while they married younger and in greater proportions than their nineteenth-century counterparts. Pickford's films, however, suggest why. Incarnating the experience of many women like herself, Pickford's screen character often rebelled against the paren-

*The Perils of Pauline* (1912–1914) identifies the new woman's greatest fear: the dangerous urbanism of ethnics, thugs, and "white slavers." (Museum of Modern Art/Film Stills Archive)

Theda Bara as the voluptuous vamp before one of her fallen victims (circa 1914). (Museum of Modern Art/Film Stills Archive)

Moral guardians become laughable: the Keystone Cops at rest, preparing for their struggle against vice and chaos. (Museum of Modern Art/Film Stills Archive)

Mack Sennett's saucy bathing beauties, showing off their sweet pulchritude at the beach. (Museum of Modern Art/Film Stills Archive)

Charles Chaplin mocks the pretensions of high art in this publicity photo
from 1915, yet enjoys a view of the new woman with a very naked eye.
(Culver Pictures)

Douglas Fairbanks, the modern cowboy, expresses the modern dilemma.
With nary a horse or "injun" in sight, he rides a divan while trapped in the
luxurious environment of the *Knickerbocker Buckaroo* (1919). (Culver Pictures)

The new energy: Pickford, Fairbanks, and Chaplin posturing at the metaphorical apex of their careers (1917). (New York Public Library/Theater Collection)

"Doug," the modern personality, shows flabby fans how to stay vigorous on the new frontier of sports (1919). (New York Public Library/Theater Collection)

### The One and Only "Doug" Himself

*Idol of countless movie fans, who thrill with delight as he leaps on and off express trains, swings from perilous heights, and finds new ways to defy gravitation in every film. An article by Doug, describing the most dangerous and daring of his stunts and giving some of his views of life, will be found on page 24*

Home Companion July 1919

"ALL very well, young man," said Madame Nellie Melba, the great singer; "but you'd better take care and not be too daring!"
"Believe me, dear lady," replied Doug, "I'm the most careful little fellow you ever saw in your life."
And then he went out and walked all about the yard on the top of a tall ladder, as you behold him at the right, a feat to make the rest of us mortals shudder.

THE most dangerous stunt he ever did—jumping the Grand Canyon. He says of this feat: "Never again!"

"Doug" lifts Jack Dempsey, equating the champ's heavyweight stardom with Fairbanks's stardom (1921). (New York Public Library/Theater Collection)

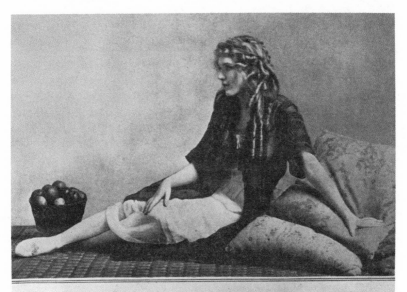

This little girl earns $100,000 a year

The Horatio Alger dream comes true for women: mass culture and the movies make Mary Pickford rich (1914). (New York Public Library/Theater Collection)

The celebrity's column offers advice to the fans who look to the star, on and off the screen, for solutions to problems of real life. (New York Public Library/Theater Collection)

DAILY TALKS

By Mary Pickford

"Little Mary" reads a feminist newspaper and lends her stardom to the struggle for women's emancipation. (Culver Pictures)

***

*Top:* A major component of Pickford's appeal: her rebellion against unjust authorities, as seen here in *Tess of the Storm Country* (1914). (Museum of Modern Art/Film Stills Archive)

*Bottom:* Tess attempts to baptize a friend's illegitimate baby: Pickford's defense of unwed mothers shows that the loss of virginity is not a sin. (New York Public Library/Theater Collection)

Pickford dramatizes the miseries of modern women's work in *The Eternal
Grind* (1916). (New York Public Library/Theater Collection)

---

*Top:* The starting point of the Pickford formula. Here the spunky girl is
entrapped by Victorian duty and propriety in *A Poor Little Rich Girl* (1917).
(Museum of Modern Art/Film Stills Archive)

*Bottom:* City streets provide a stage for the post-Victorian Pickford, here
seen dancing ragtime with an Irish youth in *The Hoodlum* (1919). (Museum
of Modern Art/Film Stills Archive)

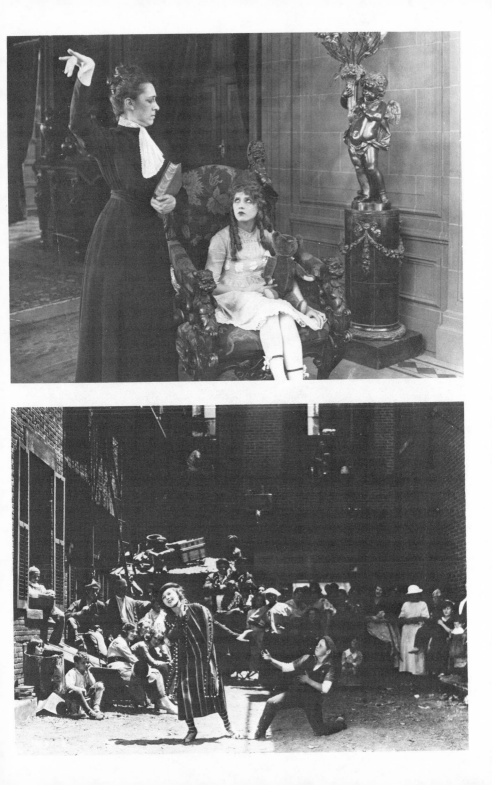

MARY PICKFORD to ap-
pear for the first time in
the role of an Italian, in
the Famous Players Film
Company's production,
"Poor Little Peppina."—
To be released some time
in February :: :: ::

In *Poor Little Peppina* (1916) Pickford assumes the style and vigor of an
Italian immigrant. (New York Public Library/Theater Collection)

Pickford epitomized the star who experimented with multiple selves, yet still remained "America's Sweetheart." (New York Public Library/Theater Collection)

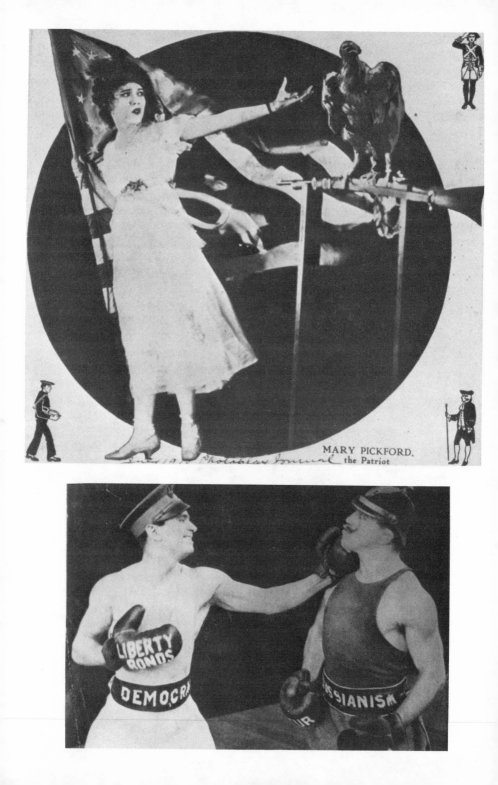

MARY PICKFORD.
the Patriot

The Garden of Eden, modern style. The golden couple enjoying their swimming pool at palatial Pickfair. (Museum of Modern Art/Film Stills Archive)

---

*Top:* "Colonel" Pickford spurs on the troops to emulate the Spirit of 1776 in this World War I poster. (New York Public Library/Theater Collection)

*Bottom:* In this World War I poster, sport becomes the training ground for war: Fairbanks knocks out the Kaiser and helps make the world "safe for democracy." (New York Public Library/Theater Collection)

tal domain. In pursuit of autonomy, she procured jobs in factories, offices, restaurants, or theaters. (Since this employment was usually regimented, the desired freedom was rarely attained, and the "slave of the machine" turned her energies toward free time.) Dance halls, movies, and lower-class neighborhoods offered environments for excitement as well as the chance to mingle with all types of men. Yet the mutual sexual attraction could be dangerous. Inevitably, one of the heroine's friends or relatives loses her chastity. Despite the star's befriending of the fallen and ostracized sinner, there is only one route to the happy ending. For "good" and "bad" girls alike, marriage must sanction the new sexual style. In essence, the huge popularity of this formula suggests that the emancipated woman's sexual tension diffused impulses toward making work more meaningful; the heroine's dominant desire was to retreat from public realms into the safety of domesticity.[51]

A girlish identity also had important economic implications. On the screen, she may convert a bad boss to righteousness; but she never questioned his right to rule. Off the screen, despite her enormous income, she was "unspoiled," as the press noted. This meant that she maintained the stance of a dependent woman in public, ultimately yielding to male or parental authority. True, the star was noted for driving a hard bargain with producers. But always behind the scenes her mother handled the money. When Mary established her own production company, she took pains to point out that Adolph Zukor was still "Papa" of the firm. He along with Mrs. Pickford tried to regulate her public demeanor. In the business office, Zukor was in charge; on the set it was the director. As one critic noted, "The director visualizes the parts for her and instructs her to imitate him. In other words, he supplies the brains." Much as Pickford resented being type-cast, she confessed, "I allowed myself to be hypnotized by the public into remaining a little girl." She knew it paid off, so she stuck with it.[52]

Exactly at this point the needs of the new man and woman fused. With a "girl" like Pickford, men such as Fairbanks could find an emancipated woman whose brief years of freedom gave her an alluring veneer that promised to revitalize his life. One of her more revealing films, *Behind the Scenes* (1914), brings out the implications of this union for the home. The story revolves around a small town girl who goes to the city. When office work proves unfulfilling, she becomes a cabaret chorus girl. Her newly found sexuality attracts a suitor who takes her to nightclubs, restaurants, and sporting events. Shortly thereafter, they marry, but the husband takes her back to his father's farm where work is endless. Lonely and restless, the heroine leaves her spouse to return to Broadway. There she gains fame, but a lecherous producer tries to rape her. Now her husband comes to the rescue, and both recognize their mutual folly. Agreeing that the marriage must change, they move to the city. There they strike a compromise. The husband will work less and spend more time with her in leisure pursuits; she in turn will implement her emancipation into their private life.[53]

With this marital transformation, the anticipated "necessities" of life escalated. The new home demanded high-level consumption to provide refined pleasures formerly scorned by the middle class. In effect, this meant that the happy ending of a Pickford film included a man for the working woman who would support her leisure needs. Furthering this message, the press constantly showed "America's Sweetheart" modeling the latest dresses and fur coats; purchasing pets and cars; and living in an elaborate home filled with eclectic foreign artifacts. Advertisers paid her handsomely to endorse cosmetics for that youthful look. This elegance let the public know that, despite her expensive tastes, the star was above vampish materialism. "Unspoiled Mary" was above all a prospective marriage partner whose "face displayed every emotion but villainy"; whose innocence elevated her above vice; who knew that "too much powder puff could destroy a dynasty." Never would Pickford's carefully groomed primitivism corrupt men.[54]

More importantly, this transformation allowed the pre-War woman to retain her older civic functions. Instead of destroying the code of self-denial, refined consumption offered the means for restoring male virtue. As special lighting surrounded her face with a heavenly glow, "Little Mary" still carried the spirituality of the nineteenth-century family with its commitment to individualism. The fact that this obviously Anglo-Saxon woman played characters from all parts of the social order suggested that these values still held the urban society together, and woman's role as moral guardian was still intact. *The Hoodlum* (1919) illustrates this message. The film focuses on a rich girl who rebels against the restraints of her grandfather, a New York monopolist. Seeking a cultural alternative, she becomes a social worker in the city's slums. There she also takes on the manner and slang phrases of the immigrants, dances in the streets, and plays with black children. In the process of her liberation, "the Little Evangelist" cares for the poor and helps a young "muckraker" with his work. Together they convert her grandfather into a social guardian. Now that reform has transformed big business, the hero and heroine are free to get married. Again, the family has provided the basis for class harmony; but this time it is *within* the corporate order.[55]

The ultimate proof that the emancipated man and woman still served the public good occurred during World War I. Both Pickford and Fairbanks portrayed the War as an extension of their efforts to transform the self as well as the world. "Before the War," explained Fairbanks, "we were as a nation, from prosperity and self-indulgence, perilously close to disaster. Now the whole world is going to be made safe and clean, including the U.S.A." Off the screen, America's Sweetheart posed for numerous War posters. The Army made her an honorary colonel who saw the troops off to war, while a "Pickford Cannon" sent shells to the "Bosch" carrying her name. To stir the fighting spirit, a Pickford film showed the Huns as the greatest white slavers of them all, bent on destroying the American home. In order to protect pure women, Fairbanks advocated closing vice districts and exporting enemy aliens. One famous propaganda poster showed the star in boxing shorts, "knocking out the Kaiser." Furthermore, Pickford and Fairbanks toured the country together in the Liberty Bond drive, and received an audience with President Wilson at the White House.[56]

After the War came the appropriate merging of their careers, when Pickford and Fairbanks divorced their spouses and married each other. As in their films, the modern home was not achieved without a struggle against confining norms of the past. Nevada's district attorney threatened to sue the couple for defying the state's residence laws; the Catholic bishop excommunicated Pickford, using the opportunity to preach against marital infidelity and separation; the Baptist minister who presided over their wedding was nearly censured for marrying a divorced man and woman; Pickford's former husband, Owen Moore, threatened to sue for adultery. Yet the criticism soon gave way to acclaim. Rather than encouraging divorce, their union appeared as the way to perfect wedlock. Neither saw divorce as an admirable thing. Yet they both felt it was the unfortunate price to pay for the domestic ideal. Pickford claimed that her former husband was an abusive drunkard, jealous of her success. Now, with Fairbanks, she had a marriage of equals. As they honeymooned in Europe, the press heralded the golden couple, and the huge crowds seemed to sanction their emancipation. Presumably, their breaks from the past had led to the happiness their films promised to millions.[57]

During the next ten years, their union was constantly in the public eye. Symbolic of the modern marriage they epitomized was their famous Hollywood estate, Pickfair. The home was now expanded far beyond the functional Victorian domicile. Modeled on a European chateau, Pickfair collected and refined elements of upper- and lower-class pleasures. It was a consumer's paradise that resembled an innocent doll's house more than a formidable, aristocratic mansion typical of the eastern elites. Swimming pools, gyms, fountains, and cultivated lawns supplied a private "vacation land." Inside, the couple decorated each room in the motif of a foreign country, so that movement from one part of the house to another provided exotic adventure. In this kingdom of eternal youth, Doug and Mary highlighted continual newness by dipping into their vast wardrobes of stylish clothes for each of the day's activities: work, sports, dining, dancing, and parties. It followed that whenever the two sat for photographs, their smiles radiated happiness. A typical reporter described the Pickfair life as "the most successful and famous marriage that the world has ever known," succeeding where "others failed." For neither Pickford nor Fairbanks envisaged the home as "the dumping ground for the cares of the day."[58]

In the attention the press and fan magazines paid to their tastes, likes, and dislikes, the modern imagery of the star was fully born. On and off the screen, they were "Doug and Mary"—ordinary folk like you and me who were blessed by opportunity. Yet as European royalty and the American rich visited Pickfair, and Doug and Mary emulated in small the styles formerly reserved for a Vanderbilt, Astor, or Rockefeller, they showed the aspiring urbanite that upward mobility could be expressed in this new realm of leisure even more than on the job itself. Instead of being resentful of the wealthy, they demonstrated how modern consumption allowed one to emulate the styles of the high and mighty. In real life, "Doug" was the smiling, youthful hero whom Mary described as "always on the jump." Fairbanks himself extolled "sunrises over sunsets, beginnings over endings," and never spoke of failure, death, or depressing things.[59] Pickford recalled that he had an endless habit of writing "success" on scraps of paper—a code that he both lived and preached in self-improvement pamphlets for the boy scouts, as well as fan magazines. In his partner, Mary, he found the new woman with the old values. She participated in charity and orphanage work, yet radiated a modern consumer ideal. Together, their common touch appeared equal to any nobility.

The golden couple eventually divorced, and each went on to a third spouse. Yet in the period from 1914 to 1918, their importance as cultural reformers cannot be overemphasized. Every major player before them suggested that the crisis of the age was not so much status decline or a search for order as it was the dissolution of the family values of the past. Unlike vice crusaders, and early film makers like Griffith, who had tried to hold on to traditional domesticity in the face of the forces that were tearing it apart, Pickford and Fairbanks pointed to the twentieth century. True, they rebelled against the constraints at work and the sexual roles of the past; but they showed how to resolve these potentially explosive  issues in private ways. Instead of trying to contain the fruits of the corporate order within a Victorian framework, they tried to make high-level consumption a means for restoring family stability. The idea was not to resist the modern organizations, or to question its rationality with counter-cultural values. Rather, they tried to find freedom in the realm of leisure, which would then offer an uneasy accommodation to the new order. By carrying her moral emancipation into the home, the new woman hoped that an expanded domestic realm might compensate for the inadequacies of public life, and strengthen relations between the sexes. In turn, men would think of success more in terms of the money that would provide the good life. Although there was no conspiracy of big business to foist this formula on the public, the movie industry had synthesized consumption to Progressive ends, which perfectly suited the needs of the emerging corporate era.

*Chapter Six*

# YOU ARE THE STAR:
# THE EVOLUTION
# OF THE THEATER PALACE,
# 1908–1929

Equal opportunity came to mean not merely that each of us
had a right to protect his interests with his vote, but that each
of us had a right to stalk around in public places and live
vicariously the life of the rich.

CHARLES FERGUSON, "HIGH CLASS"
*Harper's Monthly Magazine*, 1932[1]

Charles Ferguson's observations concerning the movie theaters
spreading over the cities in the late teens and twenties captured a
key ingredient of our story. Powerful and innovative as Pickford
and Fairbanks were, they alone were not enough to validate the rise
of a new economy and morality. Going to a movie meant much
more than merely watching the screen. It was a total experience
that immersed the fans directly in the life they saw in celluloid.
Gradually, theater owners began to realize that they could heighten
the immediacy of moviegoing. If entering the theater felt like coming into the star's home, the viewers could become part of that high
life they watched in the darkened room. For a brief period during
the day or evening, the happy ending was theirs, too. Nowhere
was this more obvious than in the cathedrals of the motion pictures, which democratized the styles of elite estates or hotels on an
unprecedented scale. A close examination of this phenomenon can
help us understand why the masses could so closely identify with
the stars. Who went to the movies, and what did they expect from
them?

In the early period, theater owners catered to the immigrants'

tastes for foreign films, pure entertainment, and shorts portraying
their political and economic situation. Yet after 1908, they faced a
quandary in attracting a more affluent audience for their recently
uplifted product. They saw that movies were spreading. But they
also knew that the nickelodeon was merely one among many
amusements appealing to the urban workers. Amid the hurly burly
of the streets in 1910 there were 9,000 saloons and just 400 movie
houses. An average poorer neighborhood in those days might have
twenty nickelodeons which captured the attention of the respectable press and social workers. Still, the same areas might also have
nearly a hundred saloons and twenty dance halls. Yet as the movie
house moved uptown, it was not just one of many entertainments
for the bourgeois. Rather, it was the only legitimized arena where
the classes and sexes mingled. But it was left in an ambiguous situation. How could theater owners sanction an amusement that drew
audiences precisely because it had been forbidden? Shrewd theater
owners realized that if they could remove this unease without losing the allure, they could reap handsome profits.[2]

Theater managers thus did everything possible to raise movies
above their disreputable origins. The municipal codes and censorship board played an important role in this process. Like the
movies themselves, the theaters benefitted from these reforms. For
once the movie house earned a license, a more affluent clientele
could enter the arena with some sense of safety. As a result, between 1908 and 1914, as films went from shorts to photoplays,
nickelodeons changed from store fronts to more sumptuous buildings. Describing this process of elaboration, Adolph Zukor recalled
that the "nickelodeon had to go, theaters replaced shooting galleries,
temples replaced theaters, cathedrals replaced temples." Another
exhibitor, Marcus Loew, refurbished his Brooklyn store front, and
changed its name from the Cozy Corner to the Royal. In Chicago,
the future head of Universal Pictures, Carl Laemmle, transformed
his chain of nickelodeons into prestigious "White Fronts." Still
others, such as A. J. Balaban of Chicago who would soon put
together a large chain with Samual Katz and merge it to Paramount
Pictures, made the most of the synthesis of movies and reform. On
his marquee he displayed a magnified copy of a letter from Jane
Addams:

It is unfortunate that the five cent theaters have become associated in the public mind with the lurid and unworthy. Our experience at Hull House has left no doubt that in time the moving picture will be utilized for all purposes of education. The schools and churches will count film among its most valuable entertainment and equipment.[3]

Balaban's tactics clearly reflected the wisdom of a shrewd businessman, ever ready to change his product for the better market. In New York, Boston, St. Louis, and Chicago, the pattern after 1908 was to open refined theaters in neighborhoods higher up the social order. As movie houses in Boston increased from thirty-one to forty-one in 1914, all the new ones opened in the wealthy suburbs of Roxbury, Dorchester, Cambridge, and Somerville. "For the first time in the history of the town," observed a reporter in the industry's major trade journal, "the selectmen of Brookline, Massachusetts, have decided to grant a license to a photoplay show." In the city's major cultural area of Brighton, three movie houses opened, despite the opposition of Mayor John F. Fitzgerald, grandfather of the future President Kennedy. Another opened across from the Boston Symphony, and the exclusive opera house at Potter Hall converted into a cinema. The same thing was happening all over. In Atlanta, for example, Walter P. Eaton noted in 1914, "You cannot of course draw any hard and fast line which will not be crossed at many points, but in Atlanta, Georgia, for example, you may often see automobiles parked two deep along the curb in front of a motion picture theater, which hardly suggests exclusively proletarian patronage."[4]

Well-heeled motorists spurred theater owners to do everything in their power to keep the wheels pointed toward the movies. In this effort, they developed a whole literature on how to charge higher prices and bring in more wealthy patrons. Among the primary criteria were seating capacity and location. A high-class movie theater had to be located on a well-lit major thoroughfare. In part this was done to make it visible to a wider population. But it was also important to assure patrons of security. Patriotic symbols on the imposing marquees contributed to this respectability. Presumably, a packed house with a "crowded look" indicated that movies were acceptable to everyone, and no longer located in "dirty dives." It was equally crucial to raise the status of the proprietors themselves.

One method was to have the well-dressed owner greet patrons at the door. Another was to raise the license fee from $25 for a "common show" to $500, the same as for a legitimate theater. At the same time, seating capacity was increased from a limit of 300 to over 1,000. With large investments at stake, exhibitors did everything to clean up their establishments, for they wanted no "trouble with the police." Finally, operators were cautioned to encourage a "mixed house" by avoiding programs slanted to one nationality, by eliminating ethnic vaudeville acts, and by discarding all songs in foreign languages. By 1916, New York had ten luxury houses, which the trade journals of the industry described as alternatives to the "gay and fatuous forms of degeneracy" among the rich and the "jaded appetites of the unwashed poor."[5]

Theater architects also sought a middle ground between decadence and shabbiness. Between 1908 and 1914, proprietors saw that ladies and gentlemen would come to their establishments if movie houses mirrored the designs fashionable for public buildings at the time. Traditionally, this had required classical forms from Greece and Rome. Democrats equated the balance, clarity, and angularity of these styles with the order so necessary for a self-governing polity. During the Progressive era, the classical designs advocated by the Founding Fathers, combined with their French and Italian derivatives, infused a great architectural revival. Designers for the Chicago World's Fair as well as the City Beautiful movement all contributed to a proliferation of these motifs. When this was applied to the early movie theaters, at times it became a hodgepodge. But the Gothic, Romanesque, and romantic genres were usually framed by the Doric, Ionic, or Corinthian pillars associated with classicism and reason. While this suggested that movies too were in line with the spirit of reform, it also reflected continuity with historical progress. Upon entering, the patron encountered an atmosphere that made no distinction between public and private values.[6] Like libraries, state houses, and public buildings, the movie house would educate as it entertained.

A major director like Griffith considered these theaters ideal frames for his photoplays. In sober contrast to the ornate feudal styles popular among the very wealthy of New York and other large cities such as San Francisco and Chicago, classical architecture symbolized the moral middle. It also stood out with grandiose pretention against "low-life" structures housing saloons and penny arcades. Both of these high and low cultural styles reflected the values of a feudalistic, European tradition; but Griffith saw that Doric or Ionic styles remained true to "American sentiment and setting." In contrast to Gothic romanticism, classicism fit a public-spirited citizenry, radiating the designs of the early Americans "who drew their spirit from the Greeks and Romans" who "lived their lives with the same severity." Presumably, these theaters would inspire the self-discipline of the founding fathers, stoic men like Washington, Jefferson, Lee, and Patrick Henry. With such places complementing the democratic spirit of Griffith's own work, he explained that "if I had a son I would let him see pictures as he liked, because I believe they would keep his character along the most rigid lines of conduct. No one need fear it will deviate from the Puritan plane."[7]

Classicism also fused the goals of the early film makers to those of the exhibitors. The trade journals in 1910 began calling for better films and more luxurious theaters in which to exhibit them. On the outside of such theaters as The Empress in Owensburg, Kentucky, The Superba in Grand Rapids, Michigan, The Star in Cherry Valley, New York, and The Elite in Carthage, Missouri, Grecian pillars graced the façades, and patriotic symbols and flags adorned the marquees. Inside one might find the Statue of Liberty or American Eagles. Soon each had orchestras, a far cry from the pianos, organs, or even silence that accompanied the nickelodeons. Now operators hired professional musicians; and film makers such as Griffith synchronized their productions with specific pieces. The ride of the Klan in *The Birth of a Nation*, for example, followed the crescendo of Wagner's "The Ride of the Valkyries." Adding to the prestige value of classical music, the better theaters also featured conductors advertised as having studied with European maestros. Patriotic music such as "The Star Spangled Banner," "Yankee Doodle," "Dixie," and "My Country 'Tis of Thee" commonly heralded the openings of new theaters or special films in the period before the War. When these refined orchestras played jazz or ragtime, the honky-tonk quality associated with urban vice evaporated.[8]

Best of all, these refinements were offered on an egalitarian basis. In contrast to the playhouses of the nineteenth century, all peoples mingled at the movies. Even when theaters moved into wealthier neighborhoods, the seating arrangements still were not sharply differentiated by rank. Although loges were slightly more expensive and the balconies still reserved for blacks, even the most expensive seats were not beyond the reach of patrons of modest means. In 1913, when it cost from 40¢ to $1.40 to see stage drama, movie admissions averaged a mere 7¢. There were two prices for cinema tickets, ranging from five to fifteen cents; but people of modest incomes could afford both. While this openness seemed dangerous in the store fronts, owners of refined movie houses encouraged a family crowd, safe even for unchaperoned females. During intermission, the screen often showed a picture of a startled woman being harassed by a strange man, with the caption, "If annoyed, tell the management." In addition, proprietors provided "kindergardens" where children would be supervised during the picture. All this contributed to a sense of democratic morality. In 1913, one critic commented on the modern film house, which unlike the uptown stage theater had "emancipated the gallery" and created the "great audience" which was "none other than the people without distinction of class."[9]

One of the most successful theater owners of New York City, William Fox, perceived that this required merging low life with high life. Like much of the early audience, Fox was a Jewish immigrant from Eastern Europe. At first he worked as a garment cutter and "sponger" in Manhattan's Lower East Side. Soon this skilled entrepreneur realized that those with a nickel or dime to pay for a show "outnumbered those willing to pay a dollar by a hundred to one." Beginning with nickelodeons, he graduated to store fronts and then luxury houses of classical design. Fox recalled that "the motion picture when it started did not appeal to the native born who had their own forms of recreation . . . its appeal was to foreigners who did not understand our tongue." But when vice crusaders cleaned up the movies, Fox turned New York's notorious Haymarket Saloon—the most famous pub in the vice district—into a white, Grecian-styled movie house. In this symbolic gesture, the up-and-coming theater magnate captured the aura of popular mingling and brought it into a proper atmosphere. As he wrote in 1912,

Movies breathe the spirit in which the country was founded, freedom and equality. In the motion picture theaters there are no separations of classes. Everyone enters the same way. There is no side door thrust upon those who sit in the less expensive seats. There is always something abhorrent in different entrances to theaters . . . in the movies the rich rub elbows with the poor and that's the way it should be. The motion picture is a distinctly American institution.[10]

A clear testimony to the power of this appeal came in 1913 when *Harper's* magazine asked Olivia Harriet Dunbar to go among the "riotous joy of the multitude" and describe the "lure of the films." While the editors of a prestigious magazine may have questioned the propriety of sending a woman to see the hurly-burly of the movies, they soon discovered that Dunbar actually liked the chaos. Patrons, she observed, flowed in and out of the theaters without paying any attention to formality. Once seated in front of the screen, they seemed to leave their status concerns and social roles behind. Inside the darkened room, the diverse audience was part of one crowd sitting passively "amid the strange turbulence of a nightmare." The half-slumbering viewers were drawn into one "oddly literal dream" after another. In a society noted for energy and order, these theaters seemed to "offer thousands of cases of disproof of all that has been fallaciously said regarding the restless energy of the American." Crowds came and went, films danced on the screen, yet through it all, there was protection for "endangered girlhood" and a refined atmosphere, evoking "emotions in conformity with the orthodox code."[11]

Gradually, theater managers realized that movie patrons wanted more than a perpetuation of civic proprieties; they wanted a release from daily concerns as well. In this, fans appropriately looked to the movies for a new and glamorous facet of urban culture: nightlife. Perhaps the best example of this after 1910 was New York City's Broadway. As the largest thoroughfare of mid-Manhattan, it had long brought together the upper middle-class from the east side and the immigrants from the west. In the twentieth century, this common meeting ground was complemented by perhaps one of the most unique developments of the period, the ability of electricity to turn the night into day. Even though gaslight had been available earlier, the brilliance of electricity was magical. Now it was possible for groups to escape the cares of the day on the "Great White Way" at night. Advertisers lit up the evening darkness with huge billboards; and ambitious theater managers capitalized on this electrifying atmosphere by using multicolored bulbs on their mar-

quees. A reporter for *The Atlantic Monthly* described the scene in
1910: "When I walk down Broadway, I want to shout for joy it is
so beautiful." Charles Chaplin also appreciated the magnificence of
Broadway. Seeing it for the first time as a young immigrant in
1912, he recalled that "it began to light up with myriad colored
lights and electric bulbs that sparkled like an electric jewel. And in
the warm night, my attitude changed and the meaning of America
became clear to me: the tall skyscrapers, the brilliant gay lights, the
thrilling display of advertisements stirred me with a sense of hope
and adventure." [12]

Realizing this appeal, managers started consciously to identify
moviegoing with the atmosphere of nightlife. The dancing marquee
lights foreshadowed the medium itself. Seated in a darkened room,
the audience participated in an experience that was, in an often
quoted phrase, "hypnotic." While a legitimate theater divided the
story with a rising and falling curtain, the film continued without
break from beginning to end. Instead of actors and actresses performing on an artificial stage, events on film took place in real surroundings. The director "brought the players right into your lap,
not the least flicker of emotion was lost." Magnified so many times
larger than life, the star seemed to have unusual qualities of emotional power. The viewer entering the theater, consequently, expected to *feel*, as well as see, the star's charisma. As *Reel Life* explained this vicarious thrill, "To have world famous celebrities
brought to your very door, to meet people of great renown face to
face, to be able to observe their little everyday mannerisms and
become really acquainted with them on the motion picture screen,
is of absorbing interest to everyone." [13]

After 1914, theater owners were more conscious of infusing their
movie houses with these same emotional and personal qualities. [14]
This appeared most symbolically in the slow decline of theaters
built with classical design, which had been linked to the rational
concerns of daytime. As the popularity of film makers such as Griffith gave way to the rebellious quest for newness of Pickford and
Fairbanks, owners started to integrate more elaborate foreign
motifs into their buildings. Commenting on the decline of classic
balanced forms, one theater architect wrote, "It is difficult to reconcile gaiety of architectural expression with the style of ancient
Greece." In other words, no longer could an owner simply imitate

the pragmatic, rational look of public buildings. New theaters had to radiate unique exotic qualities capable of standing out in sharp juxtaposition from the surrounding businesses. As one builder explained, "An exterior design in which the curves of graceful arches predominate provides a pleasing contrast to the cold, straightforward lines of the usual service buildings."[15]

One way to heighten the appeal of night time play was to draw on designs of northern Europe, and make the theater a magnificent palace that emulated the hotels, restaurants, and estates of the very rich. Although hotel proprietors of the nineteenth century had utilized this concept to attract settlers to boom towns, or to highlight the splendor of their cities, the quest for magnificence found its greatest model in the innovations pioneered by John Jacob Astor III's son, who built the Waldorf Astoria in New York. This glittering hotel graced the society pages of newspapers in the eighties and nineties, showing urban readers the life of those who had money. Corridors and dining rooms adorned with marble, mahogany, and mirrors gave rich men an opportunity to show off their women laden with fine clothes and jewels. Yet there was no doubt that the wealthy had exclusive entry rights to this prohibitively expensive Renaissance playground. Here and in other French and Italian-styled edifices up and down Fifth Avenue, the industrial titans and their families could "lead an expensive, gregarious life as publicly as possible."[16]

One of the great innovations of theater owners was to bring "big rich" opulence within the reach of millions of urbanites. Precisely at the time when Broadway players were entering the movies, perceptive proprietors were converting luxurious playhouses into cinemas. It was obvious that nothing brought people downtown like a first-run house which emulated the domains of the wealthy uptown. Indeed, the idea was to make aristocratic splendor a modern necessity. The head of New York's largest theater chain, Marcus Loew, articulated this philosophy: "The gorgeous theater is a luxury and it is easy to become accustomed to luxury and hard to give it up once you have tasted it." Given this expanding demand, it was easy to raise prices, for managers knew that the middle-class audience would pay for prestige, as long as it was not prohibitive. "If the patrons don't like it," wrote Carl Laemmle as he raised his entry fees, "tell them that's the way they do it in Europe." In other

*[margin note: if so expensive how mass.]*

*[margin note: Coney Island]*

words, the lavish, expensive environment increased the allure of the movies. It may have been as important as the film itself.[17]

As the movie house drew on extravagant styles, it went even one step further in capturing the appeal of mass culture: it signaled a release from everyday inhibitions, tapping the quest for post-Victorian freedom. In this transformation, motifs became more "barbaric" or "primitive." At first, managers tried to capture the ambiance of the film by filling the theater with artifacts from the movie's era. Pickford's *Ali Baba and the Forty Thieves*, for example, might be shown in an auditorium laden with Arabian decor. Soon the entire edifice would exude this romance. The exoticism of ancient lands, the Far and Near East, American Indians, India, Latin America, or the "Dark Ages" began inspiring downtown houses in the late teens. Undulating spires, curving pillars, and floating or towering ceilings were a far cry from classical balance and proportion. Another device for accomplishing a similar effect was to duplicate nature inside of the auditorium. In these "atmospherics," explained one designer, the idea was to create the Italian countryside with murals, piazzas, and gardens, complete with artificial shrubbery and domes painted like the sky. In one of the first theaters to employ these devices, the Riviera in Chicago, the interior duplicated the Mediterranean. Here the viewer could feel free from the limits of time and space, similar to the celluloid itself. "With a little architectural hocus-pocus," wrote Lewis Mumford of these theaters, "we transport ourselves to another age, another climate, another historical regime, and best of all to another system of aesthetics."[18]

Everything in the theater palace heightened the break from the "machine-like world." Entering the lobby, patrons beheld a "world of nations," filled with fine furnishings, tapestries, statues, and rugs from the four corners of the globe. Mirrors covering entire walls let the fans see themselves amid this luxury. Descending the sumptuous staircases in the huge lobby, patrons entered like announced guests at a grand ball. As the stars appeared amid luxury on the screen, the viewers saw their own images framed in elegance in the carefully angled mirrors in the halls. Even one's private moments were graced with the trappings of wealth, for the gilt and tile ladened restrooms were equally lavish. Ladies could adorn themselves under lights that complimented their complexions, so they might resemble their sisters on the screen. Inside the auditorium itself, proprietors utilized a "science" of colored lighting to set the mood: red for Latin passion, pastels for Scandinavian idealism. Fans blowing over ice to "banish the summer heat" further closed out the discomforts of the real world.[19]

Above all, the lavish theater had to be a personalized place where the fan felt unique and important. One of the most successful theater owners, A. J. Balaban, realized how crucial it was to provide a contrast to the anonymity of the city. In 1905 Balaban left his job as a factory laborer and entered the entertainment business. After vice crusades closed his dance hall, where wives and single women often fraternized with foreign males, Balaban opened a movie house approved by the reformers. Soon he became the most successful theater owner in Chicago, and standardized his techniques for the hundreds of first-run cinemas owned by Paramount Pictures in the twenties. First he taught employees how to behave. As extensions of the proprietor, they had to greet patrons at the door. Uniformed ushers served as the palace guard for the democratic nobles. Each young man "picked for educational and home discipline" greeted the customer with a smile and a respectful "Ma'am" or "Sir." He controlled the flow of the crowd, and escorted ladies and gentlemen to their seats. Lights on the side aisles that allowed the ushers to evict disorderly elements contributed to this sense of safety.[20]

Most important, Balaban's ushers had to be young and friendly. This was necessary because, for all its appeal, there was a slightly uncomfortable aura of luxury and status surrounding the theaters. In America, this look of aristocratic splendor had been reserved for the industrial titans or mercantile elites, groups disdained by much of the populace. Since the theaters were indeed filled with "fine furnishings" and "fountains fit for mansions and kings," Balaban warned that ushers had to soften the sense of pretension and power that went with this atmosphere. So the youthful ushers were instructed to act without condescension, and to treat all customers as friends as well as ladies and gentlemen, equal to anyone in the outside world. Smiles and cordiality presumably would dissolve any connotations of snobbishness; and the youthfulness promised that moviegoing would be relaxing, free of the power relations and corruptions of the everyday world. The well-stroked patron by this time felt like "somebody," and was now ready for some good, clean fun.[21]

Typical of this ethic were the theaters run by Samuel Lionel Rothafel, the future "Roxy." His establishments clearly showed how the styles of the rich mansions and cabarets were trickling down the social order. Rothafel knew that in an atmosphere of luxury it was necessary to dissolve the upper-class pretension. To stimulate wide participation, the public had to know it was "their theater." At the Regent in 1915, Rothafel first applied the formula he would later take into more elaborate New York theaters like the Capitol and the Roxy. Built near Columbia University, a solidly middle-class area, the Regent was noted for its French Renaissance decor, spread over an elaborate, brightly lit façade. The auditorium included colored lights, a flowing fountain, an elaborate orchestra, and aristocratic furnishings, with "not an ounce of dust." Each patron was made "to feel wanted" by the usher. In his competent hands, the customer was freed from the responsibilities and cares of the day. This formula was duplicated across the country in "Million Dollar" cinemas. As one insightful observer noted, "They offered a gilded mansion for the weekly invasion of those who lived in stuffy apartments, a gorgeous canopy to spread over a cramped and limited life, a firmament for cliff dwellers, a place where even the most menial can stalk about with the vague feeling for the moment that we have taken hold of romance."[22]

Contributing to the illusion of status was the movie premiere. Long a practice among the elite, the premiere of an opening play provided the opportunity for wealthy and famous people to promenade in public. This idea was brought to the movies almost without alteration starting about 1913. At first trade journals argued that by getting the local leaders to attend a film, they could gain legitimacy for moviegoing itself. Gradually, however, it became more than this. True to their growing conception of themselves as democratic rulers, the Carnegies, the Lodges, Roosevelts, Vanderbilts, and other members of the Four Hundred accepted invitations to opening nights. In 1914, Mrs. Vanderbilt even wrote a letter of commendation to Harry Aitken of Triangle Company, complimenting him on his fine theater and the patriotism in his films. Aitken advertised throughout the countryside other big names who had commended his movie, gathering even wider interest. When his

In this San Francisco nickelodeon of 1898 little tempts the customer except Edison's intriguing kinetoscope. (Museum of Modern Art/Film Stills Archive)

A storefront theater in 1912 attracts an immigrant audience, in this case Eastern European Jews of New York's Lower East Side. (Culver Pictures)

A 1913 theater draws a more affluent clientele with a potpourri of classical façade, Moorish trappings, and printed assurances to "refined" customers. (Museum of Modern Art/Film Stills Archive)

---

*Top:* At intermission, screens assured viewers that the management would not tolerate advances to unchaperoned women. (Museum of Modern Art/Film Stills Archive)

*Bottom:* At New York's Paramount Theater in 1928, the patron is king. An army of well-groomed, uniformed ushers stand at attention in the lavish lobby. (Culver Pictures)

Exoticism contrasts sharply with everyday reality at Grauman's Chinese Theater in 1929, where imprints of the modern saints cover the patio. (Museum of Modern Art/Film Stills Archive)

Grauman's interior wraps the customer in the romance of the screen. Fans sit in surroundings as exotic as the world of the stars. (Museum of Modern Art/Film Stills Archive)

productions opened to the public the day following the premiere, fans thronged to partake of what the big rich had sampled, for only fifteen or twenty cents. One shrewd observer recognized how this phenomenon tapped the desire for vicarious status:

> Up to the capacities of our tastes and incomes, the rest of us followed in the footsteps of our financial overlords; for whenever we can break from our anonymous cubicles, our standardized offices, our undifferentiated streets, we abandon ourselves to Pure Romance.[23]

By the 1920s, the stars themselves were the notables attending premieres at even more extravagant theaters like the Roxy and Radio City Music Hall in New York. Perhaps the most elaborate example of stardom fused to opulence was Sid Grauman's Chinese Theater in Los Angeles. Grauman, the son of an immigrant vaudeville manager, built the Chinese in 1927, modeled on a Mandarin palace from a time when the "world was young." In a grand synthesis, this Jewish entrepreneur borrowed a tradition from European Catholics and placed it in an Oriental setting in the middle of Hollywood: it was Grauman's brainchild to invite celebrities of the industry to place their hands and feet in the wet cement of the theater's patio. Significantly, Pickford and Fairbanks were the first players to be so honored. This served a dual purpose. As the cement dried, leaving an indelible print, it gave the stars a sense of immortality. But it also allowed the patrons to measure their own features against these relics of their saints. After touching the sacred indentations, the viewers entered a mammoth auditorium where they saw these same idols moving before their very eyes. Grauman made certain that everything in the theater provided an "atmosphere in which the patron actually lived with the characters on the screen."[24]

Grauman's Chinese culminated a trend that had penetrated northern urban centers for two decades. Beneath the evolution of the theater palace from 1908 to 1929 lay one key development: from a pariah nickelodeon, the motion picture had become a major urban institution for the middle class. And the sheer number and size of movie houses reflected the overwhelming popularity of the mature movie industry. In New York City, ninety-seven nickelodeons held licenses in 1900. All observers agreed that they were located either in the cheap business sections or in the poorer amusement centers, and usually frequented by men. Nine years later there were 400, including several "store fronts" which were hastily converted shops showing "flickers" on a screen. Seating capacity was limited to 400. By 1912, movies could show to a 1,000-plus audience, and more luxurious, classically designed theaters began to spread up and down main thoroughfares, catering to men and women of all classes.[25] Over the next fifteen years, the number of cinemas grew to over eight hundred, averaging 1,200 seats each, or one for every six people in the entire metropolis. In other words, while the population of New York doubled between 1910 and 1930, the capacity of movie theaters increased more than eight times. Such growth in less than two decades testifies to the enormous appeal of the movies, and to the advent of a truly new public arena with phenomenal popularity.[26]

Furthermore, this expansion reflected the creation of America's first *mass* amusement—but it was clearly geared toward middle-class aspirations. A number of studies over time verify this pattern. As we have seen, early examinations found that the 1908 patrons were workers; by 1912 25 percent of the audience was clerical and 5 percent was business class of both sexes.[27] Detailed examinations from the twenties and forties show that this expansion continued. Polling the audience, investigators found that high school and college graduates went most often, although they comprised only one fourth of the population in 1920. Likewise, people with higher incomes went more often than workers or farmers; and those under thirty-five comprised the bulk of the audience. Men and women attended in equal numbers; but females were the ones who read the fan magazines, wrote letters to their idols, and knew the film plots by heart. In essence, the core of the new audience was made up of precisely those people who would have not appeared in the neighborhood of a nickelodeon.[28]

It was also no accident that with theaters glorifying mass consumption, moviegoing was unquestionably an urban phenomenon. The theaters were overwhelmingly situated in cities, at a time when half the nation's population lived in rural areas. There were 28,000 theaters in 1928; and over half of them were in the industrial centers of New York, Illinois, Pennsylvania, Ohio, and California. The major cities in these states contained most of the large luxury cinemas. San Francisco, New York, Chicago, and Los

Angeles each had from five to eight hundred theaters, averaging over 1,000 seats each, or one for every five to seven people. These movie houses stayed open seven days a week, twelve hours a day, while those in the small towns were only open on weekends. In contrast to a place like New York, whose 800 theaters could contain one sixth of the city's residents, the Southern city of Birmingham, Alabama, had only thirty-one theaters. Although it had a much smaller population, the combined capacity of its movie houses was only one seat for every thirty-two people in the city. All in all, this "mass" media was geared to a Northern and West Coast urban market—precisely where the work week was shortest and the per capita income largest.[29]

The phenomenal popularity of the movies during these years was also unique to the United States. Although other countries had films, the United States was clearly the cinema capital. The audience was between twenty and thirty million weekly; and movies absorbed the largest portion of the average American's recreation budget in the 1920s. During the decade, the number of theaters in the United States grew from 21,000 to 28,000. By comparison, in Germany they went from 2,826 to 5,000; and in France from 1,500 to 3,900. European houses were probably smaller as well. Yet the combined populations of these two countries equalled that of the United States. Moreover, this country had more movie theaters than all of Europe. Part of the explanation lies in economics. America was the most industrialized and wealthy country, particularly after the War had devastated the economies of Europe. Also, American affluence was probably more widespread, making it possible for more people to spend their excess funds at the movies.[30]

Beyond this economic explanation lies a deeper cultural cause. Most western European nations industrialized within a more aristocratic, hierarchical tradition. Consequently, the movies did not become identified with the perpetuation of egalitarianism. Nor were they part of a moral revolution that was eroding Victorian behavioral codes. In twentieth-century America, however, movies and mass culture were key elements in the transition from nineteenth-century values of strict behavior toward greater moral experimentation. As the economy consolidated, the leisure arena preserved a sense of freedom and mobility. Both on the screen and in the theater, moviegoers tasted the life of the rich as it was brought within reach of the masses, breaking down the class divisions of the past. Here was a revitalized frontier of freedom, where Americans might sanction formerly forbidden pleasures through democratized consumption. One theater chain manager noted why the luxury movie house could perpetuate the spirit of the old West in a new age. Using an apt metaphor, he wrote,

> Our movie houses have collected the most precious rugs, fixtures and treasures that money can produce. No kings or emperors ever wandered through a more lavish environment. In a sense they are social "safety valves" in that the public can partake of the same environment of the rich and use them to the same extent.[31]

Yet the creation of the lavish theaters suggested that Americans were divided on the meaning of the new life. The "cathedrals" of motion pictures seemed to offer secular salvation; the classless seating and sexual mingling of both sexes in a former lower-class arena suggested a break from formality. After 1914, this break was intensified as classicism gave way to architectural styles that mixed foreign, high and low culture together. Managers heightened the effect of an escape from time and hierarchy of the outside world through the friendly ushers, the nightlife, and the premiere. Here was a place where people could presumably mingle on equal terms with the top people in society. Nevertheless, the ambivalence in this release from restraint required that it be surrounded with all the symbols of high culture which gave status. In order to afford this style of leisure, both sexes would have to pursue success even more diligently. While the "cathedral" of the motion picture glorified consumption and play, it thus kept alive very traditional values. But this experience did not end when the patrons exited. They could see that the message of the movie and its palace was alive and well in the last great component of the motion picture universe: Hollywood.

*Chapter Seven*

# THE NEW FRONTIER: "HOLLYWOOD," 1914–1920

All their lives they had slaved at some kind of dull, heavy
labor, behind desks and counters, in the fields and at tedious
machines of all sorts, saving their pennies and dreaming of the
leisure that would be theirs when they had enough. Finally,
the day came . . . where else should they go, but to California, the land of sunshine and oranges.

NATHANAEL WEST
*Day of the Locust*, 1939[1]

No matter how exaggerated his account may have been, Nathanael
West caught the spirit of a modern vision, unique to America. Fans
in the sumptuous movie house did not merely sit in an oasis of luxury in a barren land. Rather, it was possible to take much of the
celluloid experience home with them. Yet they needed experts to
show them how. In response to that need, the motion picture industry began to build a film capital on the West Coast. Other countries also centralized studios; but in America the production site
was surrounded by a community where the stars really lived the
happy endings, in full view of the nation. Here moviedom became
much more than something seen on the screen, or touched in the
theater. At a time when the birth of a modern family and consumption ideals might have remained just a cinematic fantasy, Hollywood showed how it could be achieved in real life. Out in California, stars participated in an exciting existence, free from the
former confinements of work and Victorianism. With this leisure
utopia before the viewer's eyes, they might learn how to regenerate
the frontier in new ways for the twentieth century.

To grasp the significance of this West Coast creation, we have to
first confront earlier explanations of why the movie industry came

to Southern California. A generation of film scholars have offered two basic reasons.[2] One was that the climate was ideal for film making. In this region, Mediterranean balmy weather made it possible to film outdoors all year round, without the hindrance of snow or rain. Moreover, the area included deserts, mountains, and seashore, all near by. The second argument claims that, to escape Edison's trust, independents moved to the far end of the continent where they could flee quickly into Mexico if confronted with court subpoenas or demands for their pirated cameras.

Yet on examination, neither of these factors can explain the move. Film makers had survived Eastern weather for over twenty years, going to Florida, the Caribbean, or other winter filming locations including California, if sunny weather was required. In 1913, there were twenty film companies in New York, Philadelphia, and Chicago, and only four on the West Coast. Two of these were in California, but only one was in Los Angeles. On top of that, if proximity to Mexico had been a decisive factor in the patent war, independents would have gone to San Diego, two hundred miles closer to the border. But none did. There was also a violent and bloody revolution in Mexico at the time, which would have discouraged eager film makers. In fact, the first permanent studios in Los Angeles were established by solid members of the trust. More recent scholars offer an alternative to these views by pointing out that economic factors pushed the industry westward.[3] Though this is certainly part of the reason, it still does not explain why it took so long for moviemakers to see their interests in moving from east to west. No, something else was happening in Los Angeles besides escaping winters, trusts, and high costs.

To fathom this problem, we must realize that Hollywood emerged relatively late—over twenty years after Edison invented the camera, and over a decade and a half after the movies acquired a mass market. In retrospect, it is also clear that the West Coast production site would become more than merely a place to make films. Fan magazines, newspapers, and movies themselves would spotlight the comings and goings of movie stars—a life-style that was dramatically different from that of the nineteenth or even early twentieth century. Shortly before there was a Hollywood, this imagery had just begun to be projected on the nation's screens, catering to the tastes of the newly found middle-class audience adjusting

to the corporate order and a new morality. The new code generated the promise that if immigrants, as well as those rebelling from
Victorianism, had money and white skin, the consumer ideal
would be available to them. Another related phenomenon was the ✓
audience's demand to see this cultural mixing made real. It was not
enough to see it on the screen, or to touch it in the movie house.
Stars had to make the happy ending an extension of their own
lives, for fans had to see that their idols could make it a reality.
Was it not possible, then, that profits could be enhanced by creating a modern utopia where the dream could come off the screen
and into real life?

It took a new breed of producers to pull all of this together. In
their business skills, backgrounds and aspirations, they were ideal
generators of the move west, for that involved a total transformation of themes, stars, and theaters after 1914. Unlike the American
Protestants who first made films, these men began as small proprietors, and entered the business not as inventors, film makers, or
even entertainers. Rather, they were theater owners from immigrant backgrounds. A few came from Germany, most from eastern Europe, but virtually all were Jews who entered the country as
part of the late nineteenth-century wave of immigration. They
proceeded to set up nickelodeons in their own neighborhoods, and
went on to build store fronts and luxury theaters in better neighborhoods as the market expanded. By 1913, several had become so
aware of the new desires of the viewers, as well as the opportunities available in this marginal industry, that they entered production themselves, and moved to Los Angeles. In the process, they
expanded and consolidated casting, filming, and exhibiting until by
1920 they held the reins of the "Big Eight" companies, and virtually monopolized the market.[4] (See Tables II, IIIa, and IIIb.)

Why were the Jews able to realize fully the potential in the third
stage of the industry's growth, from 1914 to 1920? In the first
place, these recent immigrants brought cultural baggage to
America that gave them several advantages, in the film industry as
well as in the process of upward mobility. A number of scholars
have shown how this group experienced more movement up the
social ladder than any of their fellow immigrants. The film moguls
participated in this ethnic success story, and benefited from the
traditions and circumstances that fed into it. Paradoxically, it was

their outsider status in Europe that gave rise to many of these advantages. Discriminatory policies in Russia and other countries had
made land ownership difficult, and encouraged these outsiders to
enter commercial trades. For hundreds of years, they lived in
towns and cities of the Pale or eastern European ghettos, serving as
small merchants or craftsmen for a rural hinterland. When industrialization spread from western to eastern Europe in the late nineteenth century, Jews were affected in two ways. It disrupted their
status as small property owners and stimulated violent pogroms.
Acutely aware of the power arrayed against them, and accustomed
to gauging it for centuries, many immigrated to America. And
unlike Italians, Greeks, or other Southern Europeans, they came in
family groups and did not look back nostalgically to a homeland.
While others went back and forth, the Jews settled permanently
with their kin in American cities. To facilitate matters, their experiences as shopkeepers and skilled workers gave them trades that
could be utilized in a rapidly urbanizing country. At a time when

most other immigrants, and Americans for that matter, came from
rural backgrounds, the Jews as literate urban entrepreneurs had a
great advantage. They quickly compensated for their relative lack
of capital and began to climb the economic ladder.[5]

For the Jews who entered the movies, there was another element
in their experience that contributed to their success. Because they
had been outsiders, they were conditioned to seize new commercial
opportunities that were not already monopolized by people of the
host culture who might discriminate against them. In eastern and
central Europe the landless Jews functioned as tradesmen on the
margins of an agrarian society. In addition, since they were occasionally subject to removal, often forced to leave their homes at a
moment's notice, many found it in their interests to have occupations not tied to land or solid property. European Jews thus became skilled at meeting the secondary or consumption desires of
the surrounding group, and finding opportunities on the fringes of
society. In America's expanding economy, particularly in eastern
cities like New York, these immigrants used their former skills to
succeed in ready-made clothing, entertainment, and other entrepreneurial endeavors. Little wonder that moguls like Adolph Zukor
started by selling furs, Samuel Goldwyn made gloves, Louis B.
Mayer owned a burlesque house, and Carl Laemmle often com-

pared selling movies with his experiences selling clothes. The garment trades in particular required a sensitivity to current styles.
Critically important in all these skills was the ability to suspend
one's own tastes and calculate the desires of others. These movie
executives cultivated this art, giving them an advantage in a
marginal industry which appealed to consumer styles. Since film
was a product geared to subjective rather than material needs, the
Jews moved into the field with ease. To sharpen his perceptions,
Samuel Goldwyn would sit in the front of the audience with his
back to the screen, watching the viewers' reactions to the celluloid
images. He explained the methods this way:

> If the audience don't like a picture, they have a good reason. The
> public is never wrong. I don't go for all this thing that when I have a
> failure, it is because the audience doesn't have the taste or education,
> or isn't sensitive enough. The public pays the money. It wants to be
> entertained. That's all I know.[6]

Using skills like these, the moguls gained spectacular success in
the movies. But their rise was not merely the realization of American individualism. Rather, these leaders combined a strong sense of
commercial opportunity with the realization that, as in the shtetl,
they could only make it if they cooperated. Abraham Bisno, an
organizer of garmet unions in New York and Chicago, articulated
this tendency. In the old country, he argued, the aristocracy lived
for the past, the peasants for the present, and the Jews for future
opportunities. That spirit carried in the new world as well. Nicholas Schenck, who became head of United Artists, admitted,
"Yes, I've done all right for an immigrant boy, it could only happen in this country . . . unfortunately it is not always greatness
that takes a man to the top. It is a gambling spirit. I used every bit
of my ability at dangerous times, while other men slowed down at
the curves." Yet linked to this risk-taking drive was a strong sense
of group cohesion. Even the reckless Schenck never abandoned his
ethnic or family ties: he and his brother Joseph often worked
together. Following the same pattern, Sam and Jack Warner were
brothers and partners; Jesse Lasky and Samuel Goldwyn, Sam
Katz and A. J. Balaban were brothers-in-law and partners, and
Carl Laemmle became famous for what was probably typical, hiring scores of relatives to work in his Universal Studio.[7]

Each of these producers made films and statements filled with patriotism. Obviously this was good for business. But it also helps explain their rise, for America appeared to offer the full flowering of aspirations that were often thwarted in the old country. Perhaps the strongest impetus flowed from secularization and enlightenment. Late in the nineteenth century, a number of European countries granted civil rights to Jews, providing the first step toward full participation in the host culture. When emancipation merged with the deep millennial traditions within Judaism, the result was a cultural renaissance that yielded a tremendous potential to change both Jewish life and the wider world. Some Jews responded to this promise through movements like Hassidism or reinvigorated orthodoxy. Other theological innovations involved a move towards liberal and conservative brands of the faith. Still others reached out for the secular world. In artistic circles, a flowering of rich poetry and literature occurred in Yiddish as well as the host cultures' tongues. Jews who saw a sharp contradiction between poverty and pogroms, and the promise of a new life, became Zionists, radicals, or enlightenment thinkers, in the new world as well as the old.

In America, all these tendencies would flourish, for those who wanted an individualized secular millennium might see the promised land. Discrimination existed, but unlike Europe there were no strong anti-Semitic politics; and a separation of church and state encouraged Jews to enter the wider society. In addition, the religious structure of Judaism contributed to this process, for those who wished to make the choice. As one contemporary perceived, it was easier for these European pariahs to tap this opportunity than Catholic immigrants, accustomed to a hierarchical church and state, for "in its ecclesiastical institutions, no religion is more democratic than the Jews'. Among them there is no authority comparable to the Roman Catholic Pope, no denominational supervision, no ordained clergy. Any ten Jews can organize a synagogue or minyan, choose their own members and employ a rabbi." A decentralized structure also fostered assimilation into the expanding economy. Many had shed their Yiddish dialect, their distinctive clothes, and even their names in the process of Americanization and upward mobility. Every movie mogul went through at least part of this process. Some married Gentile women, and retained their heritage not through orthodoxy, but through liberal synagogues or charity organizations. Each might have agreed at one time or another with the highly assimilated hero of Abraham Cahan's brilliant novel, *The Rise of David Levinsky,* who saw that in the new country, provided one had the money, public equality at least appeared possible. Entering a dining car on a train where he joined a group of American businessmen, David remarked,

> But I was aware that it was "aristocratic" American food, that I was in the company of well dressed American gentiles, eating and conversing with them, a nobleman among noblemen. I throbbed with love for America.[8]

Optimism, however, only partially explains why Jews were so successful in the entertainment industry. Movies, after all, were not just another consumer product. They exemplified not just fun but the way the class order was changing. To seize this opportunity, the moguls combined business with their inherited traditions of expressiveness. In contrast to the dominant elements of nineteenth-century American culture, which were permeated with a code of self-denial, Jews were accustomed to a life that included a great deal of festivity. There is no question that Jewish tradition emphasizes a strong moral code and condemns hedonistic indulgence. Yet at the same time Yiddish folk culture encouraged celebrations distinctly different from the rituals of the Protestant middle classes, and more in tune with their fellow immigrants. A rich tradition of humor formed a layer to soften the acute awareness of outsider status, and was often used against the dominant group's pretensions and discrimination. Many religious holidays and Sabbath observances included music, singing, dancing, and did not forbid drinking—no small matter in a Victorian society often committed to blue laws and sobriety. Although Jews shared with Americans a taboo against premarital sex and a strong dedication to marital fidelity, women were considered sexual beings, a contrast to the ideals surrounding their Victorian sisters. Moreover, Jewish women of eastern Europe were never put on a pedestal; they functioned in the economy and participated in religious rituals in the home. Finally, Jews did not share the frugality of their Protestant peers. Money was not to be continually poured into business at the expense of enjoyment; rather, it was to provide the means for a life of comfort, even extravagance when it could be afforded.

With this heritage, the Jewish film moguls were prepared to

confront the changing moral values taking hold in the cities. The key to this process was timing. It was not enough that the Jews had skills in consumer trades, and sensitivity to new trends, or that they drew on a festive tradition. These advantages would have meant little fifty years earlier or later. But at the turn of the century, Jewish producers provided the missing link in the development of the motion picture industry. For the urban areas where the immigrants landed were soon to be the hotbeds of the revolution in manners and morals. Shrewd businessmen in the immigrant entertainment zones could see that as white collar men and women incorporated the styles of foreigners and blacks, danced to ragtime, and patronized formerly working-class amusement parks, there was money to be made. As the press and vice reports asked whether this would lead to the disintegration of the home and the disorganization of the community, Jewish entrepreneurs could face this upheaval with optimism. According to the editor of the *Jewish Daily Forward*, the Lower East Side had become

> a place where one descended in quest of esoteric types and local color; as well as for the purposes of philanthropy and uplift work. To spend an evening in some East Side cafe was regarded as something like spending a few hours at the Louvre; so much so that one such cafe, in the depths of East Houston street, was making a fortune by purveying expensive wine dinners to people from uptown who came there ostensibly to see how the "other half lived" but who saw only one another eat and drink in freedom from restraint of manners.[9]

Cultural mixing also suggested the opening up of the class order, and thereby drew on the Jews' millennial hopes in the new world. Formerly, middle-class values emanated from a Victorian heritage which in America was closely linked to a secularized, evangelical spirit. Newcomers from European countries who wanted to move up had a distinct advantage if they were also Anglo Saxon Protestants, for their common background with the host culture provided few restrictions on assimilation. By the same token, Catholic or Eastern and Southern Europeans who wanted to rise had to shed many of their traditions, which the dominant group portrayed as vice-ridden and decadent. Only now, as modern Americans, symbolized by the movie stars, borrowed the dances, styles, and sports associated with immigrants, aspiring foreigners could elevate them-

*(handwritten margin note: "no shedding' rise in staying the same")*

selves without shedding all of their cultural past. In essence, as Anglo Saxon city dwellers became more like their former "inferiors," it facilitated mobility from below. As this unfolded in the early stages of the motion picture industry, it could easily become linked to the utopian potential, the promise of a new America.

In their position as immigrants with bourgeois values, the Jewish film moguls were ideal middle men for realizing a fusion of styles. None of these producers made movies before 1912 and the advent of the vice crusades. Yet as the reformed photoplay brought movies into better neighborhoods after 1914, they confronted the full implications of cultural mixing. It was thus not the American film makers but rather the Jewish theater owners who were able to seize the potential for better markets. (They did this by searching for ways to sanction the group mingling and consumption desires for the middle and working class audiences.) Each mogul first built luxury theaters and formulated the techniques of catering to a new audience. Soon proprietors realized that the allure of luxury, fun, and freedom from everyday restraint was what drew patrons. So they moved into production in order to extend this appeal to the screen. Almost every future mogul perceived that films portraying values different from those of Victorianism would draw bigger audiences. Setting up studios of their own, they began to produce photoplays that would match the appeal of their movie houses.

Surely the future moguls were not the only ones to seize this opportunity; but they had several material advantages which lead to success. Adolph Zukor, the head of Paramount Pictures, exemplified the pattern. Coming to America from Hungary in the late nineteenth century, Zukor turned to his relatives for help in getting started in the clothing and fur business. Financial success came to Zukor along with secularization; discarding strict orthodoxy, distinctive clothing, and kosher food he was very much a part of the assimilation trend. With the spread of nickelodeons in New York City, he opened several small theaters in commercial districts and gradually expanded into luxury houses. Even more importantly, while the early film makers continued in their old ways, Zukor made a major break. Entering production in 1914 with his friends Jesse Lasky and Cecil B. DeMille, he formed Famous Players in Famous Plays. Soon they brought noted Broadway stars into the movies, one of the symbolic events of the era. The New York theater had been geared to the tastes of the wealthy. By bringing players such as Sarah Bernhardt, Dustin Farnum, Douglas Fairbanks, and even Mary Pickford from Broadway, Zukor made the film industry a vehicle for fusing high and low culture. Furthering this trend, Zukor made only photoplays and capitalized on the star as a personality who could synthesize moral experimentation with traditional virtues: significantly, Mary Pickford was his greatest find.[10]

In addition to pereceiving the key psychological needs of the audience, the fact that men like Zukor started as theater owners made it easier for them to get crucial financing in these early years. Ultimately this allowed them to gain control of the industry by merging supply (the stars), production (the studios), and distribution (the key theaters). Initially producers, even after several successful films, had to pay exorbitant interest rates for loans. Bankers still saw the enterprise as new and disreputable, and a film maker without outlets had only his camera and studio to offer as collateral. Financiers' money was thus guaranteed merely on the rights to an individual film. If it failed, they were left with nothing but useless celluloid. Yet when Zukor, as well as other future moguls, went into production, they had the advantage of owning theaters which had value as property, regardless of the films. Confident that his photoplays would yield a profit, in 1913 Zukor approached banks for low-interest loans, offering his buildings and land as security. Nevertheless, several Wall street bankers hedged, and Zukor, as he phrased it, by-passed the "loan sharks." He then turned to ethnic financiers who were more willing to take risks. With the help of A. H. Gianini's Bank of Italy (the future Bank of America), and the German-Jewish firm of Kuhn and Loeb, Zukor could soon boast to Charles Chaplin in 1919,

> Remember it was I who first had the vision! Who swept out your dirty nickelodeons? Who put in your plush seats? It was I who built your great theaters, who raised prices and made it possible for you to get large grosses for your pictures.[11]

Bigger and better theaters and productions also served to edge out competitive film makers. In the years from 1912 to 1920, the future moguls merged mass production to mass distribution for the first time in motion picture history. Between 1910 and 1914, over seventy production companies sold their films on an open market to hundreds of exhibitors. Despite the attempts of the original Protestant producers to monopolize the market through a patent trust, it was virtually impossible to thwart the newcomers, for two reasons. First, a company with money to make modernized photoplays, with well-known players such as Zukor's Mary Pickford and Douglas Fairbanks, William Fox's Theda Bara, or Carl Laemmle's Florence Lawrence, had a distinct advantage. In the long run, only the successful firms could afford the stars' growing salaries and the process of trial and error whereby the producers discovered just what the public wanted to see. As Samuel Goldwyn noted, by 1918 it was possible to give the public a formula geared to Douglas Fairbanks, and then predictable profits followed. This was expensive, for along with paying for high-priced players, producers also poured money into "bigness" and "elaborateness." In 1913, it cost between $1,000 and $10,000 to make a film. By the 1920s it ranged from $100,000 to $500,000.[12] Clearly, only giant firms could compete at this level. As a result, from 60 firms making over 2,000 movies in 1912, the "Big Eight" made 90 percent of the 800 films made yearly in the twenties. Universal, which had alone absorbed fifteen independents as early as 1915, was one of them.[13]

The other side of the coin involved the exhibition of films. Each major film mogul had entered production with a string of theaters. This gave them outlets for first-run films. But more important, these were usually lavish theater palaces which lent prestige value to the films shown inside. As early as 1913, movies released in a downtown house, often with a gala premiere, allowed producers to charge more for their photoplays and admissions to their theaters. Knowing that this increased demand, the largest firms began to build and absorb thousands of downtown luxury houses. Balaban and Katz, owners of Chicago's major theaters, joined Paramount in the mid-twenties; Marcus Loew brought his New York chain into Metro Goldwyn Mayer; by 1920 William Fox was able to borrow enormous sums from Wall Street financiers to build over a thousand bigger and better cathedrals of the motion picture in major cities. Ultimately, every big company with the exception of United Artists held from 500 to 1,000 theaters. Remarking how this followed patterns established in countless other American industries, Marcus Loew explained to a business group in the mid-twenties,

"Chain store methods in the movies are just like what you have in railroads, telephones, and automobiles."[14]

The Big Eight were not even limited to their own theaters. Because they monopolized the big name players and most elaborate productions, they could virtually control independent movie houses as well. In the early period, a single producer had used middle men to distribute his product to thousands of small theater owners. Now a big company could build up prestige for a film through national advertising and openings in sumptuous movie houses, and then sell it directly to the independent exhibitors, with no need for an agent. In order for any proprietor to gain rights to the films of a Pickford, Fairbanks, Chaplin, or other major stars, a producer such as Zukor would insist that he contract for the studio's entire yearly output— a procedure known as "block booking." This meant as many as seventy or eighty films by the 1920s. Nevertheless, the studios presented a convincing argument in favor of this system. The big company built up support for a film through promotions, which comprised half the cost of a production. Obviously, small theater owners could not afford to advertise on this scale. The producer also guaranteed that it would be distributed quickly, before its "timeliness" wore off—usually six months. Prompt delivery of a pre-paid package prevented the bidding wars that had previously lowered profits. Finally, studios altered endings to fit local tastes. If a story had a pessimistic finale for the more sophisticated, cosmopolitan urbanites, it could be changed so as not to offend the sensibilities of audiences in the countryside. In this way, everyone seemed satisfied; predictable profits flowed from "up to the minute" films.[15]

Clearly, the new film moguls had no nostalgia for the old entrepreneurial economy so dear to the independent producers. Rather, they followed the lead of other American firms that combined production, supply, and distribution. Like other major corporations, they too saw that these various parts could best be coordinated under one administrative office, complete with vice presidents and boards of directors. New York City offered a number of advantages for these functions. By the turn of the century, most large national corporations centered their business in New York. There they were close to Wall Street and the banks where they could go for financing. By 1920, the shares of the Big Eight were traded on the stock market and gathered investors including American Tobacco, Du Pont, and the Bank of America. New York was also near the Eastern urban centers, facilitating monitoring of many of the movies' major markets. Big producers had access to the publishing and entertainment capital of the country as well. Here they could gauge mass tastes and purchase popular stories and players for their films. And with the bourgeoning advertising industry nearby on Madison Avenue, national promotion was readily available.[16]

By the late teens, the Motion Picture Producers and Distributors Association had emerged to coordinate the movie industry. The Big Eight hired William Harrison Hays in 1921 to run the Association. Hays would gain fame as the in-house censor. But equally important were his administrative tasks. Before coming to the film industry, he had been a railroad executive and ally of the Progressive Senator Beveridge from Indiana. In 1920 he gained national fame as the chairman of the Republican Party and President Harding's Postmaster General. Reflecting the corporate side of Progressivism, he believed in business and government cooperation, a persuasion that made him an ideal administrator well worth his $100,000 a year salary.[17] From his lavish New York office he lobbied against tariffs on exported American films, and helped make the film industry into an "orderly business thoroughfare." He secured large loans from New York banks, especially the Federal Reserve, enabling his clients to buy more theaters and undercut smaller firms. With the power to arbitrate conflicts over block booking, Hays could deny recalcitrant independents access to films or theaters. Perhaps most important of all, Hays coordinated a unified front against labor unions in the studios, quelling a number of strikes in the late teens and twenties.[18]

Precisely at this time, the movies began to center production in California. While administration and marketing remained in New York, the studios moved out of the Eastern cities into Los Angeles. It was not so much the need for sun, or an escape from the now nearly defunct trust that pushed the Big Eight west. More important was the need to find a complementary locale for the innovations taking place in the film industry after 1914. In terms of costs alone, it paid to move to Los Angeles. This city on the far edge of the continent offered the advantages of a great boom town well into the twentieth century. Unlike the older urban areas of the East, it was still in its early stages of growth. Starting in about 1900, local elites began to transform the sleepy agricultural town from its Spanish origins into a modern American metropolis. Technology helped surmount the difficulties of no natural harbor or adequate source of water. As the population multiplied, Los Angeles leaders built the Owens River Aqueduct and the San Pedro Harbor in 1913. These improvements allowed the city to expand rapidly beyond its old economic base of mercantilism. Yet it remained a region without heavy industry, where boosters could tempt eager businessmen with the promise of new markets, cheap labor, and plentiful land. "Here were 50,000 people," wrote one observer of this new frontier in 1899,

> suddenly gathered together from all parts of the union, in utter igno-
> rance of one another's history. It was a golden opportunity for the
> fakir and the humbug and the man with a past he wished forgotten.[19]

One booster who was quick to tap this potential realized that the movies and the city could gain a great deal from each other. This was Harry Culver, a local politician, airport builder, and land-holder who happened to be head of the state real estate board. He owned a number of huge lots in an area soon to be known as Culver City. As the population of Los Angeles multiplied six fold in two decades, Culver as well as others saw how to make a fortune by bringing film makers west. The formula was simple: movies brought people who then bought more lots. This was not an origi-nal idea, for ever since the nineteenth-century boom towns like Los Angeles had flourished by giving lands to railroads, which then brought settlers.[20] Early in 1913, Culver gave enormous tracts to Triangle Studios, headed by Harry Aitken. But soon Triangle was bought out by Metro Goldwyn Mayer; Louis B. Mayer made this the site of his studio, complete with a mammoth Corinthian gate and imposing façades. These sorts of land deals were attractive to the peculiar kind of industry film making was. It did not matter that Los Angeles was not industrialized, for unlike other manufac-turing, the making of reels of celluloid did not require nearby min-ing, iron mills, or processing plants. Rather, all a film maker needed was a camera, site, and laborers. A finished film could be shipped to the major cities of the country without spoilage, now that an efficient rail system spanned the continent. Samuel Goldwyn summed it up when he explained why he left administration in New York and moved production to Southern California:

> Los Angeles is more efficient for us, more cheap. In Manhattan the movie waits on the community and not the community on the movie. Los Angeles has no other interest save real estate and climate. The climate takes care of itself, and we keep the real estate booming, so Los Angeles gives us all her interests and resources.[21]

Another climate was also conducive to film makers in quest of high profits, and that was the political climate. Before the 1870s, the Spanish and Mexican population had dominated civic affairs. Yet as the great migrations of midwesterners flooded the area, they changed the tenor of the town. In 1910, over 60 percent of the population had come from the Midwest. These settlers brought Progressive reform, and won out easily over their adversaries. In the big cities where the film makers began, Protestants might control professions and businesses, but city hall usually remained in the hands of immigrant machines. In contrast, Anglo Saxons dominated both commerce and civic life in Los Angeles. The local elites were aligned to the major Protestant churches, and the majority of the voters were Republicans dedicated to open opportunity and individualism. Like other Progressives, they believed in assimilating individuals who conformed to the melting pot ideal—such as the Jewish film makers. But they were hostile to group power incarnated in monopoly, political machines, organized vice, and labor unions. In order to further these ends, they passed prohibition and blue laws as well as instituting city-wide nonpartisan elections which served to undercut the strength of the Mexican and working-class wards. Civic administration was also freed from the threat of group manipulation through civil service reform. Instead of patronage, "expertise" determined by objective tests became the hiring criteria for autonomous police or city agencies.[22]

Similar impulses for open opportunity fueled an attack on monopoly and labor power. City reformers mobilized the citizenry against the Southern Pacific Railroad which had dominated City Hall prior to reform. Throughout this battle, Los Angelenos aroused the population by pointing with scorn to San Francisco, where immigrant machines and labor unions dominated the city, inhibiting low costs and business expansion. Local leaders in the City of the Angels waged a militant war against all types of unions as well as Socialist parties. Support for the open-shop town reached an all-time high when the area's largest newspaper's office, the Los Angeles *Times,* was bombed. When local and state anti-trust laws passed, effectively crippling labor and presumably monopoly as well, the Chamber of Commerce and the *Times* boasted that the city had the lowest costs in the nation. With all these inducements, producers hoped to film without harassment, and identify their product with this American bastion. They were not disappointed. Along with cheap land, they found a civic administration that helped break strikes in the studios and protected their interests as well.[23]

Los Angeles was thus an ideal place for the movies to continue on the road to reform. Yet by now the thrust had definitely turned away from the old entrepreneurial side to the corporate wing of Progressivism; for the moguls coming west were consolidating the various parts of the industry. Giving a sense of harmony to this drive, the major firms surrounded themselves with an aura of bipartisan consensus. Democratic and Republican movie moguls added to their credentials by bringing in noted reformers of both parties as executives. In 1920, William McAdoo, former Secretary of the Treasury and Woodrow Wilson's son-in-law, became head of United Artists; Joseph Tumulty, Wilson's personal aide, became chief consul for the Motion Picture Producers and Distributors Association, or the Big Eight; and as we have seen, William Harrison Hays, Republican National Chairman, came into the industry as a chief executive. Furthering this public image, Mary Pickford might visit the White House or entertain Wilson's daughter at Pickfair. All in all, the motion picture industry began to build a public image as the good citizen writ large, catering to the needs and desires of the American people.[24]

In fact, one way the industry served the public was by showing how to preserve individualism in the midst of the very corporate system it helped create. In the modern movie business where all parts were integrated, no producer could hope for the kind of autonomy Griffith had in the early years. Yet independence and freedom could be found elsewhere; and the movies would show how. Articulating the core of this awareness was a young star,

Stephan Stills. In 1925, he was asked to join several film executives on a panel at the Harvard Business School, sponsored by Joseph Kennedy—film executive and father of the future president. Adolph Zukor, William Fox, William Hays, and others all charted the growth of the movies from a small pariah business to one of the largest consolidated industries in the nation. Then Stills explained the source of the market demand. Modern men, he argued, still pursued achievement; but as large organizations removed some of the challenges of free enterprise, they turned their energies to free time. By diffusing frustration, movies helped "avoid any revolution against our economic system." Because people now needed a release from "monotonous work," the motion picture had become an "indispensable industry." Since Stills, too, was part of a large organization, he could identify and locate the problem:

> Never before in the history of civilization has there been felt such a need for entertainment. It is a disquieting fact that very few of the men and women who do the world's work find compensating joy in that work. Sadly enough, it lacks enjoyment. It has become standardized and specialized. The jobs of the factory workers and the shop girls, the clerks and the miners are routine jobs, they represent so much drudgery.[25]

As Americans turned toward leisure, it was appropriate that the film industry moved to Los Angeles. Other Western and Southern cities grew at the same pace, had an agreeable political environment, land, climate and labor situation; indeed, winter studios had been established in these places. Yet only Los Angeles offered the vision of a new West. This was crucial for the image the movies wanted to create. For ever since the mid-nineteenth century the frontier symbolized freedom from the hierarchical, industrial East. In both political and popular literature, the West appeared to hold the promise of a future democracy without greed or class enmity. Yet at a time when the dream of independence seemed to be receding in the wake of a rising corporate order and class conflict, anxious Americans might look to Los Angeles, the farthest point on the frontier, to recreate the vision of a virgin land.[26] Here was a city with no physical remains of an Anglo-Saxon tradition, where individuals could once again be free of Eastern difficulties. As Frank Fenton wrote in *A Place in the Sun,*

This was a lovely makeshift city. Even the trees and plants did not belong here. They came, like the people, from far places, some famil-iar, some exotic, all wanderers of one sort or another seeking peace or fortune or the last frontier, or a thousand dreams of escape.[27]

In the Mediterranean climate, the twentieth century quest for free-dom from the past now took a romantic turn. Ever since the late nineteenth century, Americans coming into the area were struck by three things: the Spanish heritage, the climate, and the lack of in-dustry. In this wide expanse of vacant land, evidences of the Span-ish were visible all around. Besides the Mexican population, and the proximity of that Latin country, the Spanish-style architecture of haciendas and missions spread a romantic aura over the land-scape. When this was coupled with the mild weather, and proximity to beaches, mountains, and desert, the city offered a powerful drawing card to potential settlers. With no heavy manufacturing center or tenements, the population was less densely settled than in Eastern urban centers. Planners encouraged this through zon-ing and developing outlying tracts and linking them together with streetcar lines. In the unique urban-suburban mixture that resul-ted, developers lined the streets with imported palm trees. Boosters were careful to point out, however, that this romance and fair climate was "mediterranean"—the center of a sophisticated civiliza-tion—not "tropical" like savage lands.[28] As one of the city's major designers expressed it, Los Angeles should not be dissipating, but "natural—for here nature and the trees are the thing. It should in-vite family outings, lovemaking, and a forgetfulness that cities are at hand."[29]

Given this vacationland potential, it is no wonder that the city's main developer noted as early as 1909 that Los Angeles was "al-ready the tourist metropolis of the country, the indirect profit through the attraction and retention of outsiders is certain and enormous."[30] No doubt the first testimony to this City Beautiful movement was in Pasadena, where wealthy Easterners built lavish winter homes. The crowning glory of this trend was Henry Hunt-ington's Georgian palace, and its mammoth estate, complete with expansive lawns, statues, fountains, and dozens of gardens com-prised of exotic plants from all over the world. As the homes in the city began to emulate this style in small with Spanish or Moorish motifs, a real estate developer, Abbot Kenney, took the next logical

step. Near the Pacific Ocean he created an entire community modeled on Venice, Italy, complete with canals, gondolas, and a doge
palace, surrounded with flamboyant homes he wished to sell to
newcomers in search of fun and safe living. Developers then exploited this "site extraordinarily beautiful in topography and lavish
in extent" by creating huge parks all over the city. Gradually, these
elements combined to give Los Angeles the aura of a vacationland
where families could settle in the sun, live, work, and play.
Shrewd businessmen like Kenney were quick to capitalize on this:
beach resorts, amusement parks, and restaurants proliferated.
Movie houses cropped up everywhere—from none in 1900 to over
500 by 1928. Finally, reformers in the Progressive era used vice
laws to make these areas safe, so Los Angeles would become "the
city most sought in the United States by pleasure lovers."[31]

Little wonder that movie makers were drawn to this "man made,
giant improvisation." If "there was never a region so unlikely to
become a vast metropolitan area as Southern California," as its
most perceptive historian, Carey McWilliams, noted, what better
place for the movies? Besides the economic and political environment, it seemed an ideal locale where creative imaginations could
flourish. Adolph Zukor led the way when in 1913 he brought his
Famous Players in Famous Plays to Los Angeles. In his company
was William de Mille, a noted Broadway producer and playwright
who was captivated by the traditional imagery of the West. As de
Mille crossed the Rockies, he found himself becoming "younger,"
for in the "new state" of California men could still escape the hierarchy and traditions of the East. In addition to "choosing one's inheritance," de Mille also saw that amid the sunshine and beauty,
one could find a new life of freedom. Charles Chaplin, fresh from
the slums of London in 1913, was even more enthralled. Los
Angeles appeared truly the "land of the future, a paradise of sunshine, orange groves, vineyards, and palm trees. I was embued
with it." Still another could link this new frontier to the old imagery, and see it now open to the children of immigrants like himself.
As Jesse Lasky read a western tale on a train going to the land of
sunshine, he wrote,

> I became again a child at my grandfather's knee. . . . And every time
> I glanced out of the train window at the rolling prairies, the moun-
> tains, the desert, I saw the vast panorama of sky and earth forming a

backdrop for those heroic souls whose first wagon train actually took much of the same route three quarters of a century before . . . a migration but for which I myself would not have been born in my beloved California. Superimposing the past on the present . . . was an emotional, almost mystical experience.[32]

Film moguls brought this "mystical" atmosphere directly into their new studios, which differed dramatically from the ascetic and mundane production sites of the East. In New York, Chicago, Philadelphia, and Long Island, the studios sat primarily in downtown business sections or manufacturing areas. Producers used cheaply made warehouses and factories which were barren looking and almost indistinguishable from the surrounding commercial or industrial enterprises. Internal managements also reflected the strict Victorianism that tried to contain the dangerous potential of the movies. Griffith was not alone in his concern for propriety. At Vitagraph Studios in Brooklyn, the chief executive, Albert Smith, recalled that formality and full names were essential, for "this was part of a plan to exert every precaution in favor of our young actresses. While it may be regarded as unusual precaution on our part, we nevertheless ordered all couches removed from the dressing rooms and make-up areas."[33] In contrast to these entrepreneurial establishments, the modern corporate studios in Los Angeles created an atmosphere where moral experimentation could blossom.

Perhaps the best example of this was Universal City, built in 1913 by Carl Laemmle, the theater owner and former clothing salesman from Chicago. Surrounded by the hills and palm trees of the San Fernando Valley, the white, Spanish-styled studio buildings glowed in the sun. Touching base with romanticism, the administration building followed the Spanish revival style. Yet it reflected a new America. Appropriately, Laemmle called his weekly column in the 1915 trade journal the "Melting Pot," for he glorified the Universal stars who rose up the ladder of success, shed their ethnic or Victorian pasts, and assumed a modern, healthy personality. Articles on current films hailed the sporty life. One starred Christy Mathewson, a pitcher for the New York Giants, who played a man bored with office work who turns to sports for fun and fortune. Other stories featured players having fun on the back lots, which included Roman, Athenian, Egyptian, or Parisian sets. Pictures showed the many exotic animals used in Universal films. In this cosmopolitan environment, as a studio flyer proclaimed, "Mexicans, Chinks, Indians and good Italians work, and such is the soothing climate of California that all these contrary entities live in harmony." All this rested on the high salaries and affluence that the new studios could provide, for the Los Angeles playland cost money.

Assembly line techniques and specialization encouraged high production, and yielded seventy films a year. Much of this work was routine; however, there were high compensations. Studios capitalized in the millions offered salaries for top executives and stars ranging between $100,000 and $900,000 yearly. Opulent dressing rooms and offices mirrored one's rank in the organizational hierarchy. In spite of labor strikes in the late teens and early twenties, which the city of Los Angeles helped the studios to quell, executives claimed that all employees had life, health, and retirement insurance. In addition, as early as 1914, Universal provided a veritable leisure paradise for its workers in the plant itself, complete with a free gymnasium, tennis courts, a steam room, and pool—with equal access, presumably, for all.[34]

More than most industries, the studio also had a personnel turnover which suggested that the "new life" was open to youth and talent. Clearly, the studios existed in the corporate world, but they blended modern and traditional business styles. In other firms, upward mobility by no means ceased; but here, fame and success could happen quickly, without long apprenticeship or professional training. Film relied heavily on imagination, rather than heavy investments in elaborate machinery or scientific processes. After all, it took only a story, talent, and a camera to make a movie. But without the personal touch in advertising and selling, there could be no profits. Since the product also had to be in touch with the latest tastes and psychological needs, it was an ideal place for individuals to make it on their own ideas and talents. Then, with the children of immigrants in power, movie making appeared to offer a place where all newcomers could rise on ability, without having to face discriminatory employers or a rigid seniority system. Precisely because a volatile market encouraged mobility in the midst of bureaucratic hierarchy, one noted observer could describe the modern movie industry in nineteenth-century terms:

the gold rush was probably the only other set up where so many people could hit the jack pot and the skids together. It has become a modern industry without losing that crazy feeling of a boom town.[35]

Yet this boom town opened to a much wider group of aspirants
than the older variety. For above all, Hollywood was an urban
mobility ideal which had a much broader base than the traditional
Protestant middle classes. Coming into the Los Angeles studios to
create a modern life to spread to the nation's cities were a new
breed of people. The trade journals for the industry in 1920 list the
personnel for the West Coast studios, and show that most of the
movie creators came from those places where the film audience was
largest. Over two-thirds of the American film makers were born in
the 1890s in metropolitan areas, compared to less than one-third of
their non-movie peers. Over half of the writers, directors, editors,
and players came from urban centers containing over 100,000 people in 1890, at a time when there were only twenty-eight such
areas in the entire nation. The majority of the remainder came
from Canadian or European cities. Thus, with five-sixths of the
movie people coming from cities when most of the nation was still
rural, they had a head start on their audience, and were ideally
qualified to create, propagate, and live a vision of modern urban
life.[36] (See Table IV.)

It is well to keep in mind that this was a young cosmopolitan
group. With the Jewish moguls on top, and a large ethnic component among the rank and file, the creative personnel were already
one step removed from the Victorian restraints holding earlier film
makers. As the middle-class audience groped for ways to absorb
foreign exoticism and youth, this collection of people was well
suited to serve these needs as well. Those who created the aura
—producers, directors, cinematographers, and set designers—came
largely from European or Canadian backgrounds. Undoubtedly,
this foreign contingent would appear larger if the trade journals
had listed the parents' place of birth as well. Those who provided
the models—actors and actresses—were overwhelmingly young.
Two-thirds of them were under thirty-five. Moreover, three-
fourths of the industry's female performers were under twenty-five.
This suggests that the youth cult so necessary for uplifting
"foreign" elements concentrated most heavily on women, who were

responsible for making sensuality innocent.[37] (See Tables IV and V.)

The industry's employees looked to Los Angeles for a vision of the new life, which included foreign touches filtered through an ever-widening Anglo-Saxon lens. One way to gauge this is to look at the writers who actually formulated the stories. Over 90 percent of them were born in America and had either higher education or journalism experience. This suggests an affluent group, since less than 10 percent of the population during the teens went to college, and publishing was not usually a commoner's trade. This was also the group most likely to include morally emancipated women, a factor also reflected in the industry. During the twenties, women comprised from one-third to one-half of the screen writers. Although their numbers declined sharply in the following decades, they held prominent and influential positions during the early Hollywood heyday.[38] In 1920, the forty top female writers were of middle class Anglo-Saxon stock. None were of poor or worker origin. Like their male counterparts, most were college educated or had publishing backgrounds. Maturing in the Victorian twilight, they were captivated by urban life. From the memoirs of several, we can see that they were in the vanguard of moral experimentation, forging into dress reform, new sexual styles, and consumption. It is no accident that these forty females created over seventy percent of the stories written by women. Their plots overwhelmingly revolved around heroines like themselves.[39] (See Tables IV and VI.)

The movie personnel were thus well prepared to participate in one of the most striking features of modern filmdom. When the large contingent of urbanites, youthful players, foreigners, and women scenarists left studios like Universal, they went home to "Hollywood." Before 1916, Hollywood had been nothing more than a sleepy community of orange groves. But after the industry moved west, it came to symbolize the fruits of the screen and the Los Angeles paradise. It was not the locale of the studios; rather it was an almost mythic place where the movie folk spent money on personal expression. This consumption encouraged individual creativity and freedom, while it also served as a mark of success. A shrewd observer of the industry, producer William de Mille, saw that the movie people's "conspicuous consumption" gave status to

an often routine job, and reflected on the "company that paid you."
As huge sums of money rolled in, the stars—who after all did not
make a tangible product—used spending to validate their almost
magical success. Mary Pickford saw her vast salary increases as the
way to prove that she really had made it. Charles Chaplin had similar emotions, but also envisaged extravagance as an exciting break
from bourgeois restraints. He recalled that in 1914,

> I was reconciled to wealth, but not to the use of it. The money I
> earned was legendary, a symbol in figures, for I had never actually
> seen it. I therefore had to do something to prove I had it. So I pro-
> cured a secretary, a valet, a car, a chauffeur. Walking by the
> showroom one day, I noticed a seven passenger Locomobile . . . the
> transaction was simple; it meant writing my name on a piece of paper.
> So I said wrap it up.[40]

Because the consumption allure was the key to the Hollywood
image, the star's life took on more than a private importance. In
contrast to earlier stage personalities, film idols presented national
models as leisure experts. As early as 1915, fan magazines showed
how the star's domain reflected the Southern California style. In a
city that contained few monuments or buildings reflecting the nineteenth-century Anglo-Saxon culture, there seemed to be a release
from the restraint of tradition. Amid a virgin land of constant romance, it was easier to create a life-style frowned upon in the East.
One tangible example was the expansion of domestic enjoyments
and accoutrements far beyond their Victorian limitations. As Mary
Pickford said of the estate that would soon be Pickfair, "Maybe this
summer I will take a vacation, but if I do it will be right here in
Los Angeles. I can't see why anyone would leave Los Angeles for a
vacation." There were good reasons for this. Celebrity domiciles
were located in the farthest reaches of this suburban city, removed
from ethnic groups and business centers. The vague, mythic term
"Hollywood" connoted a way of life unfolding in the exclusive
neighborhoods of Beverly Hills, Santa Monica, and Brentwood.
Freed from any nearby reminders of social responsibility, in areas
cleansed through vice crusades, the stars could create a new, uplifted life without the inhibitions of the past. Usually homes drew
on styles of European, African, or Asian aristocracy, reflecting not

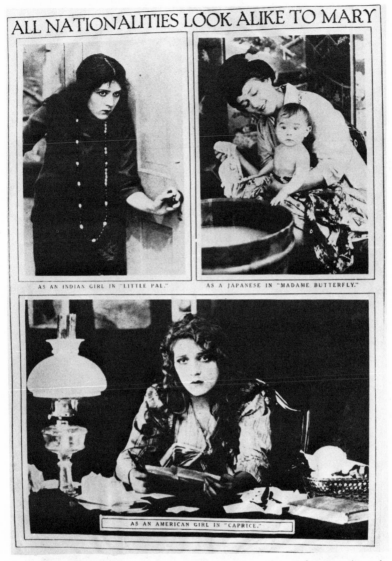

ALL NATIONALITIES LOOK ALIKE TO MARY

AS AN INDIAN GIRL IN "LITTLE PAL."

AS A JAPANESE IN "MADAME BUTTERFLY."

AS AN AMERICAN GIRL IN "CAPRICE."

As "America's Sweetheart" goes cosmopolitan, so the modern movies subvert the Anglo-Saxon ideals of middle-class life. (New York Public Library/Theater Collection)

The Biograph studios in the Bronx, circa 1912. The factory-like appearance amid the city streets typified Eastern production sites. (Museum of Modern Art/Film Stills Archive)

Universal Studios, Los Angeles, California, circa 1914. The expansive vistas of nature and the West pose a sharp contrast to the drab structures of the East. (Museum of Modern Art/Film Stills Archive)

In Hollywood, luxury is no longer the exclusive domain of the powerful. Here Douglas Fairbanks's first Hollywood estate replicates the mansions built for the nineteenth-century elite at Newport. (New York Public Library/Theater Collection)

Promise of the new life: the romantic Spanish revival style popular in Southern California carried to a Baroque extreme in the administration building of Universal Studios. (Museum of Modern Art/Film Stills Archive)

# Everybody's Doing It Now

You have never really danced until you have learned the fascinatin' rhythm of the Charleston. Here's a lesson by Hollywood's champion.

IT took place at a party given recently by Mr. and Mrs. Rudolph Valentino—the great Charleston Contest of Hollywood. The two contestants were Ann Pennington and Bessie Love. Now Ann is the undisputed champion of the stage and her fame had spread before her to Hollywood. However, Hollywood backed its own Bessie Love and the movie colony votes that Bessie has a slight shade of advantage on Penny.

When PHOTOPLAY heard of the contest, it asked Bessie to give its readers a few lessons in the intricacies of the steps. Bessie consented to pose for pictures illustrating the most important steps. There are, of course, many variations but if you have mastered the principles of the dance, the rest will come easy.

# The Swimming Pools of Hollywood

*The Carter de Havens bathe in tropical luxury—palms and weeping willows and all that sort of thing. They—there are four of them, including the two children—look surprisingly unaesthetic. But we wouldn't be surprised to learn that a Hawaiian orchestra was drumming away, concealed somewhere in the background*

*Norma Talmadge's pool, on the other hand, is almost puritanical in its chaste dignity. Edged with white it is; and very, very simple in design*

World War I brings full respectability to Hollywood, as major stars campaign for the war effort. Here Chaplin and Fairbanks urge Wall Street crowds to buy Liberty Bonds. (New York Public Library/Theater Collection)

---

*Top:* Bessie Love does the Charleston at the Valentino home, demonstrating the ideal of fun-loving, but respectable, domesticity to the readers of *Photoplay* in 1925. (New York Public Library/Theater Collection)

*Bottom:* In *Photoplay*, the home has moved far beyond the functional needs of Victorianism. Now it has expanded into playland, complete with pools and jovial friends. (New York Public Library/Theater Collection)

only high culture, but the quest for a more exotic life. Before the
War, they were stately and classical. Always they were opulent,
and mirrored cultivation and success.[41]

A double-barreled aspiration came from this model. To the ambitious Anglo-Saxon urbanite, it suggested that achievement might
yield a release from Victorian asceticism. To the equally ambitious
person of immigrant stock, it suggested that upward mobility was
no longer aimed toward a temperate Anglo-Saxon norm. Rather,
here was a cosmopolitan eclecticism, though still dominated by
American values, fit for the new order. Pickfair was the pinnacle;
but fan magazines gave frank testimony to the mammoth extent of
the style and its allure. A typical article extolling the Hollywood
life entitled "Everybody's Doin' it Now," featured Bessie Love, a
former Griffith player, in her lavish home. What "everybody" was
doing, including Bessie, was a black dance called the "Charleston."
But as Bessie gyrated in a tight-fitting, revealing dress, the backdrop of her magnificent classically designed abode signaled that
money made it all right. Along the same lines, another article described the rewards success had brought Fannie Ward, a former
Ziegfeld chorus girl who entered the movies in 1915. Photographs
showed her in Hollywood basking in the sun beneath a large Italian
chateau, complete with flowing fountains, Doric pillars, expansive
gardens, and a "Napoleonic" bedroom. Well before the 1920s,
these widely publicized homes made Hollywood a household word
with connotations far beyond the geographical. Indeed, as this
world seemed to create glowing personalities, it diffused resentments formerly directed to the wealthy. As one of the few scenarists with an immigrant, working-class background wrote of her
move to Hollywood in 1919,

> My life-long hatred of the rich and successful turned to servile grati-
> tude for their friendliness. In my eagerness to be like them, with the
> ardor of a convert to a new faith, I repudiated all that I had been. The
> poor I thought were too submerged in their own fight for bread to in-
> dulge in the amenities of life . . . this was Zion on earth.[42]

As this quote suggests, one reason why ordinary people could
identify with the stars' life was that the stars did not have the authority the industrial titans had. True, Hollywood was a "society"
community setting the pace for modern life. Yet, in replacing the

industrial titans of New York or Chicago, or the local gentry, as the nation's new aristocracy, the movie folk could be universally loved because they were not socially powerful: they were purely a status group. Unlike politicians or manufacturers, they did not hold authority over large groups of employees or constituents. Studio executives did manage large firms and were involved in politics; but they were not in the limelight. The force of the stars as popular idols lay in their leisure, rather than work lives. Much of their mystique was that they presumably rose from meager beginnings to become models of success. Yet on their jobs, they had no control over fellow employees; they, too, had to answer to the boss. Nor did they hold political clout. During the first four decades of the century, none of the industry's rank and file served on a Los Angeles school board, or held civic office or commission. Power would have been antithetical to their image as playful, friendly people.[43]

More importantly, the stars offered a number of solutions to modern problems and a reformulation of dominant myths for the twentieth century. When combined with the Hollywood life, the total added up to a clear mosaic. For one thing, it showed Americans how to adjust to the corporate order. Starting as early as the mid-teens, Hollywood became an institution which offered viable proof that the new economy could be a blessing rather than a burden. In the long periods of prosperity during the late nineteenth and early twentieth centuries, a number of businessmen, reformers, and intellectuals believed that America's "excess production" would have to be exported abroad. Behind this was the quest for a larger market. Yet a potentially large market existed internally, provided the purchasing power of the masses could be expanded. Rarely was this course followed, in part due to fears of traditionalists like Josiah Strong, who believed that unleashing abundance could destroy Victorian principles as well as the work ethic of the laboring classes. For should the workers gain the luxury that was beyond their grasp, presumably they would have no further motivation to toil. But through the late teens, Hollywood showed how this scarcity psychology could be overcome, and consumption become a positive force. Rather than luxury eroding the achievement drive, or a society based on open opportunity, it flowed into rising expectations. For as success took on new rewards, as the stars became consumption idols, excess production had a purpose. Farsighted manufacturers like the film moguls could make large profits by stimulating the purchasing power of the prosperous. In this way luxuries became necessities. Abundance, therefore, would not undercut a class order based on competition or civic concerns; rather, it would give it a different emphasis.

At the same time, Hollywood kept alive a key cultural myth. As the nineteenth century drew to a close, many Americans realized that the frontier was gone, and perhaps with it went one of the main utopian aspirations in American life. For nearly a century, people had kept alive the hope that sectional divisions, or class conflicts created by industrialization, might be eased by the existence of a safety valve. On the far frontier, people could start out anew and establish an egalitarian order, free from the hierarchies of Europe and the East. Presumably this would serve as a model for the future and set the tone for all of America. In the late nineteenth century, however, the rise of big business and the influx of "new immigrants" intensified conflicts that had already been present. Heightening the sense of chaos was women's increasing restlessness concerning their place in society, and the emergence of an industrial elite with unprecedented power. The need for an outlet seemed even more urgent than before. Yet now the frontier was conquered, and the promise of an egalitarian order seemed to vanish. Americans at the turn of the century asked themselves: would men and women be able to find personal fulfillment in a conflict-ridden, hierarchical society that had spread all over the continent?

A partial answer to this bubbled up from the masses and poured out of the popular culture. Initially, it seemed that the moral revolution would subvert the home and class order even further. Yet the motion picture firms growing up after 1914 soon showed the way out of this dilemma, without returning to Victorianism. It was not just that they catered to audience needs. After 1914, the film industry itself was part of the corporate order, and film makers created a style to ease the pressures of the era that they were also feeling. Pickford and Fairbanks, then the theater palaces, and finally Hollywood showed how middle-class ideals could be regenerated to fit the modern age. Now the Victorian synthesis gave way to a less puritanical culture more amenable to non-Anglo Saxons, provided they had white skin. Consumption on a mass level showed that resentment of the rich could be lessened, and that women could find happiness in an expanded home. The mobility ideal of the stars, theater palaces, and Hollywood thus offered a new twist on the traditional success ethic: men and women would work for money to buy the trappings of the good life. With this reborn West, the Hollywood frontier promised to solve some of the major public problems facing reformers, and thus set the stage for the culmination of the consumer culture in the twenties.

# Chapter Eight

# POLITICS DISSOLVED:
# CECIL B. DEMILLE
# AND THE CONSUMER IDEAL,
# 1918–1929

> D. W. Griffith is an idealist and his love scenes on the screen
> were idealistic things of beauty . . . but his pictures are not
> successful today because modern ideas are changing. The
> idealistic love of a decade ago is not true today. We cannot sit
> in a theater and see a noble hero and actually picture ourselves
> as him. . . . In contrast to D. W. Griffith is Cecil B. DeMille
> . . . I know his attempt to appeal to current thought is not
> haphazard.                             IRVING THALBERG, 1927[1]
>             Production Chief Metro Goldwyn Mayer Studios

Irving Thalberg perceived that in the twenties the era of Griffith
was gone and something new emerged with the most successful
film maker of the decade, Cecil B. DeMille. Before the War, Pickford and Fairbanks had furthered this move away from Victorianism by demonstrating how moral experimentation became acceptable within the context of Progressivism. These stars showed
how to break from the asceticism of the past, provided one never
lost the sense of civic virtue. Flirtation and consumption were thus
ultimately held in check by the values that lay at the heart of corporate reform. Yet after 1919, devotion to a large-scale political
movement declined, and film makers like DeMille began to project
even more radical changes within family and sexual life. Impulses
for public duty waned, and reform would be focused within the
private realm of manners, rhetoric, and taste. To a generation of
historians, this aspect of the "roaring twenties" seemed to be a
sharp break. Yet in a number of ways, it merely extended the
trends of the past two decades.

    The most important factor in this exaggerated sense of a "revolu-
tion in manners and morals" was the widening acceptance of a new

economic order. In this we must consider the twenties as much more the result of continuity with the reformist era than a radical break. True, small entrepreneurs, workers, and farmers could feel oppressed by the rise of big business hegemony; and others might be disillusioned by the War and League of Nations. Yet there was a strong sense of optimism among the urban middle classes. After all, the corporate wing of reform had not failed, but succeeded only too well. In a nation still dominated by Anglo Saxons, the political arena had been saved from radical parties and unions. A host of federal agencies had been created to regulate business and appease some of the social welfare demands of immigrant machines and Progressives. Moreover, moral crusaders had expurgated saloons and legitimized healthy recreation. Now there was a new area where big business could presumably serve the public good. Local control and voluntarism faded; but there were plenty of reasons to hail the advent of an organizational age.

In the popular literature of the cities during the 1920s, the corporations no longer loomed menacingly. To the new generation, they were indeed a fact of life. Between 1880 and 1930, the number of salaried employees increased eight fold, coming to compose over 60 percent of the entire middle class. Soon the white-collar ranks became the largest single group in the labor force; and by 1939 1 percent of all the nation's firms employed over half the people in business. Women were heavily involved in this new economy. From 1890 to 1930, the proportion of females in the work force rose from 19 to 25 percent, with the greatest rise occurring among sales, office, and clerical work. Not only were these positions the most routine and menial, but the percentage of women in the prestigious careers of medicine and law had actually decreased.[2] For both men and women, then, the expansion of the more bureaucratized realms in government and commerce meant that the top would be much harder to reach; but there were compensations in the form of security and affluence.[3]

Throughout the 1920s, a measurable increase in wealth appeared. Although over half the nation's population still had substandard incomes, the vast increases in productivity yielded unprecedented growth. From 1897 to 1930, the net national product climbed from $15.8 billion to $70.3 billion, and per capita annual income rose from $231 to $719. As a result of increased wages and salary, household expenditures tripled between 1909 and 1929. The most dramatic rise was for consumer goods: amusements, leisure pursuits, clothes, appearance, furniture, and automobiles. The amount spent on cosmetics, beauty aids, and home decorations increased eightfold from 1914 to 1924. All of this was centered in the urban industrial North, where the work week was shortest and the per capita income greatest. And mobility was still alive among the middle ranks, which continued to grow and absorb newcomers from below.[4] Even more important, these people used their free time and wealth to explore more private, rather than public, concerns.

A number of indicators suggest this pattern. For one thing, voter turnouts declined from approximately ninety-five percent in the 1890s to less than fifty-five percent during the twenties. Poll taxes and literacy tests in the South explain some of this; but the electoral decline was just as pronounced in the North. At the same time, studies of major cities show that participation in civically concerned church and voluntary organizations decreased, and Protestant ministers preached less the code of social duty and more the means toward personal satisfactions. The economy was another public institution that involved people less and less. Between 1900 and 1950, the work week shrank four hours every decade; paid vacations began for employees; the old and young left the work force in increasing numbers; and life expectancy increased, allowing people to spend a greater part of their lives away from work. At the same time, family resources and energy were less geared toward raising and supporting kin. From 1900 to 1930, the size of the average household declined from 3.82 children to 2.82, and more and more individuals lived alone.[5]

As the urban family lost some of its nineteenth-century functions, so did the expectations surrounding it change. In real life as well as on the screen, young middle-class women were no longer learning solely the role of Victorian motherhood and its attendant moral duties. Indeed, the historical evidence suggests that the highly publicized "flappers" who appeared more alluring than their general forebears were, in fact, discarding Victorian sexual morality. In spite of the continuing taboo against premarital intercourse, the Lynds discovered that single men and women in Muncie, Indiana, did much more unchaperoned dating and petting than the previous generation. Louis Terman surveyed over seven hundred college women in 1939, finding that 74 percent of those born between 1890 and 1900 had been virgins at marriage. But of those born after 1913, the proportion dropped to thirty-one percent. The historian Daniel Scott Smith studied pre-marital sexual patterns and found that the number of pregnant brides rose steadily after 1900. Institutions may not have condoned this behavior, but they did encourage new marital ethics to legitimize it within wedlock. By the late twenties, the liberal Protestant churches sanctioned birth control as a way to free sexual pleasure from fears of conception, and thereby strengthen rather than weaken the marital bonds.[6]

Given the changing assumptions about marriage, it is no accident that wedlock was becoming more popular. In spite of the increasing divorce rate and the growing economic independence of females, both men and women married younger and in greater proportions than in the nineteenth century. Perhaps—as the films suggest—because labor was not emancipating and premarital sexual experimentation was restrained, the ideal of matrimony was all the more appealing. The median age for brides in 1890 was 22.0 years; but it fell to 21.2 in 1920 and continued to decline until after World War II. For males, the drop was also dramatic, from 26.1 years of age in 1890 to 24.3 in 1930. Likewise, when spouses did divorce more readily, it was not necessarily because they had rejected the idea of marriage; rather it was because a particular spouse had failed to live up to expectations surrounding the new home. As a study of divorce in Los Angeles suggests, a major cause for separation was the fact that women did not want to work, and men had failed to provide the new "necessities" of life.[7]

In many ways these marital expectations mirrored the themes Hollywood and popular literature radiated in the late teens. The hero and heroine were to shed Victorian sexual inhibitions and take on "fun" morality and a consumer life-style.[8] Giving this quest for private fulfillment a real basis was not just increased sexual freedom. In fact, during the twenties, government, sociological, and business reports began to verify that the prime audience of middle-class urbanites was modeling its purchasing habits on images spread by the movies. One such report found that as the fashion capital moved from New York to "Hollywood," there was a "revolutionary change" in buying at the major department stores of the Northern cities. Adults were now enhancing married life by purchasing victrolas, clothes, and cars geared toward leisure fun. What is more, they looked to "youth" as the trend setters. In the youth-oriented items, they hoped to find a constant newness which might free them from the inhibitions of public propriety, or the restraints of the Victorian family.[9]

Yet while these alterations in work, family, and consumerism did continue pre-War trends, the mass media spread their meaning to the public in a much different context. Now that reform had lost its political edge, the motion picture industry learned almost immediately that the old formulas would not work. Shortly after the War, the screen stars, who were expected to show the public how to handle moral experimentation, became involved in a series of sex scandals: Jack Pickford, Mary's brother, found his wife, a former Ziegfeld chorus girl, dead in their Parisian hotel room. As the press broadcast suggestions of adultery and suicide, a Mack Sennett comedian, Fatty Arbuckle, was implicated in a sadistic murder of an actress. Not long afterwards, an English director ended up murdered in his hotel room, and several actresses were suspected as paramours and possible murderers. Yet undoubtedly the most significant episodes surrounded Mary Pickford and Douglas Fairbanks. Their initial liaison and subsequent divorces carried overtones of adultery. When, added to the other scandals, these incidents evoked an enormous public outcry, the studios realized the need for continuing the cultural side of reform.[10]

Ironically, the problem was tackled by the establishment of an industry-wide censor. In 1920, the Big Eight brought in the solid Republican reformer, William Harrison Hays, to coordinate their ethical and economic interests. We have already seen his important economic function. But he was also in charge of transferring the old moral guardianship of the small city and town to the movie corporations. Hays created continuity by bringing into his censorship board local groups formerly aligned to the National Board of Review. Yet without local bases in settlement houses and political alliances, the social and church groups became completely dependent on the Motion Picture Producers and Distributors Association, where they received high salaries, but very little power. With their backing, Hays blackballed the less powerful individuals involved in the scandals, such as Fatty Arbuckle, set up an agency to supervise players, and included moral turpitude clauses in actors' and actresses' contracts.[11]

Once it appeared that Hollywood had cleaned up its own act, Hays worked diligently to make the movies of the Big Eight respectable enough to guarantee wide markets, without losing the titillating overtones that drew the audience. One of his most successful efforts to overthrow local restraints on his clients' products occurred in Boston, where he thwarted the election of municipal censors. Yet at the same time, he furthered the appeal of the movies by sanctioning a morality that even went beyond Pickford and Fairbanks. As he assured Carl Laemmle, he had no desire to ignore the public's interest in sex; rather, films had to be made "passionate but pure . . . giving the public all the sex it wants with compensating values for all those church and women groups." In other words, sensuality might be acceptable if it would sell goods and not disrupt any institutional functions. Only now, sex and its associations with women and family were somehow to be separate from the symbols and meanings of public life.[12]

Fortunately, Hays did not have to look far for the formula, since one of those instrumental in hiring him had been putting it on the screen for four years already. This was Cecil B. DeMille. Along with his partners Adolph Zukor and Jesse Lasky, DeMille helped form Paramount Pictures, which began as Famous Players in Famous Plays in 1914. It was their brainchild to bring Broadway stars into the movies. During the next fifteen years, DeMille became a vice president of the Bank of America, a militant anti-union Republican, and a founder of the industry's major trade association. Appropriate to his corporate interests, he made over fifty films between 1914 and 1929 that visualized more sex and displayed more consumption than any previous photoplays. The most innovative spurt in his creativity came between 1918 and 1920. While these films set the tone for the twenties, an approving censor like Hays was crucial for sanctioning the questionable morality in these extremely profitable films. Much as Griffith presented images appropriate for the 1908 to 1914 era, and Pickford and Fairbanks for 1914 to 1918, DeMille's work tapped the post-War public imagination.

DeMille was well suited to reassessing the impact of affluence

on the dominant Protestant culture. Unlike Griffith and most of the
Jewish studio founders, DeMille was the scion of an eastern elite
family with a long tradition of merging social betterment to the
dramatic arts. Cecil was the younger of two sons born in the 1880s
at Ashfield, Massachusetts, to Henry and Matilda Beatrice De-
Mille. Henry DeMille was descended from a long line of Huguenot
planters in South Carolina. Coming to New York City, he graduated from Columbia University and took orders to become an Epis-
copal priest. But in the late 1880s he shed the clerical collar and
turned to the "wider pulpit" of university teaching and the New
York stage. Writing domestic dramas geared to the tastes of the
Fifth Avenue rich, he soon aligned himself with the major Broadway impresario, David Belasco. Never did Henry shed his belief
that the stage was an educator of the public, an ethic furthered by
his wife. Beatrice DeMille came from a German Jewish family and
apparently converted to her husband's religion. Avidly working in
church affairs, reading the Bible to her children every night, she
also mingled in the circles of New York reformers. Henry George
was often a guest at their home, and her son William married the
radical single-taxer's daughter.[13]

After Henry's death, Beatrice took her two sons onto the Broadway stage, where she began her lifelong commitment to furthering
their careers. The mother became a writers' agent noted for her
belief in women's emancipation and "equality in marriage," while
her two sons, William and Cecil, took up the crusade in "reform
and betterment plays." Each tried his hand at acting, producing,
and writing. In the words of William, their most successful works
attacked "outworn institutions" and preached a "social revolution
through drama." By 1913, the DeMilles were noted stage figures,
and had thoroughly assimilated the tastes of a wealthy audience
that wanted to make their high society more spicy. The DeMilles
were thus well equipped to bring the glamor and appeal of the
stage to a movie audience eager to touch the fast life as well. Soon
they established their own studio, one of the first permanently
located in Los Angeles. Shortly thereafter Zukor brought in Sarah
Bernhardt, and Cecil DeMille acquired a famous Broadway player,
Dustin Farnum, to star in a filmed play, *The Squaw Man* (1914). In
this story, a wealthy Anglo-Saxon urbanite loves an Indian
maiden, because she offers more "red blooded" primitivism than

his genteel sweetheart. But in this early film, the twain can never meet; the hero eventually marries Lady Diana after all, and the broken-hearted squaw kills herself.[14]

In the pre-War period, DeMille hoped to bring "disasters before the public" in order to fight "sex." While these echoed themes of other film makers, DeMille's uniqueness was that he picked up where the others left off. Most early films ended in marriage, which is where DeMille began. His first plots revolved around civic order corrupted by faulty home life. *The Whispering Chorus* (1918), for example, shows a clerk in a large office "employed by another man." Dreaming of excitement, he turns to the vice dens of Chinatown, complete with opium and loose women. His guilty conscience—symbolized appropriately by his mother and wife—says "don't"; but he continues his dissipation anyway. In another film, it is not work but the new woman that threatens to destroy the hero. *What's His Name* (1914) portrays a man who marries a "sweet" girl only to have her turn to the stage where she is economically and sexually emancipated. Soon the hero loses his identity, becoming dependent on her money, and she leaves him for a millionaire. Only when their child becomes ill are they reunited. Another restless female in *The Cheat* (1915) tries to escape suburban boredom while her husband is endlessly at work. She turns to a rich Oriental for money and excitement, who brands her with a hot iron, making her his "property." In this as in countless other De-Mille films, the family is restored. But in the first phase of De-Mille's creativity, the resolution came through a revival of Victorian values.[15]

The end of the War, however, brought to an end this union of reform and morality. Now that Progressivism as a broad-based movement began to fade, there was a need for a new solution to male and female restlessness. After the Armistice, a number of extremely popular films suggested that people looked far beyond the old formulas to resolve their internal crises. It is no accident that ma .y of these productions made heroes of former villains. One was Rudolph Valentino, a handsome and talented actor who immigrated from Italy and worked as a dishwasher and cabaret dancer in New York. The other was Erich von Stroheim, the son of a Jewish hatter who passed himself off as an Austrian noble. In the pre-War period, their dark features which connoted dangerous

foreigners often made them ideal evil men whose eroticism threatened the good society. Yet a reversal occurred in some of the most
successful films of the twenties; frank sexuality made these stars
objects of hero worship for an enormous audience.

The films that launched the careers of these artists demonstrate
the source of their popularity. Valentino first gained fame in *The
Four Horsemen of the Apocalypse* (1920), the highest grossing film of
the twenties. There he played the son of an Argentinian businessman. In an electrifying opening scene, we see the sexy hero Julio
dancing the tango in a smoke-filled cabaret. Dressed in tight pants
and Gaucho hat, he clutches a beautiful woman as they sway to the
rhythm of the music. When his family moves to Paris, his father
insists that he give up his life as a bohemian painter for a business
career. But the son has fallen in love with the wife of a work-
obsessed American. Together they rebel against a passionless society. Even though World War I makes Julio a martyred hero and the
wife a contrite nurse who returns to her spouse, the foreign lover
was the unambiguous model for emulation. Valentino would carry
this aura into other films such as *The Sheik* (1920), in which he plays
an Arab who seduces an emancipated English woman.

Erich von Stroheim portrayed a similar type of hero in his two
most famous films, which he wrote, directed, and starred in. In
*Blind Husbands* (1919), the "man you love to hate" was a Viennese
noble, whose clothes and trappings were highlighted by detailed
camera work. Early in the story an American doctor is so work-
obsessed helping others that he ignores his wife. Overhead a caption explains that "in divorce the most common cause is alienation
of affection . . . we often blame the other man, but what of the
husband?" In response to her husband's lack of attention, the wife
becomes attracted to the hero, whose good manners, handsome
face, and attentiveness to her sensual side strikes a sharp contrast to
her mate. Stroheim's other major vehicle, *Foolish Wives* (1922), portrays a similar theme. It shows how a rich aristocrat in Monte
Carlo seduces the wife of a successful American dedicated to the
Protestant work ethic. Although the von Stroheim character always
pays for the sins of adultery in the end, there was no doubt that he,
like Valentino, held part of the viewers' sympathy throughout. Implicit was a criticism of the Victorian home which had been
stripped of its civic function, and now had no purpose other than

meaningless discipline. Clearly, the enormous public response to this message indicated that something had to change.[16]

DeMille's phenomenal success lay in presenting what that transformation might entail. The formula was to take the desires projected onto foreign lovers and bring them into American culture. Instead of reforming the external world to meet the Victorian ideal, now the screen depicted an internal domestic revitalization.[17] Some elements of this appeared in the Pickford-Fairbanks genre; but DeMille's beginnings were their happy endings. Heroes and heroines do not start with a great social purpose; nor are they single. Rather, the film generally begins with the couple already married, and revolves around purely personal concerns devoid of public purpose. This allowed DeMille to pioneer a set of marital ethics that the Protestant churches would not sanction until ten years later. As the director explained in 1920, by bringing passion "into the bonds that the Bible has lain down," sex between husbands and wives would stabilize rather than weaken marriage. For "the breaking of the law comes from adultery, not sex." The director knew that this rebellion held a strong appeal for women. In fact, over 90 percent of DeMille's films in the late teens and twenties were written by female scenarists, and carried such suggestive titles as *Old Wives for New* (1918), *Don't Change Your Husband* (1919), *Male and Female* (1919), *Why Change Your Wife?* (1920), *Forbidden Fruit* (1921), and *The Affairs of Anatol* (1921).[18]

In these pre-1920s plots, DeMille set the style for the next decade. The stories usually begin with a bored husband or wife trapped by routine jobs or social roles. Seeking excitement outside their institutional lives, they turn to cabarets, foreign lovers, "primitive" music, and dance. A husband might become attracted to the new "jazz babies." But when he asks his wife to participate in this new youthful playfulness, he meets a stone wall of moral condemnation. Rejecting his "Oriental ideas" and "physical music," she still clings to the old rules, saying that wives and mothers should discipline their mates and children. Leaving the "convent," the husband proclaims, "I want a sweetheart, not a governess." Often DeMille reversed the formula and had a rebellious wife demand that her work-obsessed husband become more fun-loving. Either way, the marriage dissolves.

Divorce, however, leads to an ambiguous freedom. Now both

partners can assume the "carefree qualities of youth" offered by urban nightclubs, resorts, and luxury tours. In taking on an appropriate style, one ex-wife tells her dress maker, "I've been foolish enough to think a man wants a wife decent and honest, make the dresses sleeveless, backless and transparent—go the limit . . . thank God I'm still young." Yet the hero and heroine also learn that modern life is a "Golden Calf which makes the feast of Babylon look like a cafeteria." Respectable men fall prey to nightclub performers like "Satin Synne," who insists that "the Devil is not a man but a woman, and that's what every woman knows but is afraid to tell." Likewise, the freed wives are captivated by gigolos with exciting looks, dancing, and love-making, until they extravagantly spend the heroines' money while refusing to work.[19]

*The Affairs of Anatol* (1921) highlights the dilemma. It begins with the plight of an office worker, Anatol, bored with life. Rather than trying to change society, he looks to personal reformation. Out for a night on the town with his reluctant wife, they go to a cabaret where "the management is not responsible for lost husbands." There Anatol meets an old school chum, who was "sweet as a flower" in the old days, but is now a "jazz baby" complete with bobbed hair, tight short skirts, and a fun-loving smile. Since his wife cannot get into the "swing of it," Anatol is attracted to the sexy flapper, and pledges to free her from a big spender who is a "man of iron downtown, a man of dough in the nightclubs." This effort begins as a reformer's urge to save women from white slavers; but no sooner does the hero begin to build a "temple to God" than he finds one built "by the Devil nearby." In other words, the hero's attraction wins out over his benevolence.

Slowly he degenerates. Anatol leaves his wife and supplies the chorus girl with violin lessons and education. Yet when he is not around, the girl reverts to smoking, parties, and dancing to jazz music. Anatol finds himself unwittingly drawn to this allure, for "no amount of moralizing can keep the moth from the flame." One night, he finds that she has returned to her downtown sugar daddy. In a symbolic effort to purge himself, Anatol breaks into their party, proclaims that although she has "blue-black diamonds" around her neck, her soul is "as black as ink." So he proceeds to destroy the luxurious apartment, the fine furnishings, and the presents he has given her. If the beleaguered male cannot find satis-

faction in the modern women or work, he turns to the countryside
as an alternative, only to find that women on the farm are equally
drawn to the new morality. Meeting dangers on all fronts, Anatol
suddenly announces that "if this is the gay life, I'm going back to
my wife."

The solution, however, did not involve a return to Victorianism,
as it might have in earlier films. Rather, "foreign" allures had to be
safely integrated into the American family. DeMille's favorite device was to have disillusioned husbands accidentally meet their ex-
wives, who have become exciting creatures in the meantime. In the
case of Anatol, the spouse too has gone to the Broadway night life
to "see if there was room for wives." Now that they both are beautiful and stylish, they fail to recognize each other. Yet once they
discover each other's real identity, they also find romantic stability.
For the desirable woman wants an exciting man to provide security; and the husband needs a wife who will hold his interest, but
not disrupt the drive for success. When they remarry, the happy
ending demonstrates that fun and sex can actually strengthen marriage. In a luxurious home at the end of *Why Change Your Wife*
(1920) for example, the husband has shed his obsession with work
and cavorting around town for release; and the former temperance
crusader has shed her spiritual books for a revealing dress and the
latest hair style. Instead of rejecting "Oriental music" she puts on a
record of the latest dance, the "Hindustan," and she pours him a
drink as they start to foxtrot. A final caption warns, "Ladies, if you
want to be your husband's sweetheart, you must simply forget
when you are his wife."[20]

The ideal had important consequences for women. In the pre-
War era, a heroine like Mary Pickford still carried the temperance,
suffrage, and moral impulses of nineteenth-century women. Her
characters were identified with the cult of motherhood and inspired
men to exercise Christian stewardship over economic and political
life. Given her duty, Pickford's sexual allure and emancipation had
to be held in check by girlish innocence. But because a DeMille
hero is less involved in public endeavors, he wants his wife to take
on a more sexual appeal. This meant that women had to shed the
ascetic tradition, and its civic functions as well. On the one hand,
this allows an exploration of personality, fun, and the hitherto forbidden realm of sex. As a result, the respectable women could shed

the little girl image for a more mature sexuality. This opens up a unique aspect of the twenties. Motherhood, as an ideal which had lasted for a century, virtually disappeared from films as the main aspiration for women. Now heroines become flappers or erotic wives, like DeMille's major characters. On the other hand, this expressiveness was gained at the expense of women's role as social guardian, for no longer was the home tied to larger communal endeavors.

Still the formula did not totally reject the private side of Victorianism. Clearly the heroes in DeMille films wanted sexy mates, not social workers. But as the scenes of dissipation suggest, women could not go too far. Otherwise the corporate executives, clerks, salaried professionals, and college students would not be able to exercise the self-control necessary for getting ahead. For DeMille this meant that women's potentially raw sensuality had to be made "Godlike," as he phrased it, rather than "low class." As he explained his philosophy in 1920, wholesomeness was necessary to show that the potential marriage partner would still "use every weapon to kill the beast in man through her love and purity . . . helping him to overcome that Adam of lust that eventually leads to ruin." In other words, DeMille realized that the tradition of the "fathers" had to be retained. Ironically, this meant that despite the desire for emancipated partners, males were even more committed to keeping women and their eroticism confined to private life, where they would still exercise their traditional function. "Love," wrote DeMille, "without so much of the maternal is only passion; and I know of no emotion so untrustworthy as passion." [21]

Demands for retaining part of the motherhood cult put great pressures on women, especially single ones. Not only did they have to radiate the sensuality men wanted, but they had to assure future spouses that they were not "loose." Echoing the still strong taboo against pre-marital intercourse, DeMille's films served as jeremiads against youthful sex. In fact, some of his most significant productions—*The Godless Girl* (1929), *Manslaughter* (1922), *The Ten Commandments* (1923), and *The Road to Yesterday* (1925)—sermonized against promiscuity. Typically, the films start with an ambitious man attracted to a sensual modern woman. To show how this could threaten marital order, DeMille transferred his characters to ancient Italy, Israel, or the Renaissance. There the inability of the hero to control sexuality led to the loss of will and the fall of civilization. The message was that modern progress could be disrupted by women's sexual freedom if it was not contained within the safe boundaries of the private, leisured home.[22]

To further shave away the dangers of eroticism, it had to be refined. For this, high-level consumption and the imagery of youth were all important. Working or middle-class women were supposed to think that the way to attract successful men was to surround themselves with an aura of luxury. Clothed in a Tiffany gown, or Coty jewelry, a plain woman would supposedly become not only beautiful, but high class. The famous DeMille bathing scenes highlighted this Cinderella message. In opulent surroundings, the heroine washed her bare body. Certainly this was erotically exciting to the male viewer; it also implied that sensuality can be cleansed of its potentially dirty qualities. When the heroine steps out of the water and puts on a gorgeous gown and make-up to look younger, she is made elegant, innocent, and youthful. The larger implications were clear: To afford this type of woman, a man could not shed the work ethic. For such a female did not "sell herself cheap." In fact, it was her expensive tastes that spurred men on to achieve.[23]

One DeMille film in particular dramatized how this implied a new code of success. *Forbidden Fruit* (1921) opens with an oil monopolist trying to hire a young man who has dreams of going west and becoming self-made. In order to entice the hero, the boss wants to show him the high life that can be his in the city with a nice salary. This includes introducing him to a beautiful socialite. But as the evening drew near, the bait got sick. So the boss dresses up his maid—a poor working girl married to a slimy crook—who becomes equally ravishing. As the screen flashes to the girl as Cinderella, the hero falls in love. When her husband conveniently dies in a robbery, the two are free to marry. He has indeed earned the fruits of the system; and her masquerade has yielded a new mobility ethic for women: glamor leads to a leisure-oriented home that only a man with money can buy. She quits work, they marry, and the hero is inspired to labor hard for the boss to gain the high salary so necessary for the good life. Presumably, his sacrifice of independence in the West was worth it: success can bring him a beautiful woman.[24]

By reorienting the nature of the home between 1917 and 1921, DeMille defined the limits of the moral revolution on the screen for the next decade. Formerly a director like Griffith saw an intimate connection between saving the ascetic family and transforming a corrupt society. Heroic ideals were conceived broadly; but in the twenties they narrowed. In spite of the growing inequalities of wealth or political corruption during the period, the themes of Progressivism almost vanished. Earlier stars like Pickford, Hart, or Theda Bara who were identified with Victorian images declined in popularity. Major films no longer revolved around reformist issues. Even the seeming exception highlights the rule. When producers brought the great Soviet director, Sergei Eisenstein, to Hollywood in the twenties, they eventually refused to let him make a film, for they felt his scripts were too critical of American society. Little wonder that no major artist or director identified his product with a socially transforming ideal. A comparison for the earlier period is almost impossible to acquire; but an analysis of the twenties' 6,600 films showed that only fifteen (0.22 percent) dealt with labor, fifty-one (0.77 percent) with modern politics, sixty-six (0.95 percent) with religion, and 198 (2.94 percent) with the environment of the poor or immigrants. Clearly something had changed.[25] (See Table VII.)

Nevertheless, men did not give up on achievement. Rather, its perimeters had changed. A common device in comedy, for example, was to show a man trying to be an old-fashioned do-gooder who finally learns a more modern ethic. Two of the era's major stars were masters at this. Unlike the outsider Chaplin, Buster Keaton and Harold Lloyd were insiders who fumbled in their efforts to achieve the old Protestant heroism. In Keaton's *The Cameraman* (1928), *Sherlock Junior* (1924), *The Navigator* (1924), and *Seven Chances* (1925), the central character is inept in the face of the machine age and afraid of the new woman. The typical solution was given its most hilarious form in Harold Lloyd's immensely popular *Safety Last* (1923). Playing an ambitious American youth, Lloyd goes to work in a huge department store. There we see him confined by the time clock, bosses, and the female customers who bombard him behind the lingerie counter. He is nervously attracted to a sexy girl whom he tries to impress by pretending to be the store's manager. Clumsiness in both roles leads him to realize that he must find a new way to make it to the top. This he does, literally, through an advertising stunt. The hero becomes a "human fly" in order to climb the firm's skyscraper. In some of the funniest scenes ever filmed, the hero frantically scrambles up from floor to floor, desperately waiting for his circus stunt-man friend to take over. But the real gymnast is being chased by a cop for illegal parking, so the hapless youth must persevere. Miraculously, he makes it to the top, where his ecstatic sweetheart embraces him. An odd form of upward mobility indeed.[26]

Given that the modern world was so impenetrable, the traditional code of individualism had to be reassessed as well. Now the dream of potency had to find a more romantic locale. Over 50 percent of the Hollywood films in the twenties were western, swashbuckler, detective, or gangster genres. Such traditional fare had informed dime novels of the nineteenth century, and films of the early period, but now the tone differed. Written almost exclusively by men, these new films allowed the audience to identify with heroic males. Yet it was not the old Anglo-Saxon cowboy like William S. Hart who conquered villainous symbols of current political or economic threats. One theme, perhaps best dramatized in John Ford's *The Iron Horse* (1925), used the mythological West as a metaphor for modern optimism. In this story, the building of the transcontinental railroad is seen laying the foundation for the machine age. After surmounting difficulties, the railroad is completed, symbolizing national unity, one open to immigrant workers of all nationalities. Although the film clearly shows an American hero as the dominant force, the Polish, Chinese, and Italian workers can put aside labor conflict for the great opportunities opened up by the machine-made America.[27]

Yet precisely because the dream of potency was so difficult to achieve in this machine age, the heroic image also had to change. Now the man of will needed an exotic environment, far removed from contemporary life and work, where he can revenge himself against oppressors, and win exciting females. While these allowed men to achieve in far away places, it also had a modern message. Without rejecting parental values of success, the man could transcend the moral boundaries of the past. Modern heroes were Anglo males who mingled in the urban underworld, or romantic locales. Unlike the ascetic Griffith characters, these men took on some of the foreign elements they either adopted or fought: swarthy looks, physical graces, opulent dress, and the desire for dancing and fun. And the very remoteness of the setting freed these stars from the psychological inhibitions of conventional life. In other words, the hero looked to different cultures for those traits that seemed absent from his own tradition. Consequently, he saw foreigners in almost cliché terms, projecting onto them all the grace he now wanted to acquire.

Nowhere was this transformation more evident than in the career of Douglas Fairbanks. During the pre-War era, the smiling, clean-cut Fairbanks was linked to reviving the manhood of the frontier. Films such as *His Picture in the Papers* (1916), *Wild and Wooly* (1917), *The Knickerbocker Buckaroo* (1919), *A Modern Musketeer* (1918), and *His Majesty the American* (1919) showed a white-collar worker using his athletic ability to order modern society. Yet in the twenties, the same will power emerged in exotic locales. Far from contemporary social problems, Fairbanks was a tanned Spaniard, Frenchman, Arab, or Californio in extravaganzas that far exceeded earlier photoplays: *The Gaucho* (1927), *The Mark of Zorro* (1920), *The Three Musketeers* (1921), *The Thief of Bagdad* (1924). Still preaching the Horatio Alger code of success, he triumphed over lusty villains and moved up the class order. Corresponding to the exotic locale, he assumed a swarthy appearance, won the love of an exciting female, and gained status from the aristocratic environment. In essence, success brought greater symbols of importance through high-level consumption; but it did not yield economic or political autonomy in the modern world.[28]

Realistic films taking place in modern settings showed how male heroes could assume much of the romantic ideal. Contrary to common myth, it was not found in rags to riches—only 1.5 percent of all the productions made in the twenties focused on that theme.[29] Much more common was a two-fold message. One side was projected in King Vidor's *The Crowd* (1927). The story begins with the birth of a child on Independence Day, 1900. His father proclaims that "someday" the boy will be "something big." Twenty years later the son leaves for the city to realize the paternal dream. In a magnificent shot, he stands on the New Jersey side of the Hudson River with the Manhattan skyline towering above his meager figure. A caption notes, "Like the other seven million, he believes that New York depends on him." Yet soon we see the youth amid huge buildings and massive crowds. He ends up in an office lost in a sea of desks, hardly something "big." In response, he turns to fun off the job and an exciting, youthful woman. They marry and she quits her job as a secretary. But in order for the home to offer excitement, he must work even harder. Significantly, he goes into advertising, selling goods that will enhance free time. In the end, he and his happy family go to a movie and applaud one of his commercials.

*The Crowd* also showed what was another dominant theme of the era: a transformed personality provided the means to modern success. No film dramatized this better than a charming but realistic comedy made by William Seiter, *Skinner's Dress Suit* (1925). Seiter shows his hero, Mr. Skinner, as a beleaguered male who has just married and moved into suburbia. Commuting to New York City, Skinner is lost in the crowds. At the office, he punches time clocks, and routine tasks drain his energy. Meanwhile, Mrs. Skinner buys on installment plans stylish clothes, furniture, and dancing and charm lessons. She not only lives above her means, but assumes the instruction will make Skinner a new man. Naturally, he remains skeptical, until a chance event proves to be his big break. This happens at a nightclub, where his employer holds an office party. The cabaret itself is testimony to mass culture and Rudolph Valentino's popularity. The customers sit amid Arabian architecture and eat on pillows, while "sheiks" serve as waiters. Everyone at the party remains formal, until the dancing begins. Now, the Skinners do the Charleston that they learned at dancing school. Soon Mr. Skinner shows his bosses how to do the steps, shake, and have fun. Now his employer promotes Skinner away from his desk, for they realize he has a personality that can sell goods. Indeed, as the money rolls in, Mrs. Skinner's faith in refurbishing her husband's life has paid off. In the age of cooperation, personality is a commodity that will advance one up the ladder.[30]

Once success became defined less in terms of civic improvement or job satisfaction as in the past, its rewards could become a dominant aspiration for upwardly bound rural as well as immigrant "youth." During the twenties, this theme overlapped with one that was very rare in the teens: an intense generational rebellion that permeated scores of films. *Stark Love* (1927), for example, showed a

young man in the Tennessee hills wooing a country girl who reads
fashion magazines and dreams of a life of leisure in the city. The
boy, too, wants to leave for urban opportunities—education and
money not found on the farm. But first he must win the Oedipal
battle. His widowed father lusts for his sweetheart, and connives
with her father for a marriage promise. At the same time, the patriarch demands his son's loyalty and subservience on the farm. Finally, just in the nick of time before the union is consummated
through rape in the bedroom, the youth physically battles his father and the heroine smashes the elder's head to knock him out.
The young couple then float down the river toward a new life in
the city. In a similar though less violent film, *The Jazz Singer* (1927),
Al Jolson plays an assimilating immigrant. This incredibly successful movie was the first "talkie." It showed a poor Jewish boy whose
dreams of becoming a jazz singer are thwarted by his father. Yet
his mother approves of him shedding the ghetto's religious orthodoxy. And as he gains fame as a blackface entertainer, he sings his
thanks to her, "Mammy, how I love ya'." Hence the hero discards
tradition but not the familial standards of achievement. For only
with money can he win the new woman and the exciting life he
desires.[31]

None of this quest for private fulfillment was lost on the heroines
of the twenties, whose needs perfectly complemented those of
their potential providers and husbands. Films that featured a new
woman were usually written by female scenarists and played by
one of the large number of young actresses under twenty-five who
worked in the Hollywood industry. Interestingly enough, the female heroine was much more likely to be found in contemporary
urban society, and was generally more optimistic about it than her
male counterpart. Whether she was an emancipated wife or flapper
played by Clara Bow, Mae Murray, Joan Crawford, Gloria Swanson, or Norma or Constance Talmadge, she portrayed a restless
young woman eager to escape from an ascetic home. Seeking a new
role, she could take a job in search of freedom and money, but
would never identify with the low level work available. In the rare
films where women hold economic power over men, it was shown
as a waste of a beautiful woman's true role. These and other
heroines find their real emancipation in short skirts, glamor, and
innocent sexuality. They love to go out on the town and rub

elbows with men, where they smile, flirt, and dance the Charleston to black orchestras. Yet as one title warned, they must never be *Manhandled* (1924), lest they lose the virtue so necessary on the marriage market. This pays off in the attraction of a successful man who also wants fun in leisure and can afford to support her emancipation. Consequently, over 95 percent of all films concentrating on a working girl end with her leaving employment for marriage. And over 85 percent of the decade's films resolve all difficulties by culminating in romance or the suggestion of conjugal bliss.[32]

Two films by the classic flapper star Clara Bow illustrate the allure as well as the tension in this new woman. The first coined a term for what all women should have, *It* (1927). In this story by Elinor Glyn, a bored department store clerk looks to leisure for freedom. She cultivates her youthful beauty and dancing ability in the city's nightlife. Since these actions were directed toward catching men, the heroine soon attracts her boss, who wants an alternative to the genteel women of his class. To win him, Clara has to show that she is not the mother of an illegitimate child who lives with her. In other words, she must prove that she is chaste, despite her naughty behavior. The plot charts this effort, and culminates in their marriage. Another film shows why this virtue was so important. *The Plastic Age* (1925) features Bow as a sexy coed who attracts the top college athlete and scholar. Her sexuality and wild night life, however, drain him of the energy he needs to win games and get high marks. When he begins to fail, his parents arrive and demand that he straighten up. She nobly leaves his life, so he can succeed again. This proves her goodness, and in the end she wins her man.[33]

Yet what happens to the woman after this happy ending? Rarely was this confronted on the screen. But when it was, it suggested—along with the era's comedies—that the cultural reorientation was not successfully completed. Indeed, some of the disillusionment associated with the 1930s originated earlier. The one genre where this appeared was the works starring the magnificent Swedish actress, Greta Garbo. Garbo was brought to Hollywood in the mid-twenties, when the DeMille formula was well established. Even the titles to her films evoke the passion that showed on her expressive countenance: *Flesh and the Devil* (1927), *Love* (1927), *A Woman of Affairs* (1929), *The Kiss* (1929), *The Torrent* (1926), *The Single Standard*

(1929), *Wild Orchids* (1929). In these vehicles, she usually plays a tormented wife of a man who can afford to give her everything. She is the leisured woman with sexual allure, luxury, and a mansion. Still her quest for fulfillment is stymied by her narrow role in the domestic confines and the sexual divisions perpetuated by her work-obsessed husband. Seeking an alternative, she turns to a man who appears to be what her husband is not: romantic and attentive. In scenes of remarkable erotic power, Garbo arouses her audience to the expectations of a real sexual relationship. Like no other star of her time, Garbo is definitely beyond innocence. Yet the inevitable tragedy appears in Garbo's brooding, mysterious face: her lover too is bound up in society's demand for masculine success and control over female sexuality. Implicit in all her films, then, is a sharp criticism of half-hearted breaks from nineteenth-century puritanism. Still the heroine holds on to the hope that with even greater self-beautification efforts, she will find the truly exciting man and the utopian hearth removed from the cruel outside world. [34]

Perhaps the most powerful and visually beautiful dramatization of this dilemma occurred in *The Temptress* (1926). The film opens on a masquerade ball in an elaborate European estate. In the shadows, Garbo kisses a handsome man with visible passion. Yet she is married to another: a businessman who merely uses her as a status symbol to further his career. In rebellion, she follows her lover to Latin America where he supervises a large crew of men building a dam in the wilderness. Since this is a place where males are committed to taming nature and "work, Work, WORK," as a title proclaims in large letters, the men including the hero are drawn to the temptress and ignore their tasks. Finally dissipation leads to the dam's collapse and the town's destruction. Nevertheless, the film has a happy ending. She inspires her lover to rebuild the dam and they marry, with the wife agreeing to remove her threatening sexuality from the public arena. So, despite the initial message that "emancipated" women were not really free in the economic or sexual realm, the story ends by affirming men's subordination of women, and the containment of sexuality in the leisure realm. In other words, because passion was still a threat to the work ethic, women's emancipation was to be for the benefit of men in their private hours. [35]

Corresponding to the emphasis on personalism was a new style of film aesthetics. Before the twenties, major directors used the medium to teach moral lessons and inspire the audience to change the world. Surely there was excitement, but the movement and power of the screen directed emotions to conquering the corruptions of society. In accord with this reformist goal, cinematography displayed balance, clarity, and objectivity. For the director wanted to show a realistic and accurate picture of the world, so the audience would know how to better it. Yet when artists like DeMille began to emphasize internal rather than external transformations, they used techniques in new ways. Initially, they stayed within realism; but the "Rembrandt Style" that DeMille boasted concentrated on the face and emotional struggles. Close-ups no longer showed hazy ethereal glows. Now lights and shadows highlighted the inner life.

Although the older style remained, DeMille paved the way for one of the era's great cinematic developments. Hollywood producers began to look toward Europe to import innovative directors. Film makers such as F. W. Murnau, Joseph von Sternberg, Mauritz Stiller, Victor Seastrom, Fritz Lang, and Erich von Stroheim all came from Germanic European countries and had been influenced by expressionist painters and dramatists. That mode placed less emphasis on a clear depiction of the world, and stressed how lyric and poetic states of mind could infuse the environment. When this was transformed into film, the visually beautiful products starred players like Greta Garbo; and they used the camera to alter an empirical perception of the landscape. Using mysterious lighting, dual visions of reality, and hazy focusing, they explored the inner life of their characters. The objective world was less important than the atmosphere and mood of the surroundings. Von Stroheim or von Sternberg were noted for their attention to detail, especially the body and clothing. Glimmering light would capture the "oceanic emotion of love." Or in the work of F. W. Murnau, especially *City Girl* (1929), and *Sunrise* (1927), the objective world faded before the psychic mood. Similarly, his moving camera created a sense of weightlessness on the screen, and refocused the point of view on the subjective life of the central character who was often in search of his or her true being. By the mid-twenties, the influence of these directors infused much of the Hollywood product. The quest for private fulfillment in screen plots was accentu-

Rudolph Valentino demonstrates the tango and the allure of the Latin lover in *The Four Horsemen of the Apocalypse* (1920). (Museum of Modern Art/Film Stills Archive)

In *Foolish Wives* (1922), Erich von Stroheim tantalizes an American bored with her work-obsessed husband. (Museum of Modern Art/Film Stills Archive)

Gloria Swanson and Thomas Meighan in *Why Change Your Wife?* (1920) enact the opening of the DeMille scenario: a prudish wife censures smoking in an effort to control her husband's indulgence. (Museum of Modern Art/Film Stills Archive)

The other side of the coin: the husband so concerned with public affairs that his wife (Gloria Swanson) sits bored in *Don't Change Your Husband* (1919). (Museum of Modern Art/Film Stills Archive)

The runaway wife in *Don't Change Your Husband* spurns her gigolo (Lew Cody), discovering that luxury alone will not make her happy. Note smoldering incense at right. (Museum of Modern Art/Film Stills Archive)

After marital separation, the transformed hero (Wallace Reid) learns that Bebe Daniels, as Satan Synne in *The Affairs of Anatol* (1921), will only lead to destruction. (Museum of Modern Art/Film Stills Archive)

The husband and wife (Gloria Swanson) reconcile in *The Affairs of Anatol* and bring allure into the formerly austere home. DeMille's camera lingers over sexuality and possessions, the modern elements of a stable marriage. (Museum of Modern Art/Film Stills Archive)

Agnes Ayres in DeMille's *Forbidden Fruit* (1921) embodies the solution for the modern female. Here she is a modern Cinderella: a dowdy, working-class girl transformed to an elegant lady with the aid of conspicuous consumption. (Museum of Modern Art/Film Stills Archive)

Harold Lloyd in *Safety Last* (1923) plays the beleaguered white-collar worker. Getting to the top is no easy task. (Museum of Modern Art/Film Stills Archive)

---

*Top:* The Classic DeMille bath scene from *Male and Female* (1919) shows Gloria Swanson amid wealth, cleansing her body and, of course, titillating the audience. (Museum of Modern Art/Film Stills Archive)

*Bottom:* Greta Garbo in *The Kiss* (1929), with Anders Randolph, begins with the elegance of the DeMille happy ending, yet still finds a huge gulf between her and her husband. In essence, spending has not solved the sexual crisis. (Museum of Modern Art/Film Stills Archive)

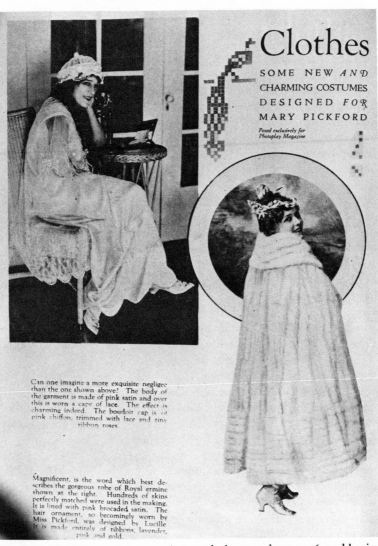

# Clothes

SOME NEW *AND*
CHARMING COSTUMES
DESIGNED *FOR*
MARY PICKFORD

*Posed exclusively for*
*Photoplay Magazine*

Can one imagine a more exquisite negligee
than the one shown above? The body of
the garment is made of pink satin and over
this is worn a cape of lace. The effect is
charming indeed. The boudoir cap is of
pink chiffon, trimmed with lace and tiny
ribbon roses.

Magnificent, is the word which best describes the gorgeous robe of Royal ermine
shown at the right. Hundreds of skins
perfectly matched were used in the making.
It is lined with pink brocaded satin. The
hair ornament, so becomingly worn by
Miss Pickford, was designed by Lucille.
It is made entirely of ribbons, lavender,
pink and gold.

Mary Pickford flaunts her expensive wardrobe as early as 1916, and begins
the reign of the screen star as the consumption idol. (New York Public
Library/Theater Collection)

---

*Top: The Crowd* (1925) demonstrates the continuing routinization of
middle-class work. No wonder the hero turns to leisure and the new
woman for excitement. (Museum of Modern Art/Film Stills Archive)

*Bottom:* Tom Mix, the modern "Rhinestone Cowboy," sheds the roughhewn look of the past, and finds romance in *The Lucky Horseshoe* (1925).
(Museum of Modern Art/Film Stills Archive)

ated by a "foreign" style that heightened the importance of the intimate self.[36]

Film makers furthered the effect through longer films and more elaborate sets. In this development, the twenties provided a golden age for art directors. DeMille began the trend by creating expensive trappings and exotic splendors. To accomplish the task he brought people directly from Broadway and the *Ziegfeld Follies*— one of the most noted being the Viennese designer Joseph Urban. Called upon to make expressive backgrounds, these art directors complemented the images produced by the camera. Instead of designing a Spanish, French, or English home directly after the original, the walls, doorways and floors might be foreshortened and entrances enlarged to create a sense of depth and endless space. Another technique was to build natural environments with curving lines and hazy backgrounds, lit in such a way that shadows and light permeated the players. The effect generated a dream world. Here was a perfect environment for utilizing the moving camera and the subjectivity of the character. Finally, films were longer and slower paced, drawing attention less to action and more to exploring the mystery of environment and individuals.

In such surroundings, there might be a release of inhibitions. "Modern audiences," explained De Mille of this new formula, "don't go to the movies to be the leading characters objectively, but subjectively. They go to have their insides Janet Gaynor, insides, not outsides. They want to feel her emotions. They want to be her, but emotionally, not physically." DeMille and other directors thus utilized a number of techniques to heighten the effect. One was to accentuate the power of what film makers thought was the most exciting emotion of the age: sex. DeMille in particular took great pains to urge American actresses to shed their Anglo-Saxon inhibitions during love scenes so the close-up would involve the audience intimately. Directors also wanted men and women players to carry themselves as objects of grace and beauty. Often this process of looking at the body as an object on display was indeed something new. One actress, Betty Blythe, recalled that she was told to practice walking in an elaborate gown. Although she was only one step removed from Victorianism, she soon "walked toward a long mirror. And I saw my body. I saw my legs, my torso, my long, long arms. I said, is that I? . . . I had never looked at my body as a piece of statuary. . . . I had this marvelous feeling; it was most extraordinary. I can still feel the chills all over my body."

A return to basic emotion and bodily grace also generated an expressive acting technique. Future generations watching some of the era's films would see an exaggerated, even laughable style. Yet it was consciously planned. Some of it was due to the need to convey emotional ideas in a silent medium, in order to explain relationships. Some of it was due to the fact that filming in silence took fewer frames per second than when run on sound projectors—so it looks less subtle today. Still the most important reason was that producers and directors wanted their players to shed Victorian or middle-class restraint. Exaggerated and intense emotions in dramatic situations were one way of conveying a release from repression, showing a psychological realism of intense feeling. As the actors and actresses heightened the level of normal expression, viewers saw how they, too, could be free of repressions. Precisely because of the effort to show life as more intense than it was, an actress like Garbo could not only project the style but even push it too far. As the Soviet director Sergei Eisenstein remarked after seeing her work before the camera, "She possessed none of the techniques learned at professional schools, acting purely by instinct. Instinct of course sometimes fails the actor. On such occasions there were hysterical outbursts and floods of tears on the set. Acting was a hard way of earning a living for Garbo."

All of this struggle, however, could be worth it if the fans elevated the player to stardom. Clearly, hero worship had been a part of American life flowing from the individualism of a democratic culture. Citizens had glorified industrial titans and military, political, and even show business personalities. Yet the celebrity gave hero worship a new twist. Producers furthered the unprecedented cult of the stars in the twenties by making their films more costly and technically superior than the shorts of the pre-War era. Sets and lighting made the star look younger, more beautiful, and taller than in real life. Romantic close-ups provided a powerful sense of intimacy, one that on the gigantic screen turned the player into an almost godlike force. When this persona met and conquered difficulties, his or her character became at one with the word "star." Like the course of celestial bodies, the stars never fell to earth's foibles. Always full of energy and warmth, the star constantly shed light on the viewers, showing them how to be dazzling as well. Audiences thus found predictable models of success. As a secular god who met and solved the problems of the current day, the hero explained Stephan Stills to the Harvard Business School, was one who

> appeals to the midriff, not the mind, and the people on the screen are people with enormous physical vitality. The player allows the spectators to live vicariously the more brilliant shadow figures of their mind. They are what people would like to be. Here there is no suppression or frustration. The film offers a Freudian reverie, geared not to the intellect, but to the mind and heart.[37]

Here progress took a new turn, from the social and historical to the private sphere. An audience looking for liberation from the past turned to the stars to learn how to be different. Producers fed this need by advertising films as bigger, more costly, and better than in the past. New players and fresh stars arose to satisfy each generation's tastes. Every major production portrayed the hero and heroine breaking from the past, symbolized by the latest outfits and hairdos, and more opulent surroundings. In accord with the Hollywood formula of "variety in clothes, faces and names," a star—unlike a nineteenth-century character actor—was a young person who experimented with a number of roles, identities, and styles. After the currency of their films wore off, they left the first-run houses to appear on local screens throughout the country. In sum, producers had learned that it paid to create images that came and went, so that the viewers got the illusion of newness, progress, and change without any alteration in the larger community.[38] As Irving Thalberg explained in 1926,

> The various stars and directors are examples of style and we can very easily trace their popularity up and down to the style of the moment. For instance, it is no accident that Clara Bow with her representation of the flapper would be a star today. If it hadn't been her it would have been some other girl of exactly the same qualities.[39]

It was no accident, then, that the screen player set up models for the consumption economy. For the twenties saw a much higher degree of personal cultivation as players took on what can only be called a slim, pasted down look. The effect was to stylize even further the playful and erotic appearance of the stars, in order to legitimize what was seen as the potential anarchy in their foreign and formerly lower-class activities. Hence unlike the heroes of old, male stars were not producers who helped build the society, but figures heavily oriented toward spending. Even that great symbol of American manhood, the cowboy, experienced this change. During the teens, the greatest Western idol was William S. Hart. As a roughhewn, plain-dressed hero, Hart portrayed the ideal of ascetic manhood which challenged institutional corruption. But as Hart's career declined, the popularity of Tom Mix rose. Indicative of a new era, "Tom" often played agents of the federal bureaucracy, such as in *Sky High* (1921), and Phillips Oil Corporation even built him a commemorative museum. Such success yielded appropriate rewards. On the screen, Mix wore spangled, opulent Western gear, rode a white horse, and sat on a silver saddle. Off the screen, he drove a huge white convertible, and lived in a Renaissance chateau noted for a neon sign blazing his name to passers-by.

In Hollywood, others followed the same pattern. Fan magazines glorified those like Douglas Fairbanks, Rudolph Valentino, Harold Lloyd, and John Barrymore who each had palatial homes and lavish wardrobes containing hundreds of suits and shoes. To an admiring public, these ever-youthful personalities could show that becoming self-made had taken a new form.[40] Although robber-barons and the wealthy had large wardrobes and palatial homes in the past, the Hollywood stars linked this not to an established elite, but to the tradition of open opportunity. Rarely was the star portrayed as born into this status or wealth. Rather, he was an average, unknown American who used his talent for expressing charisma, charm, and sex appeal. Rising from anonymity, he acquired fame, which rested not on domination of others, but on the ability to entertain and make people happy. This could indeed bring a kind of nobility, as when stars married European aristocrats or people from "high society," or when they entertained royalty as in the case of Douglas Fairbanks and Mary Pickford, Rudolph Valentino and Gloria Swanson. Yet at all times, the stars were ordinary folks whose lavish lifestyles could be democratized. Thus they were the models, not the enemies, for the middle class.

Female players who showed viewers how to attract the modern man also consumed extravagantly. The career of Gloria Swanson, the major star of the twenties, exemplified this pattern. Coming from a modest Protestant background, she first gained notice in the teens as a Sennett bathing beauty. From there she became the before-and-after wife in DeMille's matrimonial dramas. In some of the decade's most successful films, she played the flapper or the modern woman who caught successful men. Yet she was not a stunning beauty like Greta Garbo, Norma Talmadge, or Clara Bow; rather it was her ability to transform herself through clothes and cosmetics that made her so famous. Learning, as she confessed, "all my expensive tastes from DeMille," she was known as the "best dressed woman in the world." Since the "studio paid all the bills . . . never did I wear the same dress twice." Nor did she stay long with any one man. Between 1920 and 1930, she married a film star, two millionaires (one owned Hollywood's famed Brown Derby restaurant), and the Count de Falaza. Believing that "beauty is a career," she endorsed products and cosmetics that promised a similar allure to other females. For "the world holds no place for a worn looking woman these days, and admiration is so necessary for a woman's happiness."[41]

The consumption ideal overlapped with the Hollywood home, which during the twenties became even more lavish and exotic than the teens. Throughout the decade, fan magazines, films, newspapers, and radio portrayed it as the place where the stars might enjoy a thoroughly romantic marriage. In contrast to the ascetic family of the past, it was not tied to the socializing institutions of production, religion, or the state. As a private ideal, it was a place where stars could bring passion, fun, and pleasure into their formerly restrained lives. Each estate reflected the personality of its owner. There was Cecil B. DeMille's "Paradise," Rudolph Valentino's "Falcon's Lair," Harold Lloyd's "Green Acres," and of course "Pickfair." Norma Talmadge's house was typical, with "ballrooms, theaters, swimming pools, projection rooms, pipe organs, sun parlors, picture windows, pillared pagodas and every other conceivable comfort and luxury." These homes broke from Anglo-Saxon styles and took on the romance of exotic lands; Nathanael West observed that the Hollywood Hills were now filled with "Mexican ranch houses, Samoan huts, Mediterranean villas, Egyptian and Japanese temples, Swiss chalets and Tudor cottages." As the stars appeared as "commoners" rising to success, they signaled that people should work for new rewards: money to buy private fulfillment.[42]

Whatever tension existed in the ideal was resolved in the ever-present youth cult. Amid the leisure and fun, the Hollywood star would presumably stay young. When this model became the key to the consumption that fans brought to their free time in the twenties, it became a greater concern than previously. Like adolescents who were increasingly removed from the economy and filling colleges, stars and their fans were exhorted to make leisure a place for sexual mutuality and more physical attractiveness. Yet no matter how great the egalitarian potential, it was a revolution limited to the private realm. Neither sex could use the quest for expressiveness to challenge economic inequalities, routinized work, or the continuing separation of sexual roles in public life. Rather, because the twentieth-century cult of youth was ultimately seen as removed from somber concerns, the spontaneity of adolescence could not served as a lever to criticize and change the larger society. For this reason, it could offer great meaning and fulfillment in leisure time, without threatening the status quo. Instead, by constantly changing clothes, manners, and styles, adults in leisure could avoid facing their half-hearted rebellions from the sexual roles of the past.

The world of Hollywood, of course, did not emerge in a vacuum. It culminated the cultural reform of the teens, and reflected the new demands the urban middle classes were making on the economy. Clearly, this was in the interests of film makers who profited from leisure activities; but it was no manipulated conspiracy. Nor had Americans totally given up on the code of success with its high value placed on work. Yet the rise of mass culture did suggest that in the corporate era people increasingly looked outside conventional public arenas, in part for the individualism and classlessness that had been the promise of the democracy. In a society where private work and civic duties took less of one's energies, leisure became the egalitarian arena where people might find fulfillment. Now the business world became less a moral testing ground and more a supply house for new desires. From the twenties on, no leader could afford to ignore the fact that urbanites had turned away from vice crusading, and wanted a pragmatic approach to a smooth-running economy. One reason was that people hoped to indulge in a DeMille type home, which promised compensations to both sexes for the limitations and frustrations of work and civic life. In other words, despite the criticism implicit in many films, much of the modern economy would run on the same tracks as the movies, gaining steam from the unfulfilled promise of a moral or economic revolution. That is why William Harrison Hays firmly believed that in the twenties

> More and more is the motion picture being recognized as a stimulant to trade. No longer does the girl in Sullivan, Indiana, guess what the styles are going to be in three months. She knows because she sees them on the screen. . . . The head of the house sees a new golf suit. The housewife sees a lamp of a new design . . . down they go to the dealers to ask for the new goods.[43]

With this, modern mass culture truly had been born.

# EPILOGUE

I love being rich. I love playing tennis and not being cold in
the winter. I am the original Horatio Alger story.[1]

MOVIE STAR DIANA ROSS, 1977

By the twenties, the movie industry had developed into a major
urban institution. Growing out of a quest for meaning outside of
work, it was a focal point for the revolution in morals that characterized the middle class during the first two decades of the twentieth century. In the plush movie houses, the groups, at least those
with white skins, that had once maintained separate amusements,
now mingled: men and women, immigrants and natives, working
classes and affluent. The films expressed the larger implications of
this new life, focusing on familial, political, and economic issues.
Women were no longer the ascetic mothers of the past. Nor were
corporate men totally consumed by their work. Together the sexes
learned from the Hollywood life-style how to find individualism
and expressiveness in leisure. As this helped to ease the transition
from Victorian to modern life, it also helped to legitimize the consumption economy.

Perhaps the most intriguing question is whether movies caused
or reflected this reorientation. While a definitive answer is impossible, there are clear boundaries to the problem. In one sense, the
movie industry remained passive before social change. Movie
makers did not cause the breakdown in Victorianism, with its related alterations in work, sexual roles, and family expectations. Yet
because producers catered to an audience experiencing these transformations, and geared drama to their expectations, the art provides a complex form for discerning formerly hidden connections.
By merely reflecting the viewers' concerns, films reveal more about
the moral revolution than we could discover without this source. In

another sense, however, movies also generated change. Artists, like
the audience, felt that mass culture had become a focal point for
nonauthoritarian behavior and developed an appropriate form for
expressing these feelings. In the process, they created a unique
American cinema. Yet most important, movies were perhaps the
most powerful national institution which offered private solutions
to public issues. In other words, motion pictures could not change
society, but their form could infuse life with a new instinctual
dynamism and provide a major stimulus for generating modern
manners, styles, and models of psychological fulfillment.

But these solutions were not totally private. Because they had
such a profound effect on the way modern urbanites approached
consumption and leisure, there was a need for Hollywood. As the
tangible symbol of twentieth-century aspirations, it presented a new
success ethic and life-style. Undoubtedly, for this reason, future
social critics would focus on moviedom in order to expose the neg-
ative side of American life. Starting in the thirties, when artists and
novelists reassessed the consumer culture, Thomas Hart Benton
painted Hollywood as an inferno of garish sex, fame, and make
believe. Nathaniel West's *Day of the Locust* (1939) and Budd Schulberg's *What Makes Sammy Run?* (1941) examined literary heroes
who saw the Golden West as an escape from Eastern repression,
poverty, and dull work. A similar theme unfolded in a popular
genre of the movie industry itself, films focusing on Hollywood. In
a magnificent representative example, Billy Wilder's *Sunset Boule-
vard* (1950), Schulberg's and West's themes find an echo. While
the movies represent the height of happiness and success, none of
the main characters find this salvation; Hollywood is shown as
nothing beyond the rest of the world, with its unfulfilled moral and
economic revolution. If anything, disappointment resonates
through these stark, realistic tales.

Nevertheless, in a society with so few other options, even the
Depression could not dull the expectations surrounding Hollywood. Like so many other industries, the motion picture business
deeply felt the economy's collapse. Overcapitalized to build large
theaters and million dollar films, several of the major companies experienced bankruptcy, including Paramount, RKO, Universal, and
Fox Pictures. In many cases this led to further consolidation and

selling out to Wall Street conglomerates. The original moguls would still remain as executives; but power was taken out of their hands. Two of the original founders would go to jail in the thirties for jury tampering and trying to buy off labor. For it was during this decade, and with the aid of the New Deal administration, that unions finally came to the studios. The unskilled, skilled, and even white-collar workers including writers, directors, and players were organized. Some would even be part of the left wing and liberal politics then sweeping the country; and many became the targets of anti-Communism and McCarthyism in the post–World War II era.[2]

On the screen, these reassessments surfaced dramatically. Unlike other major industries, Hollywood would go through the Depression without any decline in demand for its productions. Artists closely identified with the previous era's concerns faded. Others, however, would become the major drawing cards of the day. Mirroring the rise of the immigrants in New Deal politics, as well as the population's search for roots in regional cultures, stars emerged who expressed the struggles of city dwellers and rural folk. Heroes such as James Cagney, Edward G. Robinson, Humphrey Bogart, John Wayne, James Stewart, and Henry Fonda displayed through language and manner urban toughness and the wisdom of common Americans, free of foreign or exotic dissipations. Heroines such as Jean Harlow, Bette Davis, and Joan Crawford provided the allure and stability to support themselves and their men through an era of deflated hopes. Still others could take the road of comedy. W. C. Fields and the Marx Brothers ridiculed the dominant values of the middle-class family, while Frank Capra attacked corruption in public life in a series of successful films. Yet through it all there was still the sense that the good hero might once again move up the social order and acquire affluence. As in the twenties, this was defined by the sexual expressiveness and fun of the Hollywood home. Fan magazines and happy endings of thirties movies suggest that despite the structural changes in the society, people wanted the economy to work so that they could return to the good life.[3]

Perhaps the greatest testimony to this is in one of Charles Chaplin's great films of the thirties, *Modern Times* (1936). Reflecting the comedian's continuing ability to tap the inner wishes of the populace, it opens on the tramp, Mr. Everyman, caught on an assembly line in a large factory. There dehumanized work and callous authority try to force feed him and turn him into a mere cog in the machine. After making technological values look ridiculous, the tramp leaves the factory and encounters a strike where he is mistaken for a picketing Communist. After being thrown in jail and finally released, the hero finds romance with a girl. Together they dream of a suburban home. To capture the wish, they sneak into a department store at night where toys and luxurious furnishings appear as the pinnacle of desire. As he roller skates, she lounges on a huge bed and tries on expensive gowns. Next they go to a cabaret where she becomes a dancer, and he sings playfully in Italian. Once that dream of happiness is threatened, they turn to the open road. The final shot shows them heading down a highway, moving toward a vast expanse of nature to the West. Presumably, in the future frontier the tramp will be able to find freedom and love.[4]

When the affluent society returned after World War II, under the stimulus of defense and consumer spending, Hollywood and mass culture perpetuated that dream. While the Cold War and McCarthyism considerably lessened political conflict, and commentators talked of a consensus society, the most original movies of the 1940s often presented the opposite of this optimism: a world of disappointment with American life. Nevertheless, most film makers tried to resolve these tensions through the goal of personal mobility and the affluent home. This aspiration seemed to take hold as the marriage age dropped and the marriage rate rose dramatically. In the 1950s, with suburban life becoming more popular than ever before, scholars offered several interpretations. Some saw mass consumption as a normal response to leisure. Others suggested that big business used it to buy off discontent with the nature of work. Still others examined its effects on American character and argued that abundance had been the heritage of America for over a century. The most accurate dated the change from the twenties, and perceived that Americans were still split between "the lingering tradition of abstinence . . . and the new gospel which encourages spending to make the wheels of industry run." Yet these insightful writers missed the crux of this historical development. As we have seen, the new life was not just something that happened in response to leisure, or was manipulated by businessmen. Rather, it had a dynamic of its own that carried the evolving middle-class aspirations for private life.[5] Even in the wake of the 1960s, as the black movie star Diana Ross's quote at the beginning of this chapter suggests, mass culture could continue to absorb outsiders into the modern American dream.

# HISTORIOGRAPHY AND NEW SOURCES

Through the creation of this book, my thought has been immeasurably influenced by the work of my fellow historians. Yet at the same time, my findings and the way I have used the movies as documents have led to a reassessment of central issues in twentieth-century history, as well as the discovery of relationships among work, family, and class that have previously remained obscure. Clearly, one of my major concerns has also intrigued other scholars, beginning with the Lynds in their classic study, *Middletown:* the dissolution of Victorianism and the rise of modern society.[1] What this transition meant for family life and cultural values has drawn the attention of several scholars. In their truly innovative works, Henry May, James McGovern, and John Higham pegged the period from 1890 to 1920 as the critical juncture. May focused insightfully on changes in intellectual thought, while McGovern and Higham probed the wider social context, particularly the interaction between high and low culture.[2] Exploring issues surrounding the new woman and the rise of urban leisure, these investigators noted the blurring of lines between classes, as well as the rise of new female behavior before the twenties. Others such as Daniel Scott Smith showed that the sense of a moral change had a basis in reality: single women participated in more sexual activity than previously.[3] Likewise, students of the family have documented a new perception of the home, characterized in part by divorce, "fun morality," and leisure.[4] Still, the overall explanation as to how and why these alterations occurred still remains opaque.

Most of these studies have highlighted transformations in the female role. But we also need to understand how changes in the male experience encouraged and paralleled the moral emancipation of women. Diverse scholars such as Richard Hofstadter, Peter Filene, C. Wright Mills, Daniel Miller, and Guy Swanson have noted that upper- and middle-class men at the turn of the century realized that it was difficult to become self-made in the traditional sense, for the basis of the economy had shifted from small property to large, centralized enterprises.[5] Some have argued that the result of these economic changes was a decline in job satisfaction. Others emphasize the benefits of security generated by the system. Both assertions testify to the fact that work had changed, along with material expectations. It was this development that turned males toward the leisure realm, and toward moral experimentation with women.

Initially this created a crisis within a Protestant-based culture that ramified through the major political issues of the day. By broadening our study of the movies to include the way the birth of mass culture overlapped with the vice crusading of Progressivism, we can begin to reconcile two major interpretations of this period. Historiographical trends led by Arthur Link, Richard Hofstadter, and George Mowry, despite different emphases, all suggest that the core of the reform movement centered in the "producers" of the city: self-defined artisans, workers, and small property owners.[6] Such groups objected to the hegemony of big business as well as the class conflict it unleashed. In response, their uprising led to needed regulatory agencies and welfare measures. Focusing on the "new middle classes" and businessmen, historians such as Gabriel Kolko, Samuel Hays, and Robert Wiebe have argued persuasively that much of the movement to create an expanded state was used by people involved in the large corporations, not to roll back the clock to the entrepreneurial economy, but to "order" the new.[7] The logical culmination of their argument is that the rise of big business in the twenties was due not to the failure of reformist politics, but rather to its success.

Whatever argument one heeds, questions raised by both interpretations remain unanswered. How did the old individualistic spirit which all Americans inherited acquiesce in the "search for order"? Why was the era known for vice crusading by both types of politics followed by the raucous and roaring twenties? To fathom these complexities, it is necessary to see that Progressivism was not just animated by perceived status decline or economic chaos, but by fears of family and sexual disorder as well. Urban reformers realized that as the corporations fostered alienating work along with affluence, the prosperous turned to the amusements of the laboring classes for freedom and moral experimentation. In accord with their desire to save Victorianism, Progressives expurgated saloons and brothels; but they also pioneered a new realm of mass leisure. For they looked to properly regulated entertainments like the movies as a tool for Americanizing the immigrants, stabilizing the family, and teaching the population its civic duties.

By validating new institutions of public leisure, particularly the movies, reformers created a little-understood continuity between the teens and the twenties. Social historians such as William Leuchtenberg, Gilbert Ostrander, Paul Carter, and Leo Lowenthal, as well as sociologists and economists such as the Lynds, John Kenneth Galbraith, and David Riesman have all shown how high-level production provided the foundation for the consumer-oriented lifestyle that would characterize the future.[8] Using a broader framework, Arthur Link in a very perceptive essay noted that Progressivism waned in the twenties as a political movement among the urban middle class because the high wages, free time, and security supplied by the corporations undercut hostility to big business.[9] I have tried to show that this was not because of the failure of Progressivism, but because the cultural side of reform had succeeded only too well. For by legitimizing amusements, reformers helped alleviate urbanites' anxieties as they made the transition from an economy of production to one of consumption.

The movie industry provides a valuable lens through which to view this process. Other amusements might be studied, such as ocean cruises, resorts, or amusement parks. But the film industry created not only a public arena of fun, but also a dramatic display of the new life on the screen. In seriously exploring these two sides of the movies, this study works in a much larger context than previous examinations of motion pictures. Prior to the 1970s, the field was dominated by journalists, publicists, gossip columnists, and film critics. Some of these concentrated on anecdotal history or the glamor of Hollywood life. Others had substantial merit and added to our understanding of individual artists, the industry's growth, and aesthetic innovations. At the other extreme were books written by social scientists looking to the movies for universal truths about American culture. Recent studies have broken from this ahistorical perspective and created works of real value.[10] For example, concentrating on social change in the twentieth century and using scholarly documentation, Robert Sklar and Garth Jowett examined the history of the movies from 1896 to the present.[11] While these represent an improvement over earlier efforts, neither focuses on the formative years from 1900 to 1920. Nor do they concentrate on the industry's relation to larger political issues, or changing work and sexual roles.

In an effort to comprehend these connections, this study assumes that the movie people were not just putting on the screen or in the surrounding trappings of moviedom what they thought would sell. Rather, they too were drawn to the themes of mass culture because they were living its allures from the inside. To uncover how the rank and file, the producers, and the major artists sorted out the remnants of their inherited Victorian traditions in response to new experiences, I have drawn on a wide variety of previously untapped historical sources. In the footnotes, documentation can be found for films seen at the major cinema archives: the Museum of Modern Art, New York City; the Library of Congress, Washington, D.C.; the Eastman House Film Library, Rochester, New York. For the benefit of scholars interested in pursuing the cited movies, I have included the name of the film, the year it was released, and its archival location. Besides the films themselves, two important catalogues provided descriptions of thousands of movies, including many no longer available on celluloid. The first is Kenneth Munden, ed., *American Film Institute Catalogue, 1919–1929*, published by the Library of Congress. The second is the industry's major trade journal, *Motion Picture World* (later named the *Motion Picture Herald*), which contains earlier plots and other relevant information. Along with reformers' and police reports, plus census data, these journals also provide facts on theaters, producers, and the changing nature of the audience, film genres, and content.

Material on the major players, directors, producers, and scenarists can be found in their respective files and scrapbooks at the Museum of Modern Art, the Academy of Motion Picture Arts and Sciences, or the Theater Arts Collection of the New York Public Library. In the absence of available monograph and paper collections, the scrapbooks and clipping files contain interviews, criticism, film plots, and the image projected to audiences. In addition, fan magazines, trade directories, company newspapers, and blue books provide statistics on the industry's rank and file, while also depicting the symbols emanating from Hollywood in the teens and the twenties. These primary documents allowed me to cut through the mythology and inaccuracies of most of the earlier histories of film. Any material drawn from the theater files and collections is so designated in the footnotes. Other sources I have used are in more traditional forms, and are readily available. All of these materials have been woven into a story that revolves around the rise of mass culture and the film industry from 1890 to 1929, and provide new sources for exploring unanswered questions about twentieth-century history.

*Appendix II*

---

# TABLES

---

Table I. Members of the Trust

| Company | Owner | Place of birth, death age | Religion | Previous trade, education, wealth | Organizational affiliation |
|---|---|---|---|---|---|
| Edison, NYC, 1896 | Thomas Edison[1] | Milan, Ohio 1847–1931 84 | Protestant | Noted inventor Primary school Millionaire | |
| Edison | Frank Dyer[1] | 1871–1941 70 | Protestant | Patent lawyer | Sons of the American Revolution |
| Edison | Thomas Armat[1] | Fredericksburg, Va. 1867–1948 81 | Protestant | Inventor, real estate; worth $160,000 at death | "Virginia gentleman" |
| Biograph, NYC, 1895 | Henry Marvin[1] | Jordan, N.Y. 1867–1940 73 | Protestant | Iron foundry College ed. Millionaire | Trustee, Univ. of Syracuse |
| Biograph | Wm. Dickson[2] | England 1860–? | Protestant | Inventor | |
| Biograph | Herman Casler[2] | | Protestant | Marvin's partner in iron works, Canastota, N.Y. | |
| Essanay, Chicago, 1897–1916 | George K. Spoor[1] | Highland Park, Ill. 1871–1953 82 | Protestant | Railroad concession Millionaire | |

| | | | | | |
|---|---|---|---|---|---|
| Lubin, Philadelphia | Sigmund Lubin[1] | 1851–1923<br>72 | Jewish | Small optical shop<br>Millionaire | |
| Vitagraph, Brooklyn, N.Y., 1896–1925 | Albert Smith[1] | England<br>1875–1958<br>83 | Protestant | Magical shows, mechanic<br>Millionaire | |
| Vitagraph | William Rock[1] | 1857–1920<br>63 | | Pool hall owner<br>$4 million estate at death | |
| Vitagraph | John Stuart Blackton[1] | Sheffield, England<br>1875–1941<br>66 | Protestant | Reporter, artist<br>Millionaire | |
| Selig of Chicago | William Selig[1] | Chicago, Ill.<br>1864–1948<br>84 | Protestant | Inventor | Masons, title of the "Colonel" |
| Kalem, Chicago | George Kleine[1] | ?–1923 | Protestant | Optical imports | |
| Kalem | Samuel Long | No information to date | | | |
| Kalem | Frank Marion | No information to date | | | |
| Pathé-Melies | These two French companies had their product distributed by George Kleine's importing firm. | | | | |

1. All of this information has been gleaned from these men's clipping files at the Academy of Motion Picture Arts and Sciences, Hollywood, California. These packets have obituaries, interviews, and research materials gathered by the Academy Library.
2. This information comes from Gordon Hendricks, *The Beginnings of the Biograph* (New York: Beginnings of the American Film, 1964), pp. 5–30.

Table II. Plot Types, 1907–1919

| | 1907 | 1908 | 1909 | 1910 | 1911 | 1912 | 1913 | 1914 | 1915 | 1916 | 1917 | 1918 | 1919 |
|---|---|---|---|---|---|---|---|---|---|---|---|---|---|
| Western | 17% | 0% | 3% | 0% | 10% | 10% | 4% | 6% | 2% | 3% | 4% | 0% | 0% |
| Stock melodrama (Griffith type) | 17 | 37 | 40 | 45 | 35 | 31 | 23 | 33 | 25 | 13 | 14 | 33 | 33 |
| Moral experimentation Victorian ending (Hart, vamp, serial queens, etc.) | 0 | 8 | 3 | 0 | 10 | 24 | 12 | 15 | 14 | 11 | 10 | 6 | 20 |
| Moral experimentation Modern approach to family (Pickford & Fairbanks type) | 0 | 0 | 0 | 0 | 1 | 8 | 0 | 4 | 13 | 6 | 9 | 44 | 47 |
| Social reform | 0 | 0 | 0 | 0 | 6 | 9 | 6 | 8 | 10 | 6 | 6 | 17 | 0 |
| Comedy, attack on Victorianism (Chaplin, Sennett) | 0 | 8 | 0 | 5 | 4 | 6 | 7 | 10 | 6 | 5 | 2 | 0 | 0 |
| Domestic comedy | 66 | 37 | 24 | 32 | 16 | 4 | 3 | 0 | 0 | 0 | 54 | 0 | 0 |
| Newsreel, travelogs | 0 | 0 | 18 | 0 | 3 | 8 | 41 | 20 | 26 | 55 | 0 | 0 | 0 |
| Fantasy, adventure | 0 | 10 | 12 | 18 | 9 | 0 | 4 | 4 | 4 | 1 | 1 | 0 | 0 |
| Total number analyzed: | 12 | 27 | 34 | 22 | 74 | 77 | 166 | 228 | 280 | 344 | 236 | 36 | 30 |

Prior to 1912, only one quarter to one half of the plots were described in detail. As the years advanced, more plots were fully outlined, which is why the numbers increase. After 1917, few plots were listed, probably because films were distributed through block booking, and producers listed only some of their films. Reflecting the new audience after 1914, there was a change in featured players; from farmers, workers, and shopkeepers they became artists, athletes, models, chorus girls, sons and daughters of manufacturers and stockbrokers, clerks, office workers, college students. Also, they were listed by name as "stars." Short newsreels and travelogs also increased in number, as did reform themes, in the early teens.

Sample of plots gathered by reading all the plot summaries for the first week of February and the first week of June in each year, listed in the *Motion Picture World*, 1907–1919, new releases.

## Table IIIa. Founders of the "Big Eight" [1]

| Company | Founder(s) [3] | Birthplace | Birthdate | Early career |
|---|---|---|---|---|
| Paramount | Adolph Zukor | Ricse, Hungary | 1873 | Fur trade |
| | Jesse Lasky | San Francisco | 1880 | Coronet player |
| 20th Century-Fox | William Fox | Tuchva, Hungary | 1879 | Peddler/ clothing |
| Loew's, Inc. (M.G.M.-prod.) | Marcus Loew | N.Y. East Side | 1891 | Fur trade |
| | Louis B. Mayer | Russia | 1885 | Junk dealer |
| | Samuel Goldwyn | Warsaw, Poland | 1882 | Glove sales |
| Universal | Carl Laemmle | Laupheim, Ger. | 1867 | Clothing |
| Warner Bros. | Harry Warner | Kroznashiltz, | | Bicycle repair |
| | Sam Warner | Poland | | Ice cream vendor, |
| | Abe Warner | | | fairground |
| | Jack Warner | | | barker |
| Columbia | Harry Cohn | N.Y. East Side | 1891 | Trolley conductor, vaudeville |
| United Artists [2] | President, Joseph Schenck | Russia | 1877 | Pharmacist, amusement park |

Radio-Keith-Orpheum — emerged later, outgrowth of radio.

1. By 1940, these companies virtually controlled the industry, collecting 95% of all rentals paid by U.S. theaters, and doing a business of almost $½ billion per year. (Leo Rosten, *Hollywood: The Movie Colony, the Movie Makers*, New York, 1941, p. 61.) In 1968, these companies still released most of the movies shown in the U.S. (*Film Daily Yearbook*, 1969, pp. 172–74.)
2. United Artists was originally formed by the merging of four leading movie makers (Charles Chaplin, Mary Pickford, Douglas Fairbanks, and D.W. Griffith) into one corporation. Although all the founders were presumably gentiles, the company was headed by the president, Joseph Schenck, who was Jewish.
3. All founders listed here are Jewish.

## Table IIIb. Founders of the "Big Eight"

*Harry Cohn*   Son of a German immigrant tailor, Orthodox Jewish parents. Worked as trolley conductor, vaudeville player, entered film as secretary to Laemmle, became president of Columbia Pictures.

*Samuel Goldwyn*   Born Sam Goldfish, Warsaw. At age eleven ran away to England, worked as blacksmith's assistant. Immigrated at age fifteen, entered glove business, formed Lasky Feature Players with Lasky, then formed Goldwyn Pictures with Selwyn Brothers. He then changed his name to Goldwyn and became an independent producer.

*Jesse Lasky*   Grandson of German immigrant, son of poor shoe salesman, worked many jobs. Breaking with Goldwyn he joined Zukor and became vice-president of Paramount.

*Carl Laemmle*   Son of German estate agent, worked as store apprentice, immigrated at age seventeen, worked at odd jobs, became clothing bookkeeper in Wisconsin. At age twenty-six began a nickelodeon chain, went into production, became head of Universal.

*Marcus Loew*   Son of Austrian immigrant waiter, age six sold newspapers, odd jobs, fur factory at age twelve, fur broker at age eighteen. At age twenty he started an arcade chain, formed Loew's, Inc., in 1920, bought Metro for $3 million and merged with Goldwyn and Mayer in 1924.

*Louis B. Mayer*   Son of Hebrew scholar, came from Canada and collected junk, set up Boston junk business at age nineteen, began a theater chain at age twenty-two, became rich on *Birth of a Nation* franchises, formed Metro Co., later became production head of MGM.

*Joseph Schenck*   Immigrated in early teens, pharmacist, ran Manhattan amusement park, began film concession, joined Loew, formed First National, became head of United Artists, founded 20th Century in 1933, merged with Fox, head of 20th Century-Fox in 1940.

*Warner Brothers*   Sons of poor cobbler, worked in bicycle repair, ice cream vending, fairground barking, railroad work, then exhibition and distribution, later production. Greatest success with sound.

Compiled from files at MOMAFL and AMPASL.

Table IV. Birthplaces of Movie Personnel

| Birthplace | Producers 1920 | Directors 1920 | Dirs. & prod. execs. 1923–24 | Actors 1920 | Actresses 1920 | Sc. writers/editors 1920 | Cinema-tographers 1920 | Child players 1920 | Total |
|---|---|---|---|---|---|---|---|---|---|
| Cities w/ Pop. over 100,000[1] | 7 | 99 | 94 | 197 | 193 | 61 | 63 | 15 | 729 |
| Cities w/ Pop. 2,500–100,000 | 10 | 80 | 83 | 160 | 130 | 63 | 43 | 7 | 496 |
| Towns w/ Pop. less than 2,500[2] | 5 | 28 | 26 | 68 | 28 | 22 | 23 | 5 | 205 |
| Foreign Born | 14 | 83 | 82 | 167 | 68 | 15 | 49 | 6 | 484 |
| England | 3 | 23 | 19 | 60 | 16 | 7 | 9 | 4 | 141 |
| Ireland | 1 | 6 | 7 | 18 | 3 | 3 | 0 | 0 | 38 |
| Scotland | 1 | 4 | 4 | 5 | 2 | 0 | 2 | 1 | 19 |
| W. Europe | 5 | 16 | 15 | 22 | 15 | 4 | 22 | 1 | 100 |
| E. Europe | 1 | 4 | 7 | 11 | 2 | 1 | 5 | 0 | 30 |
| Russia | 1 | 1 | 1 | 2 | 5 | 0 | 4 | 0 | 15 |
| Mid. East | 0 | 1 | 1 | 3 | 0 | 0 | 1 | 0 | 6 |
| Australia | 1 | 7 | 6 | 11 | 12 | 0 | 2 | 0 | 38 |
| Canada | 2 | 20 | 19 | 20 | 9 | 0 | 4 | 0 | 72 |
| S. America | 0 | 1 | 3 | 3 | 1 | 0 | 1 | 0 | 9 |
| S. Africa | 0 | 0 | 0 | 1 | 1 | 0 | 0 | 0 | 2 |
| Orient | 0 | 0 | 0 | 4 | 1 | 0 | 0 | 0 | 5 |

1. Since several of the biographical sketches from which these figures were compiled listed "New York" without specifying city or state, ¼ of those were considered New York City, since the population of New York City was approx. ¼ the population of the State. (United States Census 1890. N.Y.C. = 1,515,301; N.Y. State = 5,997,853.)

2. The Census defined urban as communities of over 2,500 inhabitants, thus the first two figures can be considered "urban." The proportion of rural-bred Americans in the industry is notably small; of a total of 1914 listed biographies, 1225 were urban American born, and 484 were foreign born, leaving only 205, approx. 10%, rural born.)

Compiled using population statistics from the United States Census, 1890, with personnel listed in the *Motion Picture Directory and Trade Annual*, 1920, and 1923–24.

Total urban percent, United States 1890 — 35.4%
Total urban-American born movie makers — 64.1%

## Table V. Ages of Movie Makers, 1920

| Age | Producers | Directors[1] | Actors | Actresses | Editors & sc. writers | Cinema-tographers | Total |
|---|---|---|---|---|---|---|---|
| 15–20 | 0 | 0 | 2 | 34 | 1 | 0 | 37 |
| 21–25 | 0 | 6 | 11 | 82 | 2 | 6 | 110 |
| 26–30 | 1 | 31 | 45 | 39 | 13 | 15 | 144 |
| 31–35 | 3 | 27 | 80 | 13 | 16 | 20 | 159 |
| 36–40 | 5 | 25 | 54 | 4 | 17 | 16 | 121 |
| 41–45 | 3 | 18 | 42 | 8 | 12 | 7 | 90 |
| 46–50 | 4 | 7 | 37 | 6 | 5 | 4 | 63 |
| 51–55 | 0 | 4 | 11 | 2 | 0 | 1 | 18 |
| 56–60 | 0 | 1 | 12 | 1 | 1 | 0 | 15 |
| 61–65 | 0 | 0 | 5 | 2 | 0 | 0 | 7 |

1. Including assistant directors, art directors, and technical directors

List compiled from *Motion Picture Studio Directory and Trade Annual*, 1920

## Table VI. Biographical Data—Major Female Scenarists

| Age in *1920* | *20–25* | *25–30* | *30–35* | *35–40* | *40–50* | Total |
|---|---|---|---|---|---|---|
| *Number* | 9 | 13 | 12 | 1 | 2 | 37 |
| *Class* | | | | | | |
|   Upper | 1 | 2 | 2 | 0 | 1 | 6 |
|   Middle | 6 | 9 | 9 | 1 | 1 | 26 |
|   Unknown | 2 | 1 | 2 | 0 | 0 | 5 |
| *Marital Status* | | | | | | |
|   Married | 4 | 10 | 9 | 1 | 1 | 25 |
|   Single | 2 | 0 | 2 | 0 | 0 | 4 |
|   Divorced[1] | 1 | 4 | 4 | 1 | 0 | 10 |
|   Unknown | 2 | 2 | 2 | 0 | 1 | 7 |

1. Some women in the "divorced" category were also counted as "married," if they had re-married after the divorce.

Compiled from files at MOMAFL and New York Public Library Theater Collection, in Daisann McLane, "Silent Sisters: Women Screenwriters in Hollywood, 1915–1929," Senior Thesis, Princeton University, 1976.

## Table VII. Major Film Genres During the 1920s

| Genre | Number | Percent |
|---|---|---|
| Western | 935 | 18.84 |
| Costume or foreign setting | 659 | 13.23 |
| Comedy | 521 | 10.50 |
| Flapper, actress, model | 419 | 8.44 |
| Love, romance | 378 | 7.62 |
| Crime | 365 | 7.36 |
| Central character female | 273 | 5.50 |
| High society | 233 | 4.69 |
| Family relations | 244 | 4.51 |
| Ethnic, racial | 206 | 4.15 |
| War, contemporary and historical | 178 | 3.59 |
| Northwestern | 152 | 3.06 |
| Environment of poor | 146 | 2.94 |
| Urban night life | 144 | 2.90 |
| Working woman | 121 | 2.44 |
| Political, reform | 93 | 1.88 |
| Success up class ladder | 75 | 1.51 |
| Occult | 72 | 1.45 |
| Religion, Biblical | 58 | 1.17 |
| Labor | 11 | .22 |
| Science fiction | 5 | .10 |
| Monster | 4 | .08 |

Kenneth Munden, *American Film Institute Catalogue*, 1920–1929. 4,963 plots were summarized in this catalogue, out of a total of 6,660 films made during the decade. Every plot was included in the table; some fell into more than one category.

# NOTES

## List of Abbreviations

AMPASL   Academy of Motion Picture Arts and Sciences Library, Los Angeles, California.

EHFL   Eastman House Film Library, Rochester, New York.

LCFA   Library of Congress Film Archives, Washington, D.C.

LCPAL   Lincoln Center for the Performing Arts Library, New York Public Library, Theater Arts Collection, New York City.

MOMA   Museum of Modern Art Library, New York City.

MOMAFL   Museum of Modern Art Film Library, New York City.

MPW   *Motion Picture World*

NYPLTAC   New York Public Library Theater Arts Collection.

# Introduction

1. Irving Thalberg, "Lecture at the University of Southern California," unpublished Introduction to the Photoplay, Los Angeles, Academy of Motion Picture Arts and Sciences.
2. Robert S. and Helen Merrell Lynd, *Middletown: A Study in American Culture*, New York, 1929, pp. 251–315.
3. *Ibid*, p. 82.
4. See Appendix I for an historiographical examination of this issue.

# Chapter One: The Backdrop

1. Henry Seidel Canby, *The Age of Confidence* (originally published in 1934) in *American Memoir*, Boston, 1947, pp. 4, 26, 95, 101, 105.
2. *Ibid.*, pp. 10–15, 59, 61–64, 97, 115–20, 150–53.
3. *Ibid.*, pp. 95–101; drawn from a reading of James Fenimore Cooper's *The Pioneers*, New York, 1823; *The Pathfinder*, New York, 1840; *The Prairie*, New York, 1827; and *The Last of the Mohicans*, New York, 1826. Horatio Alger sold over sixteen million copies during the century, see Frank Luther Mott, *Golden Multitudes*, New York, 1947, pp. 158–59. On the self-made tradition, see Irving Wylie, *The Self-Made Man in America*, New Brunswick, N.J., 1954; for its application to the social reality of mobility in an industrializing city, see Stephan Thernstrom, *The Other Bostonians: Poverty and Progress in the American Metropolis, 1880–1970*, Cambridge, Mass., 1973.
4. The arguments are summarized and documented in Richard D. Brown, *Modernization: The Transformation of American Life*, New York, 1976, pp. 94–121; Richard P. McCormick, *The Second American Party System: Party Formation in the Jacksonian Era*, Chapel Hill, North Carolina, 1966, pp. 350–51; Allan G. Bogue, Jerome M. Clubb, Caroll R. McKibben, "Members of the House of Representatives and the Processes of Modernization, 1789–1960," *Journal of American History* 63, September 1976, pp. 275–302.
5. Robert V. Wells, "Family History and Demographic Transition," *Journal of Social History* 9, 1975, pp. 1–19; Daniel Scott Smith, "Child Naming Patterns and Family Structure Change: Hingham, Massachusetts, 1640–1880," *Newberry Papers in Family and Community History*, 1976.
6. Canby, *Age of Confidence*, pp. 19, 22–36, 46–48, 98–99.
7. The decline of household industry after 1830 is documented by George Rogers Taylor, *The Transportation Revolution*, New York, 1951, pp. 211–14. The division of home from work in the nineteenth century is discussed by Richard Wade, *The Urban Frontier*, Chicago, 1959, pp. 306–10; Sam Bass Warner, *Streetcar Suburbs: The Process of Urban Growth in Boston, 1870–1900*, New York, 1970; Thernstrom, *Poverty and Progress: Social Mobility in a Nineteenth-Century City*, Cambridge, Massachusetts, 1964, pp. 14, 36–37. On the movement which characterized nineteenth-century life see Stephan Thernstrom and Peter Knights, "Men in Motion: Some Data and Speculations about Urban Population Mobility in Nineteenth-Century America," *Journal of Interdisciplinary History*, Winter 1971, pp. 5–31.

8. Among several who analyze the new style, see Donald Meyer, *The Positive Thinkers*, New York, 1965, pp. 28–40; William Wasserstrom, *Heiress of All the Ages: Sex and Sentiment in the Genteel Tradition*, Minneapolis, Minnesota, 1959, p. 131.

9. Barbara Welter, "The Cult of True Womanhood, 1820–1860,"*American Quarterly* 18, Summer 1966, pp. 151–74; the quote is from *Girlhood and Womanhood, or Sketches of My School Mates*, Boston, 1837, p. 293, in Welter, "True Womanhood," pp. 154–55; Daniel Scott Smith and Michael S. Hindus, "Pre-Marital Pregnancy in America, 1840–1971: An Overview and Interpretation," *Journal of Interdisciplinary History* 5, 1975, pp. 537–70.

10. For popular stage drama, geared to the middle classes, see David Grimsted, *Melodrama Unveiled*, Chicago, 1968, pp. 130, 158, 172, 228.

11. Isabelle Webb Entriken, *Sarah Josepha Hald and Godey's Lady's Book*, Philadelphia, 1946, p. 19. *Godey's* sold 150,000 copies a month in 1860, see pp. 61, 116. Sarah Josepha Hale, "Thanksgiving of the Heart," *Ladies' Magazine*, November 1829, pp. 517–28; *Ladies' Magazine*, June 1836, pp. 6–9.

12. "The Philosophy of Shopping," *Godey's Lady's Book*, January 1854, p. 32; Meta M. Duncan, "The Corner Pew," *Godey's Lady's Book*, March 1847, p. 156; or Grace Greenwood, "Aunt Maguire," *Godey's Lady's Book*, September 1846, pp. 106–8. Both of the above trace the theme of wishing for a new, more aristocratic man. See Mary Devant, "Grace Cloverling," *Godey's Lady's Book*, March 1847, p. 210, for the wish for lower-class "happiness." See also William R. Taylor, *Cavalier and Yankee*, New York, 1963, p. 131.

13. Barbara Welter, "The Feminization of American Religion, 1800–1849," in Mary Hartman and Lois Banner, eds., *Clio's Consciousness Raised*, New York, 1974, pp. 137–57; Entriken, *Sarah Hale*, pp. 10, 41, for Hale's interest in religious social groups and uplifting lower orders; Frances Trollope, *Domestic Manners of Americans*, first published 1832, recent edition edited by Donald Smalley, New York, 1949, pp. 74–75.

14. Paul Johnson, "A Shopkeeper's Millennium: Society and Revivals in Rochester, New York," Ph.D. dissertation, UCLA, 1976.

15. Page Smith, *Daughters of the Promised Land: Women in American History*, Boston, 1970, pp. 135–36, summarizes the Beecher family; Ann Douglas Wood, "The Fashionable Diseases: Women's Complaints and Their Treatment in Nineteenth-Century America," *Journal of Interdisciplinary History* 4, Summer 1973, pp. 25–52; Catharine Beecher, *Letters to the People on Health and Happiness*, New York, 1855, p. 211, in Smith, *Daughters*, p. 134.

16. Harriet Beecher Stowe to Calvin Stowe, Brattleboro, Vermont, May 17, 1847; January 24, 1847, *Beecher Papers* in Smith, *Daughters*, p. 137; Helen Papashvily's *All the Happy Endings*, New York, 1946, pp. 65–66, similarly, comments on the unhappy marriage, placing it also in the larger context of fiction; Harriet Beecher Stowe and Catharine Beecher, *The American Woman's Home*, New York, 1869, dedication and p. 13.

17. Harriet Beecher Stowe, *Uncle Tom's Cabin*, Boston, 1852, pp. 11–14, 31, 103, 432.

18. *Ibid.*, pp. 12, 47, 74, 96, 154–57, 184, 225–29, 269–84, 314–18.

19. *Ibid.*, pp. 345–46, 358–69, 403.

20. *Ibid.*, pp. 431–38. Stowe also proposed that schools and churches of the North serve to elevate blacks to "moral and intelligent maturity" and assist them to migrate to Liberia, pp. 448–49. All of Stowe's heroines and heroes radiate salvation without the aid of priests, churches, or sacraments. St. Clare's mother is a Huguenot, and one passage has George Harris condemning the blacks of Haiti for being Catholic, hedonistic, and "effeminate." See pp. 425–26.

21. Beatrice Hofstadter, "Popular Culture and the Romantic Heroine," *American Scholar* 30, Winter 1960, pp. 98–116.

22. The alliance between prohibition and suffrage was most pronounced in the nineteenth century. In the twentieth century the tie was still there, but was often "uneasy," particularly in the cities. See Andrew Sinclair, *The Era of Excess*, New York, 1962, pp. 92–98; and *The Emancipation of the American Woman*, New York, 1965, pp. 220–29; Alan Grimes, *The Puritan Ethic and Woman's Suffrage*, New York, 1967, p. 66; Susan B. Anthony and Ida Husted Harper, *The History of Woman's Suffrage*, 4 vols., Rochester, New York, 1902, vol. 3, p. 739, in Grimes, *Puritan Ethic*, p. 66.

23. On the breakdown of female occupations, see *Statistics of Women at Work*, Washington, D.C., 1900, p. 32, in Elizabeth Faulkner Baker, *Technology and Women's Work*, New York, 1964, pp. 60, 75–77. In the first year women were counted, 1870, four-fifths were in farms or domestic occupations. The rest were divided between manufacturing and the professions, where two-thirds were teachers. See Baker, pp. 22–25. The professional women were usually not married; see Francis Willard and Mary Livermore, *A Woman of the Century*, Buffalo, New York, 1893, which includes a poll of fifteen hundred prominent women, over half of whom were single. The normal pattern for a school teacher was to leave work after marriage, see Richard Sennett, *Families Against the Cities*, Cambridge, Mass., pp. 91, 148. On Mann and Thayer, see Baker, *Women's Work*, p. 56; and Wylie, *Self-Made Man*, p. 125. On the school system, see Michael Katz, *Class, Bureaucracy and Schools*, New York, 1971, pp. 32–33, 38–39; for McGuffey and the temperance requirement in schools, see Sinclair, *Era of Excess*, pp. 43–44.

24. See for example Herbert G. Gutman, *Work, Culture and Society in Industrializing America*, New York, 1977, pp. 3–79; Harold Frederic, *The Damnation of Theron Ware*, 1896. Reprint, Greenwich, Conn., 1962 edition, pp. 47–49.

25. Canby, *Age of Confidence*, pp. 59–60.

26. *Ibid.*, pp. 15–24, 91.

27. *Ibid.*

28. Grimsted, *Melodrama*, describes the separation of theaters by class. A good example of Victorian approach is Hiram M. Stanley, "A Suggestion as to Popular Amusements," *The Century Illustrated Monthly Magazine*, January 1894, p. 476. Pictures of the classical theaters are in William H. Birkmire, *American Theaters*, New York, 1901; or "New York's Magnificent New Playhouses," *Theater Magazine*, August 1903. For the etiquette book, see Mrs. Burton Harrison, *The Well Bred Girl in Society*, New York, 1904, pp. 5–6, 13–14, 39–42, 77–87.

29. The description of the audience being male and largely working class or small property owners applies to the period before 1890. The following chapter describes the gradual alteration of this pattern. On vaudeville see Albert McLean, Jr., *American Vaudeville as Ritual*, Lexington, Kentucky, 1965; on minstrelsy, for

one among several see Alexander Saxton, "Black Face Minstrelsy and Jacksonian Ideology," *American Quarterly*, March 1975, pp. 3–28; on circuses, see Neil Harris, *Humbug: The Art of P. T. Barnum*, Boston, 1973; Gutman, *Work and Culture*, pp. 45–46, describes John L. Sullivan's support of strikes and working-class causes. The description of parks relies largely on Geoffrey Blodgett, "Frederick Law Olmsted: Landscape Architecture as Conservative Reform," *Journal of American History*, March 1976, pp. 869–89.

30. Herbert Asbury, *The Gangs of New York*, New York, 1928, pp. 177–78; Richard O'Connor, *Hell's Kitchen*, New York, 1958, pp. 88–91.

31. Department of Commerce, Bureau of the Census, *Report of the Social Statistics of the Cities*, compiled by George E. Waring, Jr., Washington, D.C., 1887, Vols. 1 and 2; for New York see Vol. 1, pp. 565–80.

32. *Ibid.*, pp. 48–51.

33. *Ibid.*, pp. 38–39. The passage from one home to another in the nineteenth century was the common pattern for both middle- and working-class girls; for the former see Sennett, *Families*, pp. 90–105; for the latter see Virginia Yans McLaughlin, "Patterns of Work and Family Organization: Buffalo's Italians," *Journal of Interdisciplinary History* 2, Autumn 1971. Quote is from Canby, *Age of Confidence*, pp. 39–40.

34. Canby, *Age of Confidence*, pp. 83, 86, 77.

35. *Ibid.*, pp. 80–86.

36. *Ibid.*, pp. 120, 83, 88, 86–87; Henry Adams, *The Education of Henry Adams*, 1907. Reprint, New York, 1930, pp. 446–47. The minimization of sexuality was a common theme in standard examinations of the Victorian home, see Oscar Handlin, *Race and Nationality in American Life*, Boston, 1957, pp. 111–35, or Sinclair, *Emancipation*, pp. 127–36. Recently the monolithic nature of such a view has been questioned by Carl Degler, "What Ought To Be and What Was: Women's Sexuality in the Nineteenth Century," *American Historical Review* 79, December 1974, pp. 1467–98.

37. Henry James, *The Bostonians*, 1886. Reprint, New York, 1945, pp. 98, 99, 190–92, 252, characterizes the heroine, Verena Tarrant. Theodore Dreiser, *Sister Carrie*, New York, 1900; Mark Twain and Charles Dudley Warner, *The Gilded Age*, 1874. Reprint, New York, 1969, pp. 110–30; Walt Whitman, "Democratic Vistas," in James E. Miller, ed., *Walt Whitman: Complete Poetry and Prose*, Boston, 1959, pp. 456–89. Stowe quote in Forest Wilson, *Crusader in Crinoline: The Life of Harriet Beecher Stowe*, Philadelphia, 1941, pp. 117–18.

38. Canby, *Age of Confidence*, pp. 40–43, 93–97, 105–06.

## Chapter Two: The Decline of Progress

1. Martha Coman and Hugh Weir, "An Interview with Mrs. Thomas Edison," *Collier's Weekly*, July 18–August 1, 1925.

2. W. K. L. Dickson, "Edison's Invention of the Kinetograph," *The Century Illustrated Monthly Magazine*, June 1894, pp. 206–07; W. K. L. Dickson and Antonia Dickson, *History of the Kinetograph and Kinetoscope*, New York, 1895.

3. Edward Chase Kirkland, *Industry Comes of Age*, New York, 1961, pp. 189–93, 399–409; Philip Edelman, "The United States and the Inventor," *Harper's Maga-*

*zine*, November 4, 1911, p. 9. On more inventions in the urban North, see Allan Pred, *The Spatial Dynamics of United States Urban and Industrial Growth, 1800–1914*, Cambridge, Massachusetts, 1966, pp. 111–30.

4. Matthew Josephson, *Edison, A Biography*, New York, 1959, pp. 68, 101, 215, 376, 434–35, 477.

5. *Ibid.*, pp. 17–26, 85, 304–10, 482; "An Interview with Mr. Edison," *New York Times*, September 14, 1913, p. 14; Coman and Weir, "Interview."

6. The story of Dickson is in three works by Gordon Hendricks, *The Edison Motion Picture Myth*, Los Angeles, 1961; *Beginnings of the Biograph*, New York, 1964; and *The Kinetoscope*, New York, 1966. See *The Edison Myth*, p. 144, for the quoted letter.

7. W. K. L. Dickson and Antonia Dickson, *The Life and Times of Thomas Alva Edison*, New York, 1892, pp. 1, 91–94, 361–62.

8. Coman and Weir, "Interview," p. 26; Dickson, "Edison's Invention," pp. 208–9.

9. The business community's desire for foreign markets to soak up excess production is the subject of Walter Lafeber, *The New Empire: An Interpretation of American Expansion, 1860–1898*, Ithaca, New York, 1965. The same theme continued into the reformist era, see Martin J. Sklar, "Woodrow Wilson and the Political Economy of Modern United States Liberalism," *Studies on the Left* 1, 1960. Although real wages increased in the nineteenth century, they were much less than the rise in productivity. See Kirkland, *Industry*, pp. 399–405.

10. The financial conservatism of the financiers is discussed in Thomas Cochran and William Miller, *The Age of Enterprise*, New York, 1961, pp. 181–210; and Gabriel Kolko, *The Trumph of Conservatism*, Chicago, 1963, pp. 26–56.

11. Note by Edison in E. Muybridge, "Zoepraxography," *Edison Laboratory Archives*, 1893, in Josephson, *Edison*, p. 392.

12. See Hendricks, *Beginnings of the Biograph* and *The Kinetoscope*.

13. On the new immigrants, see Samuel Lubell, *The Future of American Politics*, New York, 1965, p. 43; on their American entertainments see Jon Kingsdale, "The Poor Man's Club: Social Functions of the Urban, Working Class Saloon," *American Quarterly* 25, October 1973, pp. 472–89; Alexander Saxton, "Black Face Minstrelsy and Jacksonian Ideology," *American Quarterly* 27, March 1975, pp. 3–28. On the pre-industrial backgrounds of the immigrant workers and their relation to factory labor, see Herbert G. Gutman, "Work, Culture and Society in Industrializing America, 1815–1919," *American Historical Review* 78, June 1973, pp. 531–88. Labor leaders' quest for free time as a primary goal in the 1890s onwards is articulated by Samuel Gompers, "Testimony Before the U.S. Industrial Commission," *Report of the U.S. Industrial Commission on the Relations and Conditions of Capital and Labor*, Washington, D.C., 1901, vol. 7, pp. 606–8; workers' disproportionate use of increased wages for leisure goods is the subject of Louis Bolard More, *Wage-Earners' Budgets: A Study of Standards and Costs of Living in New York City*, New York, 1907, p. 95.

14. The increase in amusements was calculated by comparing police licenses over time. See *Report of the Police Department*, New York, 1886–1900. For the rise of beach resorts see Charles Funnel, "Virgin Strand, Atlantic City, New Jersey, as a Mass Resort and Cultural Symbol," Ph.D. dissertation, University of

Pennsylvania, 1973. On the rise of "Raines Hotels," see *Civic Journal*, January 22, 1910, p. 2, and February 12, 1910, p. 5; *People's Institute Bulletin*, November 29, 1908, pp. 20–22. On the music see Lewis Allen Erenberg, "Urban Nightlife and the Decline of Victorianism: New York's Restaurants and Cabarets, 1890–1918," Ph.D. dissertation, University of Michigan, 1974, pp. 136–46. On amusement parks see John Kasson, *Coney Island*, New York, 1978.

15. In 1885 there were four monthly magazines with a circulation of over 100,000 and a cost per copy of 25¢. By 1910, twenty such magazines sold for ten to fifteen cents and attained a readership of five million. See Frank Luther Mott, *A History of American Magazines*, 4 vols., Cambridge, Mass., 1957, vol. 4, pp. 7–8.

16. Among many accounts see Donald Meyer, *The Positive Thinkers*, New York, 1965, pp. 21–32; and John Higham, "The Reorientation of American Culture in the 1890s," in Paul Weiss, ed., *The Origins of Modern Consciousness*, New York, 1969, pp. 25–45; Kirkland, *Industry*, p. 193; Josephson, *Edison*, pp. 339–41, 360, 364.

17. Department of Commerce, Bureau of the Census, *Historical Statistics of the United States, Colonial Times to 1957*, Washington, D.C., 1960, p. 14; Lewis Carey, "The New Middle Class," *Antioch Review*, Spring 1945; on increased wages and a declining work week see Kirkland, *Industry*, pp. 262–77; for manufacturers' first experimentation with consumption goods see Alfred Chandler, "The Beginnings of 'Big Business' in American History," in Carl Degler, ed., *Pivotal Interpretations of American History*, 2 vols., New York, 1966, vol. 2, pp. 107–38.

18. "Women's Occupations Through Seven Decades," *Women's Bureau Bulletin No. 232*, Washington, D.C., 1951, pp. 34–35; *Historical Statistics*, pp. 71–72.

19. Josiah Strong, *Our Country*, New York, 1885, pp. 5–10, 72–90, 101–36.

20. Harold Frederic, *The Damnation of Theron Ware*, 1896. Reprint, New York, 1962, pp. v–vi, 11, 22, 36–37, 47—53, 68–71, 94–96, 148–49, 191–98, 202–17, 286–87.

21. On the new hotels, parties, and public activities of the rich see Erenberg, "Urban Nightlife," pp. 26–72; John Collier, "City Planning and the Problem of Recreation," *People's Institute MSS*, Box 14, New York Public Library; Henry Seidel Canby, *American Memoir*, New York, first published in 1947, 1968 edition, pp. 146–56, contains the best description of the new college culture for the upper and upper-middle classes.

22. Little scholarly work has been done on the Broadway stage, but see Daniel Frohman and Issac Morcosson, "The Life of Charles Frohman," *Cosmopolitan*, March 1916, pp. 592–95. The obituary of David Belasco is also useful, "David Belasco," New York *Times*, May 15, 1931; Theodore Dreiser, *Sister Carrie*, New York, 1900, pp. 291–92.

23. Montrose J. Moses and Virginia Gerson, *Clyde Fitch and His Letters*, New York, 1924, in Lloyd Morris, *Postscript to Yesterday: American Life and Thought, 1896–1946*, New York, 1947, pp. 172–77.

24. On vaudeville's growing respectability for the lower-middle class, see Albert McLean, Jr., *American Vaudeville as Ritual*, Louisville, Kentucky, 1965, pp. 31, 65–75, 193. A contemporary account and source of the quote is Albert Smith, *Two Reels and a Crank*, New York, 1952, p. 15. The two vaudeville houses on Fifth Avenue can be seen in the thorough investigation of city amusements in

New York by the Russell Sage Foundation, Michael Davis, *The Exploitation of Pleasure*, New York, 1911, p. 25, where the price was five times more than a regular vaudeville show. The last quote is from *The Musical Courier*, January 1899, in James Swigert, "Gentlemen, Stand Up! The Development of Black Musical Comedies," Senior thesis, Princeton University, 1975. See also *Spirit of the Times*, February 27, 1897, p. 1.

25. Jesse Lasky and Donald Weldon, *I Blow My Own Horn*, New York, 1957, pp. 81–84; Erenberg, "Urban Nightlife," pp. 151–57.

26. On Duncan and St. Denis, see Katherine O'Leary, "No Prince Charming Was the Answer: Woman as Dancer in the Twentieth Century," Senior thesis, *Princeton University*, 1976. The quote is from Hugo von Hofmannsthal, "Her Extraordinary Immediacy," first published in 1906, reproduced in *Dance Magazine*, September 1963, pp. 36–38. The best discussion of Irene and Vernon Castle is in Erenberg, "Urban Nightlife," pp. 201–33. The quote is from "Dancing Times," untitled clipping in Irene Castle Scrap Books, Lincoln Center.

27. On the Thaw episode and the big rich lure for chorus girls see Evelyn Nesbit, *Prodigal Days: The Untold Story*, New York, 1934, pp. 60–70.

28. "Social Conditions as Feeders of Immorality," *Arena* 11, February 1895, pp. 410–11.

29. George E. Walsh, "Moving Picture Drama for the Multitude," *Independent*, February 6, 1908, pp. 306–10; Barton Currie, "Nickle Madness," *Harper's Weekly*, August 24, 1907, pp. 1246–47; Robert Grau, "The Early History and Development of the Motion Picture Industry," *Scientific American*, August 12, 1911, pp. 155–56; Abraham Cahan, *Jewish Daily Forward*, May 24, 1908, in Irving Howe, *World of Our Fathers*, New York, 1976, p. 213.

30. Grau, "Early Industry," pp. 155–56; "The Moving Picture Revolution," *Success Magazine*, April 1910, pp. 238–40; "The Movies," pp. 9–10; on license fees see *Report of the Police Department of the City of New York*, New York, 1905–1908; for the comparison of performances see Michael Davis, *The Exploitation of Pleasure*, New York, 1911, pp. 25–28; the Davis study was commissioned by the Russell Sage Foundation, and it supplies some of the most significant evidence of theater location and seating capacity that we have.

31. John Collier, "Cheap Amusements," in *Charities and Commons*, 1908, pp. 73–78, found that the nickelodeons in New York City had grown to 400 in immigrant areas. But in 1911 Michael Davis found that clerical workers and petty proprietors of both sexes attended films, see Davis's study for the Russell Sage Foundation, *The Exploitation of Pleasure*, New York, 1911, pp. 21–35; see also the excellent scholarly article on Boston by Russell Merritt, "Nickelodeon Theaters 1905–1914: Building an Audience for the Movies," in Tino Balio, ed., *The American Film Industry*, Madison, Wisconsin, 1976, pp. 59–83; John Sloan, "Nickelodeon," sketch, Whitney Museum, New York City; "The Movies," *American Magazine*, August, 1913, p. 10.

32. "A Democratic Art," *The Nation*, August 28, 1913. This calculation comes from two samples taken from the yearly film synopses listed in the *Motion Picture World* from 1907 to 1914.

33. See Merritt, "Nickelodeons," pp. 64–65; and *Motion Picture World*, February 4, 1911.
34. Calculated from a random sample of foreign film synopses gathered from the *Motion Picture World*, 1907–1914. The quote is from a description of a Pathé film, in *Motion Picture World*, July 4, 1908, p. 13.
35. Merritt, "Nickelodeons," pp. 64–65. Porter's films are in EHFL.
36. Walter P. Eaton, "Menace of the Movies," *American Magazine*, September 1913, pp. 55–60; "The Movies," *Theater Magazine*, January 1909, p. 10; Olivia Harriet Dunbar, "The Lure of the Films," *Harper's Weekly*, January 18, 1913, p. 20. For the resemblance of the store fronts to uptown houses, see *Motion Picture World*, November 23, 1912, p. 750, for contemporary pictures; Jane Addams, *The Spirit of Youth and the City Streets*, New York, 1909, pp. 75–76, 107–9; on girls dropping in alone, see "Where They Play Shakespeare for Five Cents," *Theater Magazine*, September 1908, p. 264; "Censorship in Cleveland," *American Magazine*, August 1913, p. 93; for the idea of free women and a "homeless city," see John Collier, *The City Where Crime Is Play*, New York, 1914, pp. 1–10.
37. Dunbar, "The Lure"; and "The Anatomy of a Kiss," New York *World*, April 26, 1896, p. 1.
38. William McKeever, "The Moving Picture, A Primary School for Criminals," *Good Housekeeping*, August 19, 1910, pp. 184–86.
39. Joseph R. Fulk, "Effect on Education and Morals of the Motion Picture Shows," *National Educational Association Proceedings*, 1912, pp. 456–61.
40. Herbert S. Langfeld, "Hugo Münsterberg," *Dictionary of American Biography*, New York, 1934, pp. 337–39; Hugo Münsterberg, *The Photoplay: A Psychological Study*, New York, 1916, pp. 80–83, 152, 223.
41. Hugo Münsterberg, "Münsterberg Vigorously Denounces Red Light Drama," New York *Times*, September 14, 1913.
42. Münsterberg, *The Photoplay*, pp. 83–103, 112–30, 203–10.
43. *Ibid.*, pp. 216–23.

## Chapter Three: Rescuing the Family

1. Darrell O. Hibbard, "Letter," *The Outlook*, July 13, 1912, p. 598.
2. New York *Tribune*, December 24, 25, 26, 27, 28, 1908; New York *World*, December 25, 1908; New York *Dramatic Mirror*, June 2, 1909; New York *Times*, December 24, 25, 26, 27, 1908, pp. 1–2.
3. Barton Curie, "The Nickle Madness," *Harper's Weekly*, August 24, 1907, pp. 1246–47; Jane Addams, "Introduction," in Louise de Koven Bowen, *The Five Cent Theater*, Chicago, 1909; Addams, "The Reaction of Moral Institutions on Social Reform," *The Survey*, April 3, 1909, pp. 17–19.
4. New York *Tribune*, December 26, 27, 1908, pp. 1–2.
5. On the general atmosphere of the "white slave" panic see Egal Feldman, "Prostitution, The Alien Woman and the Progressive Imagination, 1910–1915," *American Quarterly* 19, Summer 1967, pp. 192–206; Roy Lubove, "The Progressive and the Prostitute," *The Historian* 25, May 1962, pp. 308–29; Herbert G. Gutman, *Work, Culture and Society in Industrializing America*, New York, 1977,

pp. 67–78; John C. Burnham, "The Progressive Era Revolution and American Attitudes Toward Sex," *Journal of American History* 59, March 1973, pp. 885–908; Richard Hofstadter, *The Age of Reform*, New York, 1954, would also confirm this cultural war theory.

6. New York *Times*, "Editorial," December 26, 1908, p. 6, pointed out that "the demand for the suppression or stricter regulation of the shows has come from people who would not dream of visiting them in search of innocent entertainment."

7. Kenneth L. Kusmer, "The Functions of Organized Charity in the Progressive Era: Chicago as a Case Study," *Journal of American History* 60, December 1973, pp. 657–78, shows that many of the people we are concerned with had this background. All the major figures as well as the key organizations involved were Protestants of upper-middle-class status; Herbert Asbury, *Gem of the Prairie: An Informal History of the Chicago Underworld*, New York, 1942, pp. 281–320; Mark Haller, "Vice in Chicago," in Kenneth Jackson and Stanley K. Schwartz, eds., *Cities in American History*, New York, 1972, pp. 292–98. The organizations involved with the Commissions were the WCTU, Federal Council of Churches, YMCA, Civic Business League, settlement workers, and Protestant churches of all persuasions. Lists of the Chicago Commission read like a Who's Who: Edward Skinner, Association of Commerce; Edwin Sims, U.S. District Attorney; Julius Rosenwald, President, Chicago Commons; Alexander Robertson, Continental Bank; Ellen Henrotin, Federation of Women's Clubs.

8. *Annual Reports*, New York Society for the Prevention of Vice, New York Public Library; *Social Register*, New York, 1895–1910; L. R. Hammesley, ed., *Who's Who in New York City and State*, New York, 1905, 1911, 1917–1918.

9. *The Social Evil in New York City*, 1912, *The Social Evil in Chicago*, 1912, contain the alarm over spending, dress, and new female freedom. For a typical reporter's alarm, see George Kibbe Turner, "The City of Chicago, A Study of the Great Immoralities," *McClure's Magazine*, April 7, 1907, p. 575.

10. Frederic Howe, *The Confessions of a Reformer*, New York, 1925, pp. 66–69, 233–35, 266–67, 318–21, 327–38.

11. Henry Seidel Canby, *The Age of Confidence*, 1934, reprint, New York, 1968, p. 7, describes the mix of neighborhoods and the women's voluntary organizations. The older and newer city neighborhoods are analyzed in Sam Bass Warner, *The Urban Wilderness*, New York, 1973, pp. 150–200. For the settlement's ties to religious reformers, see Louise C. Wade, *Graham Taylor, Pioneer for Social Justice, 1851–1938*, Chicago, 1964, pp. 81–82, 108; their staffing by women college graduates is the subject of John Rousmaniere, "Cultural Hybrid in the Slums: College Women and the Settlement House, 1889–1894," *American Quarterly* 22, Spring 1970, pp. 45–63; Vida Scudder, "A New Departure for Philanthropy," *Xian Union* 1 and 2, May 10, 1888, pp. 508, 620, quoted in Rousmaniere, "Cultural Hybrid," pp. 58–59; Roy Lubove, *The Professional Altruist*, Cambridge, Massachusetts, 1965, pp. 5–20, 174–80, discusses the ties to business and the new state. For a study of 500 settlement workers in Pittsburgh, see Elizabeth Metzger, "Settlement Work in Pittsburgh," Seminar Paper, University of Pittsburgh, Pa., 1973.

12. The three most discerning accounts of Jane Addams are Jill Conway, "Jane Ad-

dams, An American Heroine," *Daedalus* 93, Spring 1964, pp. 761–80; Christopher Lasch, *The New Radicalism in America*, New York, 1965, pp. 56–77; Allan F. Davis, *American Heroine: The Life and Legend of Jane Addams*, New York, 1973. For her own account of entrapment in leisure, see "The Snare of Preparation," in Jane Addams, *Twenty Years at Hull House*, New York, 1915, pp. 60–74. On being filled with "shame" and "doing nothing at all," see Jane Addams to Ellen Starr, June 22, 1884, and February 7, 1886, Starr MSS, in Lasch, *New Radicalism*, pp. 16, 23.

13. Jane Addams, "The Subjective Necessity for Settlements," *Philanthropy and Social Progress*, New York, 1893, pp. 1–23. For her comments on the first generation of public women and their relationship to men and marriage, see Jane Addams, *The Second Twenty Years at Hull House*, New York, 1930. On the idea of the city as a new missionary field, see "A Function of the Social Settlements," in Christopher Lasch, ed., *The Social Thought of Jane Addams*, New York, 1965, p. 184. The extension rather than defiance of the home is explained in Jane Addams, "Filial Relations," *Democracy and Social Ethics*, New York, 1902, pp. 77–80, 82–88.

14. The general use of the home for reform and class harmony by social gospel reformers, a tradition that Addams and other settlement workers were clearly within, is explored in Donald Meyer, *The Protestant Search for Political Realism*, Los Angeles, 1960, pp. 26–54, 134–40. For Jane Addams on reformist proposals in relation to saving the family, see Jane Addams, *A New Conscience and an Ancient Evil*, New York, 1915, pp. 9–15, 101, 210–18; Addams, *The Spirit of Youth and the City Streets*, New York, 1909, pp. 28–35; Addams, *Democracy*, pp. 2–3, 78–79, 106.

15. Addams, *Democracy*, pp. 230, 255, 257–65; Addams, "Americanization," *Publications of the American Sociological Society* 14, 1919, p. 210. The idea that the physical and cultural environment had to be changed to continue the success ethic was in keeping with Theodore Roosevelt's New Nationalism and older traditions in America, see Stephan Thernstrom, *Poverty and Progress: Social Mobility in a Nineteenth-Century City*, New York, 1969, pp. 74–79. On the nature of black families see Elizabeth Pleck, "The Two-Parent Household: Black Family Structure in Late-Nineteenth-Century Boston," *Journal of Social History* 6, Fall 1962, pp. 3–31; for immigrants see Herbert G. Gutman, "Work, Culture and Society in Industrializing America, 1815–1919," *American Historical Review* 78, June 1973, pp. 531–88.

16. Jane Addams, "Introduction," in Louise de Koven Bowen, *Safeguards for Youth at Work and Play*, Chicago, 1910; Addams, *New Conscience*, pp. 206, 270–75; for the same approach by the head of the Hull House organization for policing amusements, see Louise de Koven Bowen, *The Road to Destruction Made Easy in Chicago*, Chicago, 1916, pp. 13–15, and *Growing Up with the City*, New York, 1926, pp. 1–2, 81–89, 92–98, 120–30.

17. The dynamics of social disintegration and white slavery can be gleaned from Jane Addams, *New Conscience*, as well as the two major vice reports of the era, The Vice Commissioners of Chicago, *The Social Evil in Chicago*, Chicago, 1910, and The Committee of Fourteen, *The Social Evil in New York City*, New York, 1910. The quote is from Addams, *New Conscience*, p. 206. Allan Davis shows

that the fear of women falling into prostitution was a common concern of the major settlement workers and "advanced social justice Progressives" in *Jane Addams: An American Heroine*, pp. 177–97.

18. For the fear of puberty in nineteenth-century America, see Carol Smith-Rosenberg, "Puberty to Menopause: The Cycle of Femininity in Nineteenth-Century America," *Feminist Studies* 1, Winter–Spring 1973, pp. 58–73; The Editors, "Sex O'Clock in America," *Current Opinion*, August 1913, pp. 113–14.

19. See for example the Chicago Vice Commission, *The Social Evil in Chicago*, Chicago, 1912, or Jane Addams, *A New Conscience*.

20. Anonymous Vice Investigation, New York City, in *Popular Amusements*, YMCA, 1915, p. 392.

21. John Collier, "City Planning and the Problem of Recreation," People's Institute of New York City MSS, Box No. 14, New York Public Library. For Jane Addams along the same lines, see Addams, *Youth*, pp. 75–125.

22. See Meyer, *Protestant Search*, pp. 26–54; or Davis, *Jane Addams*, pp. 177–97; Addams, *Democracy*, pp. 78, 113, 171; Addams, *Youth*, pp. 126–28. For the way these moral-industrial reforms culminated during World War I, see Allan Davis, "Welfare, Reform, and World War I," *American Quarterly* 19, Fall 1967, pp. 516–32.

23. On the passage of moral laws, see Feldman, "Prostitution," pp. 192–206; and Lubove, "Progressives," pp. 308–29; Davis, "Welfare," and Addams, *A New Conscience*.

24. Walter Lippman, *A Preface to Politics*, New York, 1913, pp. 134–35; Addams, *Youth*; "Redemption of Play," People's Institute MSS, Box 14; *Civic Journal*, December 6, 1908, pp. 2–5; Joseph E. Lee, "Play as an Antidote to Civilization," *Playground*, July 1911.

25. The earliest favorable comments appeared in the *People's Institute Bulletin*, June 31, 1909, p. 5; Addams, *Youth*, pp. 7, 20, 78–98, 107–9; "The Reaction of Moral Instruction upon Social Reform," *The Survey*, April 3, 1909, pp. 17–19; Louise de Koven Bowen, *The Five Cent Theaters*, Chicago, 1911, pp. 1–10; Donald Young, *Motion Pictures: A Study in Social Legislation*, Philadelphia, 1920, p. 40; "The Nickelodeon," *The World Today* 15, December 1908, p. 1052; *The Chicago Motion Picture Commission Report*, Chicago, 1920, p. 16; William Healy, *The Individual Delinquent*, New York, 1914, in Young, *Motion Pictures*, p. 307; Barton Currie, "Nickle Madness," *Harper's Weekly*, August 24, 1907, pp. 1246–47; Orian J. Cocks, "After the Saloon, The Movie," *The Survey*, June 27, 1914, pp. 337–38; "Moving Pictures as a Factor in Municipal Life," *Municipal Review*, October 14, 1914, pp. 708–12.

26. *New York Dramatic Mirror*, January 2, 1909; *Motion Picture World*, April 5, 1913, p. 25; May 9, 1914, p. 793, for willingness of producers to cooperate, but resist state censorship.

27. "Charles Sprague Smith," *Dictionary of American Biography* 17, p. 252; "The People's Institute of New York," *The Century Illustrated Monthly Magazine*, April 1910, pp. 850–63; John Collier, "The People's Institute," *Independent*, May 30, 1912, pp. 1144–48; *The World Today*, January 1909, pp. 175, 476.

28. The Institute's first two journals were devoted to New England and Republican heroes, William Lloyd Garrison and Lincoln. See *People's Institute Bulletin*, De-

cember 10, 1905; "Report of the Executive Secretary of the National Board of Review," November 1914, in National Board of Review MSS, New York Public Library. This includes the executive members and the viewing staff. The quote is from Young, *Motion Pictures*, p. 16.

29. "Report of the Executive Secretary," and "Minutes of the Board," 1916–1918, National Board of Review MSS, New York Public Library.

30. "An Interview with John Collier, Secretary of the National Board," *Moving Picture World*, April 5, 1913; Orian J. Cocks, "Applying Standards to Motion Picture Films," *The Survey*, June 27, 1914, pp. 337–38; William McAdoo, "The Theater and the Law," *Saturday Evening Post*, January 29, 1922, pp. 92–93; "Standards of the Board," National Board of Review MSS, Box 14, New York Public Library; Cocks, "Moving Pictures as a Factor in Municipal Life," *National Municipal Review*, October 1914, p. 708; Cocks, "After the Saloon," pp. 337–38.

31. William Plunkitt, as recorded by William Riordan, *Plunkitt of Tammany Hall: A Series of Plain Talks on Very Practical Politics*, New York, 1963, p. 22.

32. Lately Thomas, Robert V. P. Steele, pseud., *The Mayor Who Mastered New York*, New York, 1969, pp. 19, 36, 54, 91, 104–34, 303, 469–72; Mayor William J. Gaynor to Louis Fischer, April 9, 1913, Gaynor Papers, Municipal Archives, New York City, in Erenberg, "Cabarets," pp. 129–31; "William Gaynor," in Allen Johnson and Dumas Malone, eds., *Dictionary of American Biography* 7, New York, 1931, pp. 201–2; "William Gaynor," *The National Cyclopedia of American Biography* 11, New York, 1918, pp. 353–54.

33. A prime example of how the censors saw themselves as the executors of "public opinion" is in *People's Institute Annual Report, 1908*, New York Public Library, p. 7. Raising the license fee and its key to power over movies can be discerned from *People's Institute Bulletin*, December 23, 1908, p. 5. For the general requirements of the theater code, see "New York's Theater Code," *National Municipal Review*, April 1914, p. 394. In Chicago the agency for policing movies was also the vice squad for expurgating prostitution. See Haller, "Vice in Chicago," p. 294.

34. The way the censors were the prime instigators of license complaints can be seen in *People's Institute Bulletin*, November 29, 1909, p. 22, and the numerous complaint letters to the Bureau of License in the National Board of Review MSS, New York Public Library; Mayor William Gaynor, "Speech Before the Exhibitor's Convention," *Motion Picture World*, July 1913, p. 4; Frederic Howe, "What To Do with the Motion Picture Show," *Outlook*, June 20, 1914, pp. 412–16.

35. *The Chicago Motion Picture Commission Report*, p. 12, carries the opinion of the Illinois Supreme Court. For state and federal approval of censorship, see Ford McGregor, "Official Censorship Regulation," pp. 163–65; Young, *Motion Pictures*, pp. 64–72; "Censorship for the Moving Pictures," *Survey Magazine*, April 3, 1909, pp. 8–9. The differing European and American standards were pointed out in "Censorship," *Theater Magazine*, May 1908, p. 134; Judge Daniel P. Trudge, "Testimony," *Chicago Motion Picture Commission Report*, pp. 128–32. For a scholarly discussion of European censorship see Paul Monaco, *Cinema and Society: France and Germany During the Twenties*, New York, 1976, pp. 48–61.

36. Simon Patten, "Amusements as a Factor in Man's Spiritual Uplift," *Current Literature*, August 1909, pp. 185–87; William Ingles, "Morals and the Moving Pictures," *Harper's Weekly*, July 30, 1910, pp. 12–13, contains a similar interview with Patten; Richard Hofstadter, *The Age of Reform*, New York, 1955, p. 179, contains a brief portrait; for his worries about communal disintegration see E. A. Ross, "Social Control," *American Journal of Sociology* 3, 1898, pp. 151–63. Ross's concern for adolescence, sex, and family order is in "Speech Before the National Motion Picture Conference, 1926," in Harmon Stephans, "The Relation of Motion Pictures to Changing Moral Standards," *The Annals of the American Academy of Political and Social Science*, November 1926, pp. 155–57. For his hopes on leisure as a means to class and moral harmony, see E. A. Ross, "Introduction," *Popular Amusements*, pp. i–v.
37. "White Slave Films," *The Outlook*, January 20, 1914, p. 414.

## Chapter Four: D. W. Griffith

1. Lillian Gish, "Interview," *Reel Life*, Winter 1972, unpaginated clipping, Gish File, MOMAFL.
2. The Reverend Dr. Charles H. Parkhurst, "The Birth of a Nation," review reprinted in Fred Silva, ed., *Focus on the Birth of a Nation*, Englewood Cliffs, New Jersey, 1971, pp. 101–3; Parkhurst, *My Twenty Years in New York*, New York, 1920.
3. On the "savior" see Edward Mott Wooley, "The $100,000 Salary Man of the Movies," *McClure's Magazine*, September 1913, pp. 109–16. Wilson saw *The Birth of a Nation* in 1915, and Harding saw *Orphans of the Storm* in 1921. Both were shown in the White House, unpaginated clippings in Griffith File, MOMAFL. Josephus Daniels to D. W. Griffith, December 1919, and William Jennings Bryan to D. W. Griffith, May 20, 1924, Griffith MSS, MOMAFL. Griffith's admiration for Wilson and the desire to make a film in favor of the League of Nations is in Lillian Gish, *The Movies, Mr. Griffith and Me*, Englewood Cliffs, New Jersey, 1969, pp. 182–248. For an example of how the formative critics liked his work, see Louis Reeves Harrison, "David Wark Griffith, the Art Director and his Work," *MPW*, November 22, 1913, p. 847. The quote is from "Radio Speech," Griffith File, MOMAFL.
4. For the biography of an early producer, see Albert Smith, *Two Reels and a Crank*, New York, 1952, pp. 11, 79–84, 251. On "exceptionally rich" see Isaac Morcosson, "The Magnates of the Motion Picture," *Munsey's* magazine, November 12, 1912, pp. 209–29; and the memoir of John Stuart Blackton, "Lecture," unpublished collection at the Academy of Motion Picture Arts and Science Library, Los Angeles, Calif. See also "The Moving Picture Revolution," *Success Magazine*, April 1910, pp. 238–40; "Big Fortunes Made in Nickles and Dimes," *Theater Magazine*, May 1915, p. 244.
5. George Kleine, "Testimony," *The Chicago Motion Picture Report*, Chicago, 1918, pp. 42–50.
6. Jeremiah Kennedy to Anonymous, July 8, 1908, National Board of Review Box, LCPA; the cost of running each film was tabulated from the National

Board of Review MSS Box 14, New York Public Library. The theater owners also wanted censorship, see New York *Times*, December 23, 1908, p. 1.

7.  On the "frontier" atmosphere by a contemporary observer, see Terry Ramsaye, *A Million and One Nights: A History of the Motion Picture*, New York, 1926, pp. 300–20. Each week the trade journals listed the film companies. In 1906 the future trust members had the market to themselves, see *Views and Film Index*, May 5, 1906, p. 5. In 1909 the nine trust members still controlled the market, see *Views and Film Index*, January through June 1909, and the same dates for *MPW*. By checking *MPW* for the next eight years, the figures on new companies were calculated. For the total by 1917, see *MPW*, October 13, 1917, pp. 305–7; Morcosson, "The Magnates," pp. 209–29.

8.  See for example, Russell Merritt, "Nickelodeon Theaters: Building an Audience for the Masses," in Tino Balio, ed., *The American Film Industry*, Madison, Wisconsin, 1976, pp. 59–82.

9.  Condemnations of foreign films by journals can be seen in "Our Own Critic," and "Weekly Comments on the Shows," *MPW*, January 1, 1909; "Training the Public Mind," *Views and Film Index*, April 25, 1906, p. 6; Stephan Bush, "Editorial," *MPW*, March 29, 1913; Louis Reeves Harrison, "Violence and Bloodshed," *MPW*, April 22, 1911; "What Is an American Subject?" *MPW*, January 22, 1910, p. 82.

10.  The best summary of what a "photoplay" should be is Louis Reeves Harrison, *Screencraft*, New York, 1916, pp. 54–70; "Eternal Recurrence," *MPW*, July 8, 1913, p. 24; "Both Entertaining and Educational," *MPW*, September 7, 1913; "The Art of Criticism," *MPW*, January 31, 1914; and for an exemplary model see his review of D. W. Griffith's *Ramona*, *MPW*, June 4, 1910.

11.  Early in 1906, half the films released were made by foreign companies, see *Views and Film Index*, December 1, 1906, p. 5. In 1913, 410 films were released during April, but only 31 came from abroad. See *MPW*, April 5, 1913, p. 14.

12.  See Stephan Bush, "Do Longer Films Make a Better Show," *MPW*, October 18, 1911; "Feature Programs," *MPW*, November 9, 1911, p. 529; "Is The Nickle Show on the Wane?" *MPW*, November 16, 1914, p. 1065, Louis Reeves Harrison, "How To Improve the Business," *MPW*, December 24, 1910; "Editorial," *MPW*, October 26, 1912; for the independents' monopoly of photoplays, see *MPW*, April 5, 1913, p. 104.

13.  Aitkin's life, faith, and morals are described by his brother, Roy Aitkin, *The Birth of a Nation Story*, Middleburg, Virginia, 1965, pp. 27–28, 46, 65. On his self-advertisement as a "Jacksonian Man" see *Reel Life*, March 4, 1914, p. 17, and February 5, 1916, p. 2, in MOMAFL. On the cartoons and editorials for his company, see *The Triangle*, October 23, 1915, p. 1; July 22, 1916, pp. 5–7; February 5, 1916, in Eastman House.

14.  Michael Davis, *The Exploitation of Pleasure*, New York, 1911, pp. 21–43.

15.  "Browning Given in the Movies," *New York Times*, October 4, 1909, part I, p. 8; the scholarly biography is Robert M. Henderson, *D. W. Griffith: His Life and Work*, New York, 1972; Herbert Francis Sherwood, "Democracy and the Movies," *Bookman*, March 1918, pp. 238–39.

16.  Henderson, *D. W. Griffith*, pp. 16–31; the primary sources for Griffith's up-

bringing are his "Unfinished Autobiography," in MOMAFL, and a long interview with the director by Henry Stephan Gordon, "The Story of David Wark Griffith," *Photoplay*, June–October, 1916. During these years, *Photoplay* was a serious journal, rather than the gossip and fantasy publication it became by the late twenties. The state history gives the census material for La Grange: the population in 1850 was 612, one-third of the residents were slaves, and there were five Protestant churches. It also contains an account of Jacob Griffith's service in the legislature. See Louis and Richard Collins, *History of Kentucky*, Covington, Kentucky, 1878, pp. 271, 666.

17. *Ibid.*

18. The mother's piety, teaching, and David's religious experiences are in Griffith, "Autobiography," pp. 1–7. The respect for pure women, vice district allure, and his guilt over early sexual adventures are also in the "Autobiography," pp. 6–10, 13–14, 39–42. The cemetery, church, and family burial grounds are described first-hand by Seymour Stern, "D. W. Griffith of the Movies," *American Mercury*, March 1949, p. 308. On the marriage and minister supported by Griffith, see New York *Herald Tribune*, March 3, 1936, unpaginated clipping, in MOMAFL. For the fact that women encouraged success, see Hazel Simpson's interview with Griffith, "The Poet Philosopher of the Photoplay," *Motion Picture Magazine*, September 1919, pp. 28–29.

19. Gordon, "Griffith," June 1916, pp. 35–57; Griffith, "Autobiography," pp. 1–10; Griffith, "A Criticism of the Income Tax," Los Angeles *Times*, October 26, 1919, p.3.

20. Griffith, "Autobiography," pp. 40–43, 55–58.

21. The marriage situation is in Mrs. D. W. Griffith, *When the Movies Were Young*, New York, 1925. Nobody who worked with them knew they were married. See Billy Bitzer, *His Story: The Autobiography of D. W. Griffith's Master Cameraman*, New York, 1973, pp. 63–65.

22. For the quote on reform, see Griffith, "Autobiography," pp. 80–81; Bitzer, *His Story*, pp. 5, 88–89, 188–90, recalled how he and Griffith saw the need for message films and uplift for the immigrants. On his constant work and little time for sex, see an interview with Griffith by Jim Tully, *Vanity Fair*, November 1928, p. 80. On the growing acclaim of his films, see "Browning Given the Movies," New York *Times*, October 4, 1909, Part I, p. 8. On reformer's condemnation of monopoly in the industry and hope for trust-busting to improve the art, see *People's Institute Bulletin*, December 23, 1908, p. 5.

23. Griffith, "A Few thoughts for the Radio," December 1925, Griffith File, MOMAFL; "Pace in the Movies," *Liberty*, November 13, 1926, p. 19; "The Future of the Two Dollar Movie," in Silva, *Focus*, pp. 99–101. For Griffith's dislike of sound, see Fred Cox's interview with Griffith, "Screen Pace Setter," *Hollywood Citizen News*, May 7, 1947, and Gish, *The Movies*, p. 241; Gish, *Reel Life*, Winter 1971, p. 3.

24. "Interview with D. W. Griffith," New York *American*, February 28, 1915, City Life and Dramatic Section, p. 9; D. W. Griffith, "The Motion Picture and Witch Burners," in Silva, *Focus*, pp. 96–98.

25. Leonard Hall, "Interview with D. W. Griffith," *Stage*, August 1911, unpaginated clipping, Griffith File, MOMAFL; Lillian Gish, "D. W. Griffith,"

*Harper's Bazaar*, October 1940, pp. 105–6, for the style of handling actors and actresses; see also Gish, *The Movies*, pp. 76, 84, 115, 130, 358. As late as 1948 Griffith was saying that "stars" are unnecessary. See "An Oldtimer Advises Hollywood," *Liberty*, June 7, 1939, p. 18; D. W. Griffith, "What I Demand of Movie Stars, *Moving Picture Classic*, February 1917, pp. 40–41.

26. Griffith, "Youth, The Spirit of the Movies," *Illustrated World*, in Geduld, *Focus*, pp. 194–96; Griffith, "What I Demand," pp. 40–41. In his "Radio Talk," Griffith saw youth as the quality for assimilating immigrants.

27. Griffith, "What Is Beauty," *Liberty*, October 19, 1929, pp. 28–29; Gish, *The Movies*, pp. 45, 100–102, 124–28, 349. One old friend recalled that on his death bed Griffith wondered if he had lived up to his mother's expectations, see Garrett J. Lloyd, "Griffith's Life Story," Los Angeles *Examiner*, July 25, 1948. On the idea that it is woman's "greatest life work" to inspire success in men, see Hazel Simpson's interview with Griffith, "The Poet Philosopher of the Photoplay," *Motion Picture Magazine*, September 1919, pp. 28–29.

28. On the idea that a studio should be free from surrounding corruption, see D. W. Griffith, "Pictures versus One Night Stands," *Independent*, December 11, 1916, pp. 447–48. For the studio atmosphere and its relation to women, health, and morals, see Gish, *The Movies*, pp. 85, 120–28, 206–9, and Bitzer, *His Story*, pp. 208–9.

29. D. W. Griffith, "What Is Beauty"; "What I Demand"; "The Real Truth about Breaking into the Movies," *Woman's Home Companion*, February 1924, pp. 16–17; Henry C. Carr, "How Griffith Picks His Leading Ladies," *Photoplay*, December 1918, pp. 24–28; Donald Crisp, "Funeral Eulogy," Griffith File, AMPASL, describes Griffith shooting over and over to attain the right effect. Hall, "Interview," records Griffith as saying, "If we believe in these images of pure and sweet beauty, we must confess it was done by the hand of God himself."

30. Griffith, "Pace," pp. 19–23; "Pictures versus One Night Stands," pp. 447–48; Fox, "Screen Pace Setter," p. 12. For a brilliant discussion of this aesthetic as a liberal bourgeois view of the world versus a Marxist dialectic and synthesis, see Sergei Eisenstein, *Film Form: Essays in Film Theory*, New York, 1949.

31. Gordon, "The Story," July 1916, pp. 124–29, 131–32.

32. *The Avenging Conscience*, 1914, MOMAFL.

33. *Man's Genesis*, 1912, MOMAFL.

34. For a few of the historical films, see *Judith of Bethulia*, 1914; westward expansion, *The Battle of Elderbush Gulch*, 1914; the American Revolution, *America*, 1924; the French Revolution, *Orphans of the Storm*, 1921, MOMAFL. On contemporary themes, see on labor-capital conflict, *The Voice of the Violin*, 1909, which condemns Marxists; on monopolists, *A Corner On Wheat*, 1909; on prohibition, *A Drunkard's Reformation*, 1909; on vice lords, *Musketeers of Pig Alley*, 1912, all in MOMAFL.

35. *Home Sweet Home*, 1914; independent, resourceful women appear in nearly every major film. A classic working girl appears in *The Lonedale Operator*, 1911, *Musketeers of Pig Alley*, 1912, and *The Song of the Shirt*, 1908.

36. Raymond J. Cook, "The Man Behind 'The Birth of a Nation,' " *North Carolina Historical Review* 20, October 1962, pp. 519–40; Thomas Dixon, "Why I Wrote

*The Clansman,*" *Theater Magazine,* January 1906, pp. 20–22, in which Dixon explains that his motive was to convert the North to the Southern view of race and miscegenation.

37. See for example, Alexander Saxton, *The Indispensable Enemy: Labor and the Anti-Chinese Movement in California,* Los Angeles and Berkeley, 1971, pp. 19–30.

38. On Griffith's tremendous enthusiasm on making the film and "Jake Griffith's son fighting the War all over again," see Bitzer, "Interview," in MOMAFL, and *His Story,* p. 107; Gish, *The Movies,* p. 136. The quote is from Gordon, "Story of Griffith," October 1916, pp. 86–90.

39. *The Birth of a Nation,* 1915, in MOMAFL. A detailed shot-by-shot analysis is in Theodore Huff, *Intolerance: The Film by D. W. Griffith, A Shot by Shot Analysis,* New York, 1966. Wagner's "Ride of the Valkyries" was the original music for the ride of the Klan, see Francis Hackett, "Brotherly Love," *New Republic,* March 20, 1915, p. 185.

40. See *Motion Picture Almanac,* New York, 1934, pp. 16–17. This is the annual trade journal summary.

41. See Arthur Link, *Woodrow Wilson and the Progressive Era, 1910–1917,* New York, 1954, pp. 1–24.

42. *The Birth of a Nation,* especially the titles introducing the Reconstruction story.

43. Dixon, "Southern Horizons," unpublished autobiography, cited in Cook, "The Man," p. 529. Dixon also wrote to Wilson that the "play is transforming the entire population of the North and West into Democratic voters. There will never again be an issue of your segregation policy." See Dixon to Woodrow Wilson, September 5, 1915, in Arthur Link, *Wilson and the New Freedom,* Princeton, New Jersey, 1956, p. 252.

44. A full examination of the unfavorable response is Thomas Cripps, "The Reaction of the Negro to the Motion Picture, *The Birth of a Nation,*" *The Historian* 25, 1963, pp. 344–63; see also W. D. McGuire, "Censoring Motion Pictures," *New Republic,* April 15, 1915, pp. 262–63. For Frederic Howe's and Jane Addams's disapproval, and Howe's resignation from the Board for even allowing its filming, see *The Survey,* April 3, 1915.

45. On Griffith's condemnation of his critics, see D. W. Griffith, "Reply to the New York *Globe,*" New York *Globe,* April 10, 1915, in Geduld, *Focus,* pp. 77–80; and "Defense of The Birth of a Nation and Attack on the Sullivan Bill," Boston *Herald,* April 26, 1915, in Geduld, *Focus,* pp. 43–45. For no "black blood" in the actors who played leading roles, see Gordon, "Griffith," October 1916, p. 79. For Dixon's hatred of race mixing, see Dixon, "Why I Wrote," pp. 20–22; and the producers, see Aitkin, *The Birth,* pp. 60–65; and Griffith's denials see Gish, *The Movies,* pp. 162–63.

46. For his criticism of censors, see D. W. Griffith, *The Rise and Fall of Free Speech in America,* 1916, and D. W. Griffith, "The Motion Picture and Witch Burners," pp. 96–99.

47. Gordon, "Griffith," October 1916, pp. 86–90. Quote is from unpaginated undated clipping, Griffith File on *Intolerance,* MOMA.

48. *Intolerance,* 1916, MOMAFL. See also Theodore Huff, *Intolerance: The Film by D. W. Griffith, A Shot by Shot Analysis,* New York, 1966. The attempt to reproduce each era from exact historical and archeological research is the subject of

Bernard Benson, "D. W. Griffith, Some Sources," *Art Bulletin*, December 1972, pp. 493–95. For a discussion of how the charity ball in the modern story was meant to duplicate the New York "Four Hundred," see Joseph Haneberry, the assistant director, interview in Kevin Brownlow, *The Parade's Gone By*, New York, 1969, pp. 55, 68–69. That the coming of Christ and the end to war was the conscious message is discussed in Bitzer, *His Story*, pp. 137–39. Gordon, "Griffith," October 1916, pp. 86–90, has Griffith saying how the film was made from "his head."

49. Howard Gaye was the actor arrested and deported. See Bitzer, *His Story*, p. 142. On locking out the IWW, see Haneberry interview in Brownlow, *Parade*, p. 68. For the general struggle against labor, see Louis B. Perry and Richard S. Perry, *A History of the Los Angeles Labor Movement, 1911–1940*, Los Angeles, 1963, pp. 318–40.

50. New York *Sun*, September 6, 1916, unpaginated clipping, Griffith File, *Intolerance* section, MOMA.

51. *Philadelphia North American*, December 30, 1916, unpaginated clipping, Griffith File, *Intolerance* section, MOMA; on being labeled a communist see undated interview, probably 1947, Griffith File, AMPASL. One biographer records that Lenin had the film shown throughout the USSR in 1919, see Iris Berry, *D. W. Griffith: American Film Master*, New York, 1940, p. 26.

52. Heywood Broun, "Intolerance," New York *Tribune*, September 7, 1916.

53. *Hearts of the World*, 1918, MOMAFL, is Griffith's propaganda film for the war. It was commissioned by the British government and led to the director's audience with the British Prime Minister, Lloyd George. *Orphans of the Storm*, 1921, is Griffith's indirect attack, overtly proclaimed in a long opening title, on the Bolsheviks. On its showing to Harding and the atmosphere of these years, see Gish, *The Movies*, pp. 145–51, 158–61; Playbill, "Orphans of the Storm," Griffith File, MOMA. Griffith of course was not unique in making Red Scare films, and applying their meaning to the studios in Hollywood. See *Dangerous Hours*, 1919, LCFA.

54. On the new industry, see Chapter VII.

55. In his final years Griffith saw himself as the last man to make "one man pictures"; see Otis Guernsey, "A Lively Oldster, D. W. Griffith," New York *Herald Tribune*, October 4, 1942, unpaginated clipping, Griffith File, AMPASL. On his complaints that young men of the new age were being blocked from the top and self-sufficiency, see Griffith, "A Criticism of the Income Tax," p. 3. The quote is from Billy Bitzer, "Interview," MOMAFL. See also Bitzer, *His Story*, p. 235, for a similar sentiment, and Griffith Collection, MOMA, for loan receipts from banks for his 1920s films.

56. See Gish, *The Movies*, p. 324; and "D. W. Griffith," *Harper's Bazaar*, October 1940, for his alienation from Hollywood and the films he was making. The beginning of his social disillusionment occurred with *Broken Blossoms*, 1919. That women were changing and adopting sexual styles that endangered the old masculine code of success, see *True Heart Susie*, 1919, and *Way Down East*, 1920. The danger of the new cities and the retreat to small towns is in *Dream Street*, 1921, *Way Down East*, 1920, *The White Rose*, 1923, and *Sorrows of Satan*, 1926. All are in MOMAFL. Some of these films display a growing lack of aes-

thetic mastery, probably because the director no longer felt the great, socially transforming ideal as relevant. The quote is from "Editorial," *Photoplay*, December 1924, p. 27. *The Struggle*, 1931, MOMAFL.

57. Griffith, "A Criticism"; letters to Bryan, Josephus Daniels, and other Democrats complaining of the income tax are in Griffith Collection, MOMA.

58. June Glassmeyer, Interview, June 22, 1974. She recalled that Griffith drank a great deal, but occasionally would leave the bar and come back with a red rose for her.

59. Griffith to Peter Burghard Stone Company, June 6, 1934, Griffith MSS, MOMA. The Methodist cemetery is near where Griffith went to school and worshipped as a youth, see Stern, "D. W. Griffith," p. 308. The quote is from a Griffith assistant, Robert M. Farquar, "Interview," Griffith File, MOMA. On land speculation see interview with his black chauffeur, Richard Reynolds, "Interview," MOMA.

## Chapter Five: Revitalization

1. George Creel, "A Close Up of Douglas Fairbanks," *Everybody's*, December 1916, pp. 730–35; Alma Whitaker, "Mrs. Douglas Fairbanks Analyzes Mary Pickford," *Photoplay*, March 28, 1928, pp. 30–31.

2. The new audience can be seen in Russell Merritt, "Nickelodeon Theaters: Building an Audience for the Movies," in Tino Balio, ed., *The American Film Industry*, Madison, Wisconsin, 1976, pp. 59–82. Or see the changing nature of film theaters and audience in Chapter VI.

3. See, for example, Robert Wiebe, *The Search for Order*, New York, 1967.

4. Henry Seidel Canby, *The Age of Confidence*, in *American Memoir*, Boston, 1947, p. 119.

5. See, for example, Henry May, *The End of American Innocence*, Chicago, 1959; James R. McGovern, "The American Woman's Pre–World War I Freedom in Manners and Morals," *Journal of American History* 55, September 1968, pp. 315–33.

6. Canby, *Age of Confidence*, pp. 67–71, 80.

7. Through 1914–1918 the files of the National Board of Review were replete with letters bewailing the censors' inability to get prestigious names to serve whose judgment people would respect. See People's Institute Collection, NYPL.

8. See, for example, "Broadway Favorites Invade the Screen," *Theater Magazine*, August 1916, pp. 86–87; Johnson Briscol, "Why Film Favorites Forsook the Footlights," *Photoplay*, September 1914, pp. 75–76; William de Mille, *Hollywood Saga*, New York, 1939, pp. 1–60; Thomas Ince, "The Star Is Here To Stay," *Munsey's*, November 1918, p. 337–38.

9. *MPW* 1907–1918. This was gathered by examining every plot summary recorded in the months of February and July of each year.

10. Bronco Billy, or Max Aronson, made over 300 films for George Spoor's Essanay Company. See Max Aronson, Los Angeles *Times*, Obituary Section, January 21, 1971. Some of his films are in MOMA and LCFA. For a good description of Aronson's personal asceticism see Charles Chaplin, *My Autobiography*, New

York, 1964, pp. 170–71. For the comment of the immigrant, see unpaginated undated clipping in Aronson File, AMPASL. The plot for Bronco Billy's Bible is in *MPW*, December 7, 1912. On his origins see *Stage Journal*, June 1914, unpaginated clipping, Aronson File, NYPLTAC.

11. On Hart's life and social and economic beliefs, see William S. Hart, *My Life, East and West*, Boston, 1929, pp. 8–12, 25, 55–60, 94–100, 162–72, 224, 272, 305. Hart, like Griffith, often made films independently and hated the rise of the new organizations. For his patriotic and political beliefs resting behind his work see "The Real West as William S. Hart Sees It," *Triangle Exhibitor's Bulletin*, October 30, 1916, p. 8. In *The Patriot* (1916), Hart is a farmer, who is deprived of his land by a corrupt businessman and government official. See the description in *The Triangle*, August 19, 1916, p. 4; and March 25, 1916, for *The Aryan* (1916). *The Disciple* (1915) is in LCFA and is perhaps the most dramatic portrayal of militant, evangelical Christianity ever put in an American film. *Hell's Hinges* (1915) and *The Toll Gate* (1919) are both in MOMA.

12. *MPW*, July 1914; *The Clerk* (1914) is described in *Reel Life*, February 14, 1914, p. 2, MOMA.

13. See Mack Sennett, as told to Cameron Shipp, *King of Comedy*, Garden City, New York, 1954, pp. 12–65. The quote is from "Interview with Mack Sennett," *The Triangle*, March 11, 1916, p. 5. NYPLTAC.

14. Sennett, *King*, pp. 65–90. As Lillian Gish recalled, "Griffith trained Mack Sennett and when Griffith left, Sennett invented the Keystone Cops. Griffith didn't approve at all. He said, 'That will teach children disrespect for police and the law' . . . Griffith would not glorify crime and wickedness. The bad wouldn't win out over the good." See Joyce Haber, "Lillian Gish: The Iron in Innocence," *Los Angeles Times Calendar*, January 6, 1974, p. 11.

15. Sennett, *King*, pp. 116–75. Paul Harrison, "Sennett Waxes Witty," unpaginated, undated clipping, Sennett File, NYPLTAC.

16. *The Triangle*, November 1915, March 1916. *Sennett Scrapbook*, NYPLTAC. "Bedroom Blunder," *Paramount Mack Sennett Comedies*, September 10, 1917, in *Sennett Scrapbook*, NYPLTAC.

17. See Chaplin, *My Autobiography*, pp. 1–150. Plot descriptions of the cited films are in Isabel Quigly, *Charlie Chaplin: Early Comedies*, New York, 1968.

18. *A Fool There Was* (1914); "Theda Bara Interview," *Fox Exhibitor's Bulletin*, June 1917, p. 13, and June 1918, p. 1, in MOMA; "Theda Bara Interview," *Theater Magazine*, June 1917, p. 246; "Obituary, Theda Bara," unmarked clipping in Bara File, MOMA. The films of black and labor unrest are *Destruction* (1916), and *Under the Yoke* (1916), described as lost films in a complete list of Bara films in *Films in Review*, May 1968, p. 283.

19. For two among many see "Scintillations of a Youthful Star," *Theater Magazine*, December 1911, p. 93, and E. Lloyd Sheldon, "The New Profession of Beauty," *Delineator*, March 1916, p. 5. The quote is from Louis Reeves Harrison, "Ramona," *MPW*, June 4, 1910.

20. *The Devil's Wheel* (1913), MOMAFL.

21. This reading comes from clips of a "Perils of Pauline" episode in LCFA. See also Linda Harris Mehr, "Down Off the Pedestal: Some Modern Heroines in Popular Culture," Ph.D. dissertation, UCLA, 1974, pp. 119–96; Mayor

Gaynor, *Ladies' World*, June 1913, pp. 20–21, in Mehr, "Down Off," pp. 194–95, and the description of *Traffic in Souls*, MPW, November 22, 1913, p. 849. The quote is from "Our Mutual Girl," *Photoplay*, June 1914, pp. 144–45. On Pauline's Italian chateau and her new type of sporting activities see Mabel Condon, "The Real Perils of Pauline," *Photoplay*, October 1914, pp. 59–64.

22. *Social Secretary* (1915), LCFA; *Plato's Dilemma* (1914) is described in *The Universal Weekly*, February 1914, AMPACL.

23. It is quite possible that the success books were written with someone else and Fairbanks signed his name. Nevertheless, they correspond to his public and screen image. See Douglas Fairbanks, *Making Life Worthwhile*, New York, 1918; *Laugh and Live*, New York, 1917; and *Youth Points the Way*, New York, 1924. Likewise see Mary Pickford, "My Own Story," *Ladies' Home Journal*, July 1923.

24. For example see Douglas Fairbanks, "Personal Reminiscences," *The Theater*, April 1917, p. 220. The effect was obviously to link the actor directly to the main social currents of the North, heightening his public immediacy.

25. The primary source for the Fairbanks family and the star's background comes from Richard Schickel and Douglas Fairbanks, Jr., *The Fairbanks Album*, Boston, 1976, pp. 1–50. In addition, see "Fairbanks Obituary," New York *Times*, December 13, 1939, Part VII, p. 29, and his father's obituary, "Charles Ulman," New York *Times*, February 25, 1915, Part IX, p. 4.

26. *His Majesty the American* (1919), EHFL.

27. Admiration for the industrial titans and American politicians along with fear of modern "inertia," was forcefully stated in Fairbanks, *Making Life*, pp. 80–101. Entrapment in the office appears most dramatically in his book *Laugh and Live*, and in *His Picture in the Papers* (1916), *The Mystery of the Leaping Fish* (1916), *Reaching for the Moon* (1917), *When Clouds Roll By* (1919), in EHFL.

28. *Ibid*.

29. Fairbanks, *Laugh and Live*, pp. 11–17; the danger of too much wealth dissipating the Western will is in nearly every pre-War film and book. See *Reggie Mixes In* (1916), *Wild and Wooly* (1917), *When Clouds Roll By* (1919), *His Picture in the Papers* (1916), *The Mystery of the Leaping Fish* (1916), *The Mollycoddle* (1920). His need to prove himself white appears in two interviews, Charles K. Taylor, "The Most Popular Man in the World," *The Outlook*, 1924, unpaginated, undated clipping in Fairbanks File, MOMA; see also "Douglas E. (Electricity) Fairbanks," *Motion Picture Magazine*, December 1916, p. 16.

30. Fairbanks, *Laugh and Live*, pp. 23–36; *Making Life Worthwhile*, pp. 28–32, 150–55. For the new ideology, see Fairbanks, *Making Life Worthwhile*, pp. 28–32, which links sports to escape from the "big boss." Douglas Fairbanks, "Combining Play with Work," *American Magazine*, July 1917, pp. 31–37. For the new sports clothes and discipline linked to athletics, see "Douglas Fairbanks' Own Page," *Photoplay*, December 1917, p. 15. The speed and vigor of the athlete appears in almost any Fairbanks film of the era; see especially *Manhattan Madness* (1916) in EHFL.

31. *Mr. Robinson Crusoe* (1932), EHFL.

32. All his films manifest the body cult. For his articulation see "A Photo-Interview with Douglas Fairbanks," *Photoplay*, October 1918, p. 12. On sport see Fairbanks, *Youth*, pp. 1–50; and for the quote, *Laugh and Live*, pp. 31–32.

33. *Ibid.;* Booth Tarkington, "Introduction," in Fairbanks, "Combining," p. 31; Fairbanks, *Youth.*
34. All the films are in EHFL.
35. *His Picture in the Papers* (1916), EHFL. Fairbanks also endorsed products for advertisers, making the same association between products as fun, rather than necessity.
36. White slavers and saloon mobs, or the decadent immigrants are mastered in *Reggie Mixes In, His Majesty the American,* and *The Nut.* In *American Aristocracy* and *The Mollycoddle,* he conquers foreign smugglers and German agents. In *His Picture in the Papers* and *American Aristocracy,* his initial alienation dissolves as the hero protects big businessmen from criminal attack. *The Americano* (1916) and *His Majesty the American* find the hero protecting European and Latin governments from revolution. For a view of how reformers honestly approved of these imperialistic impulses as benefiting humanity and advancing "capital," see George Creel, "A Close-Up." The quote is from the final title of *The Americano.*
37. *The Nut* (1921), EHFL.
38. The desire for a new woman is in nearly every film, but to see its clearest articulation see *A Modern Musketeer* (1915), *His Picture in the Papers, Manhattan Madness,* and *The Nut* (1921). *The Matrimaniac* (1916) is in EHFL. On the need to "nail down loveliness," and advice on marrying early, see Fairbanks, *Laugh and Live,* pp. 149–55.
39. "This Little Girl Earns $100,000 a Year," *McClure's Magazine,* unpaginated clipping, Pickford Scrapbook, NYPLTAC. On the trap of the "little girl" image, see Mary Pickford, *Sunshine and Shadow,* New York, 1955, pp. 193–95.
40. Minneapolis *Journal,* March 5, 1915, unpaginated clipping, Pickford Scrapbook, NYPLTAC. The Hearst Press voted her the most "popular" in 1916, see New York *World,* 1916, undated and unpaginated clipping in Pickford Scrapbook, NYPLTAC.
41. The primary sources on Pickford's life are the clippings, writings, and interviews in the Mary Pickford Scrapbooks, NYPLTAC. Pickford details her own life in Pickford, *Sunshine and Shadow,* pp. 40–85, and "My Own Story," *Ladies' Home Journal,* July 1923. For one of the many stories concerning her screen image, see "The Best Known Girl in America—Mary Pickford—Tells What It Means To Be a Movie Actress," *Photoplay,* January 1915, p. 9.
42. *Lena and the Geese* (1911), *The New York Hat* (1912). On Pickford in *A Good Little Devil,* see *Vanity Fair,* January 25, 1913, p. 8, and *New York Dramatic Mirror,* March 19, 1913, unpaginated clipping, Pickford Scrapbook, NYPLTAC. Her comments are in Kevin Brownlow, *The Parade's Gone By,* New York, 1969, pp. 141–55.
43. Owing to Pickford's ownership of her films, and control by the estate after her death, the difficulties of seeing them are immense. Most were shown at the Los Angeles County Museum of Art in 1974. Any plots cited were also gleaned from extensive descriptions in the Pickford Scrapbook, as was *Tess of the Storm Country* (1914).
44. *The Eternal Grind* (1916), *MPW,* unpaginated clipping, Pickford Scrapbook, NYPLTAC.
45. Films which showed her rebellion from Victorian restraints are *A Poor Little*

*Rich Girl* (1917), *The Little Princess* (1918), *How Could You Jean* (1918), *Stella Maris* (1917), *Pollyanna* (1920), and *Rebecca of Sunnybrook Farm* (1917).

46. Films in which Pickford plays an expressive foreigner were reproduced also in the trade journals and appear with pictures in the Pickford Scrapbook. They are *The Little Queen* (1914), *The Eagle's Mate* (1914), *Less Than the Dust* (1916), *The Grind* (1914), *Mistress Nell* (1915), *Poor Little Peppina* (1916), *Madame Butterfly* (1915), *Amarilly of Clothesline Alley* (1918); in *Hearts Adrift* (1914) she portrays a white girl stranded on an island. For a description of this mixture of culture and virtue, see Frederic Wallace, "Why Mary Pickford Appeals," *Motion Pictures,* July 1915, unpaginated clipping, Pickford Scrapbook, NYPLTAC. On Tourneur & Rosher's innovations, see Brownlow, *The Parade,* pp. 140–48, 160–65, 253–69, 274–76.

47. *Ladies' World,* September 1916, unpaginated clipping, Mary Pickford Scrapbook, NYPLTAC. One example of the effect occurred when Frederic Wallace wrote, "She is feminine in everything she does; she stares, but not like a virago; she is coquettish, but it is never the cold-blooded type of flirting," see *Motion Pictures,* July 1916, Mary Pickford Scrapbook, NYPLTAC.

48. *Hearts Adrift* (1914), see *New York Dramatic Mirror,* February 1, 1914, unpaginated clipping, Mary Pickford Scrapbook, NYPLTAC.

49. For a discussion of Mary as one who is not a prude but combines upper- and lower-class expressiveness, see unpaginated clipping, Pickford Scrapbook, III, NYPLTAC. The "radiant image of girlish beauty" comes from unpaginated clipping, *Motion Pictures,* January 1916, Pickford Scrapbook, NYPLTAC. The clean, youthful face as a mirror of morality is in Toledo *Times,* June 1, 1919, unpaginated clipping, Pickford Scrapbook. For one of the many articles on her use of cosmetics see the Chicago *Tribune,* 1916, undated and unpaginated clipping, Pickford Scrapbook, III. The Lindsay poem is from the Cleveland *Leader,* May 14, 1916, unpaginated clipping, Pickford Scrapbook, III. That this vision penetrated even higher journalism, see Harvey O'Higgins, "Mary Pickford," *New Republic,* February 15, 1919, p. 80.

50. On the effects of her mother's hold, see Pickford, *Sunshine,* pp. 50, 68, 86, 133. A typical reporter remarked that "wherever Mary goes there you'll see her mother," see the Cleveland *Plain Dealer,* February 24, 1917, unpaginated clipping, Pickford Scrapbook, IV. The arrest of a man for insulting Mary and the quote on realism both come from undated clippings, Pickford Scrapbook, IV. On Zukor contributing to this process, see Adolph Zukor, *The Public Is Never Wrong,* New York, 1953, pp. 174–75, in which he wrote that "Mary liked an occasional drink. For her to take one in public would have been disastrous. Smoking was also taboo."

51. For one among many, see *Motion Picture,* August 1917, unpaginated clipping, Pickford Scrapbook. Sheldon, "Profession of Beauty," pp. 5–6. Pickford, *Sunshine,* p. 250.

52. Work as drudgery in the modern city, complicated by Mary's portrayal of the average menial work for women, appears most dramatically in *Suds* (1918), *The Eternal Grind* (1914), *Stella Maris* (1917), *Behind the Scenes* (1914). The similar episode in her own life is recounted in Pickford, *Sunshine,* pp. 133–37.

53. A long description of the film is in Pickford Scrapbook, III.

54. The Pickford Scrapbooks are filled with articles on her clothes, tastes, and

home. In 1918, along with Irene Castle, she was voted the "best dressed woman in the world" by the Hearst press. See, for example, an unpaginated clipping, *Photoplay Journal*, August 1917, Pickford Scrapbook, IV, p. 10. The quote is from "How Mary Pickford Stays Young, An Interview," *Everybody's*, 1926, unpaginated clipping, Mary Pickford File, MOMAFL. Consumption also applied to eating the right health foods for the body beautiful, see "The Best-Known Girl in America," p. 9.

55. *The Hoodlum* (1919), as shown at the Los Angeles County Museum of Art, 1974, from the Pickford Archives or personal collection. Other versions of this social conversionary force are in *Pollyanna* (1920) and *A Poor Little Rich Girl* (1917). In almost all the films this power works to improve the men who love her.

56. On the stars enlisted in the War effort, see *Theater Magazine*, May–June, 1917. For Fairbanks and the War effort ideology, see his chapter, "Backing Up the Flag," in Fairbanks, *Making Life Worthwhile*, pp. 153–58. On knocking out the Kaiser, see Fairbanks, "Personal Reminiscences," *The Theater*, April 1917, p. 220. On Mary and the War effort, see New York *Tribune*, April 12, 1918, unpaginated clipping, Pickford Scrapbook, III, p. 62; for the gun, see Toledo *Times*, November 1918, unpaginated clipping, Pickford Scrapbook, III, p. 85. On her seeing the War making the country "one big family," see Los Angeles *Examiner*, May 6, 1918, unpaginated clipping, Pickford Scrapbook, III, p. 72. A complete plot summary, with pictures, of Pickford's major War film, *The Little American*, is in Gene Ringold and De Witt Bodeen, *The Films of Cecil B. DeMille*, New Jersey, 1959, pp. 133–36.

57. A host of newspaper articles, a transcript of the divorce, and underlying admiration for the divorces and creation of the perfect marriage are in Pickford Scrapbook, IV. The Catholic Bishop of Monterey condemned the scandal and divorce, see the Chicago *Tribune*, April 1, 1920; the Nevada attorney general's actions are in the Toledo *Blade*, April 5, 1920; the story of the Baptist minister who married them is in the New York *Sun-Herald*, June 29, 1920; Owen Moore's threat to sue is in the Toledo *News Bee*, March 20, 1920; all the above are unpaginated clippings in Pickford Scrapbook, IV. The pictures and descriptions of their honeymoon tour are also in the above, as well as in Schickel and Fairbanks, Jr., *Fairbanks Album*.

58. Pickfair and its elaborate grounds can be seen in Schickel and Fairbanks, Jr., *Fairbanks Album*, and Fred Basten, *Beverly Hills: Portrait of a Fabled City*, Los Angeles, 1975, pp. 61–68. On their home as a "veritable earthly paradise," see the Cleveland *Leader*, May 30, 1920, unpaginated clipping, Pickford Scrapbook. The quotes are from Adela Rogers St. Johns, "The Married Life of Doug and Mary," *Photoplay*, February 1927, pp. 34, 134–36.

59. On Pickford's charity work, and civic service, see *Photoplay*, April 1920, and Chicago *Tribune*, January 25, 1920, in Pickford Scrapbooks. For Fairbanks and his desire to hear no depressing things, see Pickford, *Sunshine*, pp. 50–100.

## Chapter Six: You Are the Star

1. Charles Ferguson, "High Class," *Harper's Monthly Magazine*, March 1932, p. 456.

2. On the number of saloons in the city, see *Report of the Police Department*, New

York, 1886–1910. In 1910 the Lower East Side had seventy-eight saloons, nine dance halls, and eight movie houses. A similar pattern characterized other poor neighborhoods, see Michael Davis, *The Exploitation of Pleasure*, New York, 1911, pp. 3–10, 21–35. The same study showed that those above "laborers" and "clerks" rarely attended low-priced theaters.

3. On the Board and theaters, see Davis, *Exploitation*, pp. 1–35. B. P. Schulberg, "Adolph Zukor," *Variety*, December 1, 1926, unpaginated clipping in Zukor File, MOMA; David Warfield, "Marcus Loew, My Friend and Partner," New York *Morning Telegraph*, September 6, 1927, p. 5; A. J. Balaban and Carrie Balaban, *Continuous Performance: The Story of A. J. Balaban as Told to His Wife*, New York, 1942, p. 42.

4. Henry Archer, *MPW*'s New England correspondent, see March 14, 1914; May 2, 1914; May 16, 1914; May 30, 1914. Walter P. Eaton, "Class Consciousness and the Movies," *Atlantic Monthly* 115, January 1915, pp. 49–50, in Russell Merritt, "Nickelodeon Theaters 1905–1914: Building an Audience for the Movies," in Tino Balio, ed., *The American Film Industry*, Madison, Wisconsin, 1976, pp. 59–83.

5. Arthur S. Meloy, *Theaters and Motion Picture Houses*, New York, 1916, pp. 2, 9, 25, 28, 89. John Klaber, "Planning the Motion Picture Theater," *Architectural Record* 38, 1915, pp. 540–54; P. R. Periera, *The Cinema Architect* 106, September 23, 1914, pp. 177–84; *Report of the Police Department*, New York, 1900–1910; Davis, *Exploitation*, pp. 1–10, 30–34; Stephan Bush, "Editorial," *MPW*, March 29, 1909.

6. The classification of architectural styles over time was done by following the column that contained pictures, called "New Houses," in the *MPW* from 1908 to 1920. In this task I am indebted to Daisann McLane, my research assistant. Classical styles predominated until about 1916.

7. D. W. Griffith, "Are Motion Pictures Destructive of Good Taste?" *Arts and Decoration*, September 1923, pp. 12–13; "The Motion Pictures and Witch Burners," in Harry M. Geduld, *Focus on Birth of a Nation*, New York, 1972, p. 97.

8. "New Houses," *MPW*, April 5, 1910, p. 57; on the nationalism, as well as prestigious conductors and orchestras, see the pictures from the early teens in Ben Hall, *The Best Remaining Seats*, New York, 1961, pp. 10–16, 37. A contemporary account and the motives are found in Albert Smith, *Two Reels and a Crank*, New York, 1952, pp. 253–54; "New Houses," *Motion Picture News*, December 6, 1913, p. 30.

9. Davis, *Exploitation*, p. 28; Stephan Bush, "The Triumph of the Gallery," *MPW*, December 13, 1913.

10. "William Fox Obituary," *Box Office Magazine*, May 10, 1952; Los Angeles *Times*, May 9, 1952; *MPW*, March 17, 1929. In a lecture to the Harvard Business School, Fox described the rise up the class ladder. See Joseph Kennedy, ed., *The Story of the Films*, New York, 1927, pp. 303–5. The quote is from William Fox, "Possibilities of the Motion Picture Unlimited," *Fox Exhibitors' Bulletin*, June 1914, p. 31, in Fox File, MOMA.

11. Olivia Harriet Dunbar, "The Lure of the Films," *Harper's Weekly*, January 18, 1913, p. 20.

12. "Broadway," *Atlantic Monthly*, June 1920, pp. 855–56; Charles Chaplin, *My Autobiography*, New York, 1964, p. 122. The photos of the early plush houses are in Hall, *Seats*, pp. 10–16, 37, and echo the same atmosphere.

13. See Frank Woods, "Spectator's Comments," New York *Dramatic Mirror*, May 14, 1910, in Stanley Kauffmann and Bruce Henstell, eds., *American Film Criticism*, New York, 1972, pp. 39–41, or Hugo Münsterberg, *The Photoplay: A Psychological Study*, New York, 1916, pp. 83–103, 112–30, 203–10. The quote is from Harry Aitkin, "Editorial," *Triangle Exhibitors' Bulletin*, October 23, 1915, p. 3, in EHFL.

14. The "New Style" management and theaters are best described in Harold B. Franklin (manager of Paramount's West Coast theater chain), *Motion Picture Theater Management*, New York, 1927, and *Architectural Forum* 42, June 1925, pp. 361–432. This is a series of articles by the "experts" in all parts of the theater "palace."

15. The changes in style are evident in the column "New Houses" in *MPW* after 1917. John Eberson, "The Capital," and E. A. Bulloch, "Theater Facades," both in *Architectural Forum* 42, June 1925, pp. 376–78.

16. On luxury hotels, see Daniel J. Boorstin, *The Americans: The Democratic Experience*, New York, 1973, pp. 350–51. For the New York Astor see Lewis Erenberg, "Urban Nightlife and the Decline of Victorianism: New York City's Restaurants and Cabarets, 1890–1918," Ph.D. dissertation, University of Michigan, 1974, pp. 26–81.

17. On the rise of prices see Stephen Bush, "Is the Nickel Show on the Wane?," *MPW*, November 16, 1914, p. 1065; Carl Laemmle, "Editorial," *Universal Distributors' Bulletin*, p. 5, in AMPASL; Marcus Loew, "The Motion Picture and Vaudeville," in Kennedy, *The Story*, pp. 290–95; "Millionaire Homes in Film Land," *Theater Magazine*, April 1915, pp. 181–99.

18. Thomas Lamb, "Atmospherics," *Architectural Forum*, pp. 391–400. This is the designer for the Loew chain; see "Thomas Lamb Obituary," New York *Times*, February 26, 1942; Balaban, *Continuous Performance*, pp. 45, 51, 70, 159, 161, 170, describes the same transitions. Lewis Mumford, "The Architecture of Escape," *New Republic*, August 12, 1925, pp. 321–22.

19. Samuel Rothafel, "What the Public Wants in the Motion Picture Theater," Kenneth Krankheim, "Theater Façades," Eberson, "The Capital," all in *Architectural Forum* 42, June 1925, pp. 361–62, 370–73, 374–76; Franklin, *Theater Management*, pp. 40, 119, 259–69, 277–81, 305. For pictures of the palaces, see Hall, *Seats*.

20. Balaban's life, his handbook, and friendly atmosphere cultivated in nearly every theater of the day are described in Balaban, *Continuous Performance*, pp. 45, 51, 70, 159–70. See also Franklin, *Theater Management*, pp. 123–40.

21. *Ibid.*

22. Balaban, *Continuous Performance*, pp. 45, 51, 70, 159, 161, 170–71; "Rothafel of the Regent," *MPW*, December 1913, pp. 1401–2; Marcus Loew, "The Motion Picture as Vaudeville," in Kennedy, *Story*, pp. 264–70.

23. Loew, "Motion Picture as Vaudeville," describes this process. On the use of advertisements capitalizing on the attendance of "society" at premiers, see *Triangle Exhibitors' Bulletin*, October 23, 1915, p. 8. For a testimonial and commendation

by Theodore Roosevelt and Mrs. Vanderbilt see *Triangle Exhibitor's Bulletin*, October 23, 1915, p. 1, and July 1, 1916, p. 8, in EHFL; *MPW*, December 5, 1915, for Lodge's attendance; Mumford, "Architecture of Escape," p. 321.

24. See the Grauman Chinese File, in AMPASL. There can be found the opening night pamphlets, as well as the biographical information about the owner, designers, and architect.

25. Davis, *Exploitation*, pp. 26–27, and *Report of the Police Department*, New York, 1890–1912, has the seating capacities for New York City's movie houses, common shows, and theaters.

26. From 1927 to 1929, *Film Daily Yearbook*, New York, published the location, name, and seating capacity of every theater in the country, according to the city and population of the area where situated.

27. Davis, *Exploitation*, pp. 26–35.

28. Leo Handel, *Hollywood Looks at Its Audience: A Report of Film Audience Research*, Urbana, Illinois, 1950, pp. 94–125, draws on studies from the twenties and forties, finding continuity between the two decades.

29. *Film Daily Yearbook*, 1928. The ratio of seats per capita was calculated by dividing each city's population by the total number of theater seats.

30. Paul Monaco, *Cinema and Society: France and Germany During the Twenties*, New York, 1976, pp. 18–31, provides information on the number of theaters for 1920. On the 28,000 theaters in America for 1929 as compared to 5,000 in Germany, 3,900 in France, 4,000 in England, 2,063 in Italy, see *Film Daily Yearbook*, New York, 1929, p. 304. The *Yearbook* is the annual summary of the industry's trade journal, *MPW*.

31. Midwestern exhibitor cited in Hall, *Seats*, pp. 90–91.

## Chapter Seven: The New Frontier

1. Nathanael West, *The Day of the Locust*, New York, 1939, pp. 130–31.

2. For one among many see Arthur Knight, *The Liveliest Art*, New York, 1957, pp. 51–54.

3. Anon., *How To Write a Photoplay*, New York, 1912, listed the addresses of all studios; "A History of Production in the East and West," *Director's Annual*, 1934, pp. 25–32, 325, in AMPASL. For example, *MPW*, January 1911, had notes from Los Angeles describing production on the West Coast, but it also had "notes" from Chicago; Boston; Jacksonville, Florida; Manhattan; Brooklyn; and San Juan, Puerto Rico. On the newer economic interpretation, see Robert Sklar, *Movie Made America*, New York, 1975, pp. 67–69.

4. The assumption that they entered production after 1912 comes from their various biographies, cited below. Leo Rosten's sociological study, *Hollywood: The Movie Colony and the Movie Makers*, New York, 1941, p. 61, lists the "Big Eight." See also Norman Freedman, "Hollywood: the Jewish Experience and Popular Cuture," *Judaism*, Fall 1970, pp. 482–87.

5. On the uniqueness of the Jews, see Nathan Glazer, "The American Jew and the Attainment of Middle Class Rank: Some Trends and Explanations," in Marshall Sklare, ed., *The Jews: Social Patterns of an American Group*, Glencoe, Illinois, 1958, pp. 138–46. For their economic position, skills, and sexual demography,

as well as their status in Europe, see Simon Kuznets, "Immigration of Russian Jews to the United States: Background and Structure," *Perspectives in American History* 10, 1976, pp. 35–124. On mobility compared to others, see Stephan Thernstrom, *The Other Bostonians: Poverty and Progress in the American Metropolis, 1880–1970*, Cambridge, Mass., 1973, pp. 136–37, 142–43, 162–65.

6. On moveable trades, particularly clothing, see Kuznets, "Immigration," pp. 56–57, 104–13. *Today's Living*, August 9, 1959, p. 8 untitled clipping, Goldwyn File, MOMA.

7. Abraham Bisno, *Bisno, Union Pioneer*, Madison, Wisconsin, 1967, pp. 5–45; Alan Hynd, "Interview with Nicholas Schenck, *Liberty Magazine*, June 28, 1941, p. 8. On Jesse Lasky and Samuel Goldwyn, see "Obituary," Los Angeles *Times*, February 1, 1974; on Balaban and Katz, see Carrie Balaban, *Continuous Performance: The Story of A. J. Balaban as Told to His Wife*, New York, 1942, p. 74; for Zukor and Loew see Adolph Zukor, *The Public Is Never Wrong*, New York, 1953, p. 237. On Laemmle's policy at Universal see undated clipping, Laemmle File, MOMA.

8. For a general study of the liberalizing trend, see Nathan Glazer, *American Judaism*, New York, 1957, and Harold Rosenberg, "Jewish Identity in an Open Society," in Harold Rosenberg, *Discovering the Present*, Chicago, 1973. Abraham Cahan, *The Rise of David Levinsky*, New York, 1917, pp. 329–30. For a similar drive among the moguls, see Samuel Goldwyn, *Behind the Silver Screen*, New York, 1923, pp. 1–35. Ray Stannard Baker, "The Disintegration of the Jews," *American Magazine*, October 1909, pp. 590–603, saw the Jews' religious structure similar to American values.

9. On Jewish life and festivals in Europe, see Mark Zborowski and Elizabeth Herzog, *Life Is with People: The Culture of the Shtetl*, New York, 1952, especially pp. 409–30. Cahan, *Levinsky*, pp. 284–85.

10. For Zukor's career see Albin Krebs, "Adolph Zukor Dies at 103, Built Paramount Movie Empire," New York *Times*, June 11, 1976, pp. 1, D18, and Zukor, *The Public*; Zukor and William Fox described the new theaters they ran in Joseph Kennedy, ed., *The Story of the Films*, New York, 1927, pp. 55–58, 303–5. This is an invaluable document, for it is a series of lectures by film executives to the Harvard Business School, describing how the industry evolved.

11. See Roy E. Aitkin, *The Birth of a Nation Story*, Middleburg, Virginia, 1966, for the high rates and problems getting good financing. A. H. Giannini, future head of the Bank of America, explained that in 1914 he started to see that good loans could be made to Paramount, undercutting the "bonus sharks." See A. H. Giannini, "Financial Aspects," in Kennedy, ed., *The Story*, pp. 77–98. Zukor's elation on having received ten million dollars from the bankers in 1914 is in Zukor, "Origin and Growth of the Industry," in Kennedy, *The Story*, pp. 73–74. The Chaplin quote is from Charles Chaplin, *My Autobiography*, New York, 1964, pp. 240–41; Zukor also "admitted that he had plans to amalgamate both the theaters and the studios," see p. 240. This was in about 1920.

12. A first-hand account and estimate of the rising costs is Benjamin Hampton, *History of the American Film Industry*, New York, 1931, pp. 305–7. Hampton was vice president of American Tobacco and an early film entrepreneur with Zukor.

13. For the big firms controlling production, see William Johnston, "The Motion

Picture Industry," *The Annals of the American Academy of Political and Social Science*
128, September 1926, pp. 90–100. Johnston was the chief editor of a major
trade journal. On the number of companies in 1912, see *MPW*, December 1912.
For the merger of these several firms into Universal, see the masthead of absorbed companies for *The Universal Distributor's Handbook*, May 1915, p. 1, AM-
PASL. The number of films made in 1912 came from counting new listings in
*MPW*. For this I am indebted to Daisann McLane. The films made during the
twenties are listed and described in *The American Film Institute Catalogue*, New
York, 1971.

14. Paul Shields, "The Movie Industry Applies Chain Store Methods," *Forbes*, July
15, 1925, p. 526; Johnston, "The Motion Picture Industry," pp. 94–191. The
Loew quote is from "More Mergers in the Movies," *Commerce and Finance*, April
23, 1924. On the same process at work in the teens, see almost any edition of
the *Triangle Exhibitor's Bulletin*, 1915–1916, Eastman House, Rochester, New
York. Or see the *Universal Weekly*, 1914–1916, in AMPASL. This was the trade
journal for Universal Pictures. On the raising of prices, coinciding with photoplays, better audiences, and luxury houses, see Stephan Bush, "Is the Nickel
Show on the Wane?" *MPW*, November 16, 1914, p. 1065; Carl Laemmle, "Editorial," *Universal Distributor's Handbook*, p. 5, in AMPASL.

15. On block booking, see Loew, "Motion Picture and Vaudeville"; Robert
Cochrane, "Advertising Motion Pictures"; Samuel Katz, "Theater Management"; and Sidney Kent, "Distributing the Product," all in Kennedy, *The Story*;
Johnston, "The Motion Picture Industry," pp. 94–101. This consolidation also
made it possible to receive loans almost without collateral, see Giannini, "Financing the Production and Distribution of Motion Pictures," *The Annals*, pp.
46–49. The average number of films made by each major company yearly was
calculated from the *American Film Institute Catalogue of Motion Pictures Produced in
the United States, 1919–1929*, New York, 1971.

16. *Ibid.* The division of the industry into specialized New York bureaucracies is in
Kennedy, ed., *The Story*; the location of the administrative offices in New York
can be seen in *The Motion Picture Almanac*, 1934, pp. 547–60. This same process
as a phenomenon of the modern corporation is described in Alfred D. Chandler, "The Beginnings of 'Big Business' in American History," *Business History
Review* 33, Spring 1959, pp. 1–31. The investments of American Tobacco are
described in Hampton, *History*, pp. 150–69. On the Bank of America see "Financing the Distribution and Production of Motion Pictures," *The Annals*,
pp. 46–49. For the DuPonts, Chase Manhattan Bank, and the stock market, see
"Influential Financial Interests Identify Themselves with Goldwyn," *MPW*,
December 31, 1919, p. 781.

17. "William Hays," *National Cyclopedia of American Biography* A, New York, 1945,
pp. 254–55. On Hays's links to reformers, see Will Hays, *Memoirs*, New York,
1955, pp. 147–55, 329.

18. On the need to undercut local censors, see the New York *Times*, January 18,
1922, p. 16, or March 12, 1922, sec. IV, p. 2. Hays firmly believed that films
should be shown abroad for "ideological reasons," see Will Hays to Frederick
Herron, November 9, 1923, Hays Collection, Collected Papers of Will Hays,
Indiana State Library; on arbitrating and blackballing any firm that did not co-

operate with the majors, see "Amendment to the By-Laws of the MPPDA," February 8, 1923, Hays Collection. Hays's ties to the Federal Reserve Board is in Memorandum to Will Hays, September 16, 1922, Hays Collection. The use of the Hays Commission to buy out smaller firms for the majors is in Albert Smith, *Two Reels and a Crank*, New York, 1952, pp. 268–69, which is the memoir of a Vitagraph Company executive. For Hays's organization of a united front against labor in the West Coast studios, see Louis B. Perry and Richard Perry, *A History of the Los Angeles Labor Movement, 1911–1941*, Los Angeles, 1963, pp. 16–25, 320–40, 476.

19. The main histories are Robert M. Fogelson, *Fragmented Metropolis*, Cambridge, Massachusetts, 1968; Sam Bass Warner, *The Urban Wilderness: A History of the American City*, New York, 1972, pp. 113–53; and Carey McWilliams, *Southern California Country*, New York, 1946. The quote is from Charles D. Willard, *A History of the Chamber of Commerce of Los Angeles, California*, Los Angeles, 1899. On the boom atmosphere and its greatest boosters, see Robert Gottleib and Irene Wolt, *Thinking Big: The Story of the Los Angeles Times, Its Publishers and Their Influence on Southern California*, New York, 1977, pp. 7–144.

20. On the older pattern of Western development, the literature is vast, but see Lewis Atherton, *Main Street on the Middle Border*, Chicago, 1954, pp. 3–14. For the population growth of Los Angeles, see U.S. Bureau of the Census, *Abstract of the Fourteenth Census*, Washington, D.C., 1930. The argument is not that the growth was faster than other places, but that it coincided with the modern economic and cultural developments of the twentieth century.

21. The Culver episode is in Academy Research Project on Tom Ince, in AMPASL. See also "Harry Culver Obituary," New York *Times*, August 18, 1946, p. 47, and Los Angeles *Times*, August 18, 1946; Culver was also finance chairman of the Los Angeles Board of Commerce from 1936 to 1939. He was born in Lincoln, Nebraska. For the Goldwyn quote see *MPW*, October 19, 1918.

22. In 1910, 60 percent of the population of Los Angeles came from the Midwest. See George Mowry, *The California Progressives*, Berkeley, 1951, pp. 6–7. On the elites and connections to churches, as well as moral reform, see Gregory Singleton, "Religion in the City of the Angels, American Protestant Culture and the Urbanization of Los Angeles, 1850–1930," Ph.D. dissertation, UCLA, 1976; on sumptuary legislation in Los Angeles, see Gilman Ostrander, *The Prohibition Movement in California*, Berkeley, 1957, pp. 71, 131. For city-wide elections, see "Proportional Representation in Los Angeles," *National Municipal Review* 3, January 1914, pp. 92–95. On the police being made into a civil service organization, see Joseph J. Woods, "Police and Politics in Los Angeles, 1919–1941," Ph.D. dissertation, UCLA, 1973.

23. For reform and anti-labor, monopoly politics, see Mowry, *California*, pp. 6–7, 87, 90–97. A general discussion of these trends in the national setting, then applied to Los Angeles, is in James Weinstein, *The Corporate Ideal in the Liberal State, 1900–1918*, Boston, 1968. For the anti-union activities in Los Angeles as well as their relation to the movie industry, see Perry and Perry, *Labor Movement*, pp. 16–25, 320–42, 476.

24. On taking polls to gauge the public taste, see Jesse Lasky, "Does the Public Know What It Wants?" *Theater Magazine*, August 1918, pp. 114–15. On obey-

ing regulatory laws and being self-made men, see the numerous expressions by the major executives, directors, and actors in Kennedy, *The Story.* For a classic example, see also Carl Laemmle, "From the Inside," *Saturday Evening Post,* August 27–September 10, 1927. For Tumulty and McAdoo, see "All They Say Is See Our Lawyer," *Photoplay,* May 1919, p. 10. For Mary Pickford and Wilson's daughter, see clipping from Chicago *Tribune,* dated 1919, Mary Pickford Scrapbooks, Robinson Locke Collection, Vol. IV, NYPLTAC.

25. Stephan Stills, "The Actor's Part," in Kennedy, ed., *The Story,* pp. 175–90. Stills felt that the people in the industry needed release from their own routine and assembly line.

26. Henry Nash Smith, *The Virgin Land: The American West as Symbol and Myth,* New York, 1957.

27. Frank Fenton, *A Place in the Sun,* Los Angeles, 1949. This is a novel by an old-time resident, taking place in the city at the turn of the century.

28. Fogelson, *Fragmented;* Warner, *Wilderness,* pp. 113–53; Gottleib and Wolt, *Thinking Big,* pp. 11–53. For a contemporary account of the romantic ambiance, with photographs and an analysis of Los Angeles architecture in the nineteenth and twentieth centuries, see Reyner Banham, *Los Angeles: The Architecture of Four Ecologies,* New York, 1971.

29. Charles M. Robinson, *Los Angeles, The City Beautiful, Report of the Municipal Art Commission for the City of Los Angeles, California,* Los Angeles, 1909.

30. *Ibid.*

31. *Ibid.* For a brief account of Venice, built between 1905 and 1910, see Fred Basten, *Santa Monica Bay: The First Hundred Years,* Los Angeles, 1972. For the number of theaters in Los Angeles, seating capacity, and per-capita seats, see the elaborate listings in *The Film Daily Yearbook,* New York, 1927, pp. 100–105. In 1880 the city had only two theaters, seating 600 each, and six concert halls. See Dept. of Commerce, Bureau of the Census, *Report on the Social Statistics of Cities,* Washington, D.C., 1886, p. 781. Charles Chaplin, *My Autobiography,* pp. 129–31. Robert O. Schad, *Henry E. Huntington,* San Marino, California, 1931.

32. McWilliams, *Southern California;* William de Mille, *Hollywood Saga,* New York, 1939, pp. 113–53. This is one of the best memoirs of the era; de Mille also saw land and labor as much cheaper than in the East, see pp. 44–45. Charles Chaplin, *My Autobiography,* pp. 130–31; Jesse Lasky, *I Blow My Own Horn,* New York, 1957, pp. 160–61.

33. See "A History of Production in the East," pp. 25–32. An insightful view of the East Coast studios in the early days is in Chaplin, *My Autobiography,* pp. 170–77. See also "Essanay's New Studio in Chicago," *MPW,* July 11, 1914, p. 266. For the quote and studio policy of Vitagraph, see Smith, *Two Reels,* p. 212.

34. See "American Studio at Santa Barbara," *MPW,* July 11, 1914, p. 240; "Universal City Opens," Los Angeles *Times,* March 16, 1915, III, p. 4; *Universal Weekly,* September 1914, pp. 1–37, in AMPASL. Capitalization of the studios is documented in *Motion Picture Trade Directory, 1928,* New York, 1928, p. 211. For employee benefits see Kent, "Distributing and Selling the Product," in Kennedy, *The Story.* Salaries of executives were released by the Federal Trade Commission in 1934. In the late twenties they went from $100,000 to $900,000 for the top ten in each studio; see *The Motion Picture Almanac,* 1934, p. 963, for

a reproduction of the report. For labor strikes and their lack of success over the period, see Perry and Perry, *Labor Movement*, pp. 320–42.

35. In this regard the motion picture industry reflects more the type of organization prevalent in the clothing and cigar businesses than that of car production, flour milling, or steel. See Alfred Chandler, *The Visible Hand: The Managerial Revolution in American Business*, Cambridge, Massachusetts, 1977, pp. 209–39. Budd Schulberg, *What Makes Sammy Run?*, New York, 1941, pp. 213–14.

36. See Table III for this information. The results of this study were gleaned from the *Motion Picture Directory and Trade Annual, 1920*, a source that gave the vital biographical information on the white-collar creative workers. This was compiled by Elaine Tyler May, "Who Put the Schmaltz on the Screen?" Master's thesis, UCLA, 1970. The comparison of 1890 comes from the listed birth places and dates in the *Directory*, then comparing them to city size as well as the urbanization of the nation in Bureau of the Census, *Population*, Washington, D.C., 1890.

37. *Ibid.*, Tables IV, V.

38. *Ibid.* In *The Directory*, editors and screen writers were listed together, and one third were women. Since on the screen credits, editors were usually not women, we can assume that women writers in 1920 would constitute an even higher percentage. During the twenties, one-third of the screen writers were women; see *The Film Daily Yearbook*, New York, 1925. The same source listed only one-sixth women screen-writers in 1940, one-twelfth in 1950 and 1960. In other words, the teens and twenties were the height of female involvement as screenwriters.

39. The profile of the forty-one top screenwriters is from Daisann McLane, "Silent Sisters: Women Screenwriters in Hollywood, 1915–1929," Senior thesis, Princeton University, 1976. McLane drew on the writers' files in MOMAFL and LCPAL. That they focused on new women and consumption themes to the exclusion of others was gathered from a tabulation of listings in *The American Film Institute Catalogue*, in McLane, "Silent Sisters," pp. 60–96, Princeton University Library. Anita Loos, *A Girl Like I*, New York, 1960, p. 1–100.

40. "Movie Royalty Homes in California," *Photoplay*, June 1915, p. 23.

41. Pictures of these homes appear in Fred Basten, *Beverly Hills: Portrait of a Fabled City*, Los Angeles, 1975, pp. 61–66, 82–83. On the city free of vice and the suburban homes, see George Ade, "Answering Wild-Eyed Questions About the Movie Stars in Hollywood," *American Magazine*, May 1922, p. 52.

42. "Fannie Ward's New Home," *Photoplay*, January 1919; "Everybody's Doin' It Now, Bessie Love Shows You How," *Photoplay*, October 1925. Anzia Yezerska, *Red Ribbon on a White Horse*, New York, 1950, p. 61.

43. Political data on Los Angeles comes from a survey by Joseph J. Woods, "Police and Politics in Los Angeles, 1919–1941," Ph.D. dissertation, UCLA, 1973. From 1900 to 1950 no Hollywood men or women held office in the city. One exception occurred in the Police Commission.

## *Chapter Eight: Cecil B. DeMille*

1. Irving Thalberg, "Speech at University of Southern California," in "Introduction to the Photoplay," unpublished text, 1929, pp. 50–55, AMPASL.

2. Richard Hofstadter, *The Age of Reform*, New York, 1955, pp. 217–18; C. Wright Mills, *White Collar*, New York, 1956, or Robert S. Lynd and Helen Merrell Lynd, *Middletown*, New York, 1929, chapters IV–VIII. For women see Bureau of the Census, *Population* 2, 1920, pp. 22–23; William Henry Chafe, *The American Woman*, New York, 1972, pp. 56, 84–89. On the changing values see Louis Galambos, *The Public Image of Big Business in America*, Baltimore, 1977. By 1919, concludes Galambos, ". . . a bureaucratic or corporate culture . . . was becoming the dominant value system throughout middle-class America—on the farm and in the factory, behind the pulpit as well as the drawing board," p. 261.

3. Despite variances in emphasis, most mobility studies show that the top of the social ladder became more closed in the twentieth century, but that mobility in the middle ranks increased for everyone except blacks, so that the bourgeoisie grew larger in the corporate era. See S. M. Lipset and Reinhard Bendix, *Social Mobility in Industrial Society*, Berkeley, California, 1959, pp. 48–56; and Stephan Thernstrom, *The Other Bostonians: Poverty and Progress in the American Metropolis, 1880–1970*, Cambridge, Mass., 1973.

4. *Ibid.* See Dept. of Commerce, *Historical Statistics of the United States*, Washington, D.C., 1960, pp. 139, 179. On the per capita income by region—which was about double in the Northeast and Pacific West over the South and Midwest—see R. A. Easterlin, "Regional Income Trends, 1840–1950," in S. E. Harris, ed., *American Economic History*, New York, 1961, pp. 527–29. On the decline of the work week and its intensity in the cities over rural areas, see Joseph S. Zeisel, "The Work Week in American Industry," in Rolf Meyerson and Eric Larabee, eds., *Mass Leisure*, New York, 1955, pp. 145–53, and *Historical Statistics*, pp. 91–92.

5. See Dept. of Commerce, *Historical Statistics*, p. 91, on the declining work week. Between 1900 and 1920, life expectancy for women rose from 51.08 years to 58.3 years, and for men from 48.3 to 56.34 years; see *Historical Statistics*, pp. 23, 25. The decline in voter participation from the nineteenth to twentieth century can be seen in Walter Dean Burnham, "The Changing Face of the American Political Universe," *American Political Science Review* 59, March 1965, pp. 7–17. The decline of women's organizations is in Chafe, *American Woman*, pp. 1–75, while the same for church is in Gregory Singleton, "Religion in the City of the Angels: Churches and Urbanization in Los Angeles," Ph.D. dissertation, UCLA, 1976. On the size of the average urban household over time, see Report of the President's Research Committee, *Recent Social Trends*, Washington, D.C., 1933, p. 683. Compared with farm families, 4.21 in 1900 and 4.3 in 1930, the trend is even more dramatic.

6. Louis Terman, *Psychological Factors in Marital Happiness*, New York, 1938, quoted in Chafe, *American Woman*, p. 95; Lynds, *Middletown*, p. 123. Daniel Scott Smith and Michael S. Hindus, "Pre-marital Pregnancy in America, 1640–1971," *Journal of Interdisciplinary History* 5, 1975, pp. 537–70; on the reorientation of liberal, Protestant churches, see David M. Kennedy, *Birth Control in America: The Career of Margaret Sanger*, New Haven, 1970, pp. 158–62.

7. Dept. of Commerce, *Historical Statistics*, p. 15. In a highly technical study of marriage, one scholar has found that, rather than owing to any demographic

change, the statistics indicated a higher inclination to marriage, see Paul H. Jacobson, *American Marriage and Divorce*, New York, 1959, pp. 32–35; Elaine Tyler May, *Great Expectations: Marriage and Divorce in Post-Victorian America*, Chicago, 1980.

8. Donald R. Makosky, "The Portrayal of Women in Wide Circulation Magazine Short Stories," Ph.D. dissertation, University of Pittsburgh, 1966. A similar theme was discussed by Patricke Johns-Heine and Hans H. Girth, "Values in Mass Periodical Fiction, 1921–1941," in Bernard Rosenberg and David Manning White, *Mass Culture: The Popular Arts in America*, Glencoe, Illinois, 1957, pp. 226–34. On production to consumption heroes in mass circulation magazines, see Leo Lowenthal, *Literature, Popular Culture and Society*, Englewood Cliffs, New Jersey, 1961, pp. 100–16. On fun morality and child-raising manuals, see Martha Wolfenstein, "The Emergence of Fun Morality," in Rolf Meyerson and Eric Larabee, eds., *Mass Leisure*, New York, 1955, pp. 86–95.

9. *Photoplay* magazine study, *The Age Factor in Selling and Advertising: A Study in a New Phase of Advertising*, Chicago and New York, 1922, pp. 1–50. *The Annals of the American Academy of Political and Social Science* 128, September 1926, pp. 1–175, had government administrators and sociologists commenting on the ability to stimulate demand by the movies. For the youth cult, women, and consumption, see Agnes Smith, "How To Hold Your Youth," *Photoplay*, February 27, 1927.

10. On the scandals and aftermath see the New York *Times*, January 3, 1922, pp. 32–33; and for a first-hand account, see Benjamin B. Hampton, *History of the American Film Industry*, New York, 1931, pp. 281–304.

11. See Will Hays, *Memoirs*, New York, 1955, pp. 105, 331–34, 340, 351, 381–84, 430.

12. Will Hays, "Inauguration Speech at MPPDA, March 21, 1922," and Will Hays to Carl Laemmle, July 10, 1922, Hays Collection, Indiana State Library.

13. The careers of the DeMille family members, Cecil, William, Henry, and Beatrice, can be gleaned from the DeMille Scrapbook, Robinson Locke Collection, NYPLTAC; William de Mille, *Hollywood Saga*, New York, 1939; Cecil B. DeMille, *The Autobiography of Cecil B. DeMille*, Englewood Cliffs, New Jersey, 1959, pp. 68–74, 242–45, describes his political, economic, and social concerns. See also "Research Biography of Cecil B. DeMille," DeMille File, MOMA.

14. The story of Henry and Beatrice is in DeMille, *Autobiography*, pp. 1–50. A sample of Henry's belief in the stage as a pulpit can be found in Henry DeMille, "Letter," *New York Dramatic Mirror*, October 17, 1891, and Beatrice's similar concerns, *New York Sun*, May 5, 1905, unpaginated clippings, DeMille Scrapbook. Her belief in the new morality and women's suffrage is in "Mrs. DeMille Champions the New Morality," *New York Dramatic Mirror*, July 10, 1912. That the sons wrote plays in favor of new morals, see *The Boston Transcript*, December 28, 1912, DeMille Scrapbook. For Cecil's belief that "motion picture producing is more than a business with me, it is a religion and reform," see "Interview," *Cinema Arts*, January 1929, unpaginated clipping, DeMille File, MOMA; *The Squaw Man* (1914), EHFL.

15. *The Cheat* (1915) and *The Whispering Chorus* (1918), EHFL. Similar lessons occur in *What's His Name* (1914), *The Man from Home* (1914), *The Golden Chance* (1916),

*Temptation* (1915), described with important stills in Gene Ringold and De Witt Bodeen, *The Films of Cecil B. DeMille*, Secaucus, New Jersey, 1969, pp. 27, 41, 95, 99. On the need to "fight sex" see Adela Rogers St. Johns, "What Marriage Means, As Told By Cecil B. DeMille," *Photoplay*, December 1920, pp. 29–31. On the War, see Cecil B. DeMille, *Autobiography*, pp. 63–68; and *The Little American* (1917), in Ringold and Bodeen, *Films*, pp. 133–36.

16. *Foolish Wives* (1922), *Blind Husbands* (1919), *The Four Horsemen of the Apocalypse* (1920), are in MOMAFL. *The Sheik* (1920) is in LCFA. *The Motion Picture Almanac*, New York, 1934, gives the box office receipts for the films of the twenties, with *The Four Horsemen* being the top grosser, see p. 17.

17. The new awareness is described by William de Mille, *Saga*, pp. 239–41.

18. On Protestant churches, see Kennedy, *Birth Control*, pp. 158–62. DeMille to Adela Rogers St. Johns, "What Does Marriage Mean," and "More About Marriage," *Photoplay*, May and June, 1921, pp. 25–26. The cited films are in EHFL and described in Ringold and Bodeen, *Films*, pp. 149, 165, 181, 195. The grosses were from five to ten times the cost, see *Variety*, March 21, 1928, p. 5.

19. The quotes are from *Why Change Your Wife* and *The Affairs of Anatol*.

20. *Ibid.*

21. The quotes are from St. Johns and DeMille, "More About Marriage," p. 26. The occupations of his heroes come from the films; significantly, they are "new" middle class.

22. *Manslaughter* (1922), *The Ten Commandments* (1923), *The Road to Yesterday* (1925), *The Godless Girl* (1929), are in EHFL. Descriptions and stills are in Ringold and Bodeen, *Films*, pp. 209, 221, 243, 257. "Rome at its worst" is the description a hero gave of his sweetheart's activities in *Manslaughter*. When she goes to prison for her crimes, prosecuted by the hero, she comes out redeemed, and the two wed.

23. The best example of a lower-class but virtuous girl transformed into a desirable creature for wealthy men occurs in *Forbidden Fruit* (1921). The pinnacle of the bath scene is in *Male and Female* (1919). The look of beauty separate from vice occurred in nearly all films; but for an example of how it became common currency for all aspiring actresses, see John Emerson and Anita Loos, *Breaking into the Movies*, New York, 1921, pp. 12–21.

24. *Forbidden Fruit* (1921), EHFL.

25. This comes from tabulating over 6,000 films in Kenneth Munden, ed., *The American Film Institute Catalogue*, New York 1971; Yon Barna, *Eisenstein*, Bloomington, Indiana, 1973, pp. 154–62.

26. *Safety Last* (1923), *The Cameraman* (1928), *Sherlock Junior* (1924), *The Navigator* (1924), *Seven Chances* (1925), EHFL.

27. Munden, *Catalogue;* same tabulation as in note 25 above; *The Iron Horse* (1925), MOMAFL. I am indebted to my colleague, Professor Karal Ann Marling, for this insight.

28. The major swashbuckling films of the twenties for Fairbanks are *The Mark of Zorro* (1920), *The Thief of Bagdad* (1924), *Don Q, Son of Zorro* (1925), *The Gaucho* (1927), *The Iron Mask* (1929), in EHFL, as well as Richard Schickel and Douglas Fairbanks, Jr., *The Fairbanks Album*, Boston, 1976, pp. 102–80.

29. From a random plot sample of 10 percent of all the films made yearly, taken from Munden, *Catalogue*.

30. *The Crowd* (1927); *Skinner's Dress Suit* (1925), MOMAFL.

31. *Stark Love* (1927), *The Jazz Singer* (1927). Parental battle also occurs dramatically in *The Big Parade* (1925).

32. The pattern discerned here comes from several sources. First are the major flapper films; second is Munden, ed., *Catalogue;* for a classic statement of what the new woman is to be, see Anita Loos and John Emerson, *How To Write Photoplays*, New York, 1920. A clear exposition of how Hollywood portrayed career women as those who wasted youth by working is *Smoldering Fires* (1925), EHFL.

33. *It* (1927). Two other films by Bow clearly show that sex could be dangerous to men's success; see *The Plastic Age* (1925) and *Call Her Savage* (1931), both in EHFL.

34. The Garbo films of the twenties are in EHFL; plots with pictures are in Michael Conway, Dion McGregor, and Mark Ricci, *The Films of Greta Garbo*, New York, 1968, pp. 45–84.

35. *The Temptress* (1926), EHFL.

36. The pinnacle of the new form appeared in Murnau's beautiful *Sunrise* (1927) and *City Girl* (1929); Seastrom's *The Wind* (1928), and Stiller's *The Temptress* (1926) and *Hotel Imperial* (1927). For the expressionist style in Europe and the United States, see Lotte H. Eisner, *The Haunted Screen*, Berkeley and Los Angeles, 1969.

37. Quote from Stephan Stills, "The Actor's Part," in Joseph Kennedy, ed., *The Story of the Films*, New York, 1927, pp. 175–80. Canonization of the "star" came with the footprints in front of Grauman's Chinese Theater, see Chapter VI. William de Mille, "Lecture at the University of California," unpublished manuscript, AMPASL, pp. 170–80; Barna, *Eisenstein*, pp. 154–55. On art direction and Betty Blythe see Kevin Brownlow, *The Parade's Gone By*, New York, 1969, pp. 269–79, 436.

38. For constant newness see Hampton, *History*, pp. 305–7, or William Johnston, "The Motion Picture Industry," *The Annals of the American Academy of Political and Social Science* 128, September 1926, pp. 90–100. On its relation to selling, see Carl Laemmle, "From the Inside," *Saturday Evening Post*, August 27 and September 10, 1927; and Sydney Kent, "Distributing the Product," in Kennedy, *The Story*, pp. 220–30.

39. Thalberg, "Lecture," p. 56.

40. This profile comes from the clippings in Tom Mix File, MOMA. *Sky High* (1921), MOMAFL, is a good example of the cowboy as government agent. One clipping asked, "Can a man who wears fancy clothes and bejeweled clothing be all man?" Another showed Mix looking like a "million, and rightfully so." The Lloyd, Barrymore, and Fairbanks material came from their respective files in AMPASL, and Arthur Knight and Eliot Elisofon, *The Hollywood Style*, New York, 1969, pp. 25–71.

41. The major source on Swanson is Swanson File, MOMA, and LCPAL. See also Gloria Swanson, "Hollywood," *The Saturday Evening Post*, July 22–29, 1950, unpaginated clippings, Swanson File, MOMA.

42. Knight and Elisofon, *Hollywood Style*, pp. 25–71; "Close-Ups of Norma Talmadge," *The Saturday Evening Post*, June 25, 1927, p. 46; Nathanael West, *The Day of the Locust*, New York, 1939, pp. 10–11.

43. William Harrison Hays, "Supervision from Within," in Kennedy, ed., *The Story*, pp. 33–40.

## Epilogue

1. Diana Ross, *Time* magazine, April, 1977.
2. For the Hollywood industry and the Depression see F. D. Klingender and Stuart Legg, *Money Behind the Screen*, New York, 1937; Robert Sklar, *Movie-Made America: A Social History of American Movies*, New York, 1975; on labor, Louis B. Perry and Richard Perry, *A History of the Los Angeles Labor Movement*, New York, 1963; on the Cold War in Hollywood see Les K. Adler, "Hollywood and the Cold War," in Robert Griffith and Athen Theoharis, eds., *The Specter*, New York, 1974, pp. 242–60.
3. Andrew Bergman, *We're in the Money*, New York, 1971; John Baxter, *Hollywood in the Thirties*, New York, 1968; Nathaniel West, *Day of the Locust*, New York, 1939; Budd Schulberg, *What Makes Sammy Run?*, New York, 1941.
4. *Modern Times* (1936) is owned by the Chaplin family and periodically shows at major theaters around the country.
5. Stuart Ewen, *Captains of Consciousness*, New York, 1976; David Riesman, *The Lonely Crowd*, New York, 1956; John Kenneth Galbraith, *The Affluent Society*, Boston, 1958; David Potter, *People of Plenty*, Chicago, 1954, especially Chapter VIII. The quote is from Robert Lynd, commenting on the twenties, in President's Research Committee on Social Trends, *Recent Social Trends*, New York, 1933, Vol. 2, p. 867.

## Appendix I

1. Robert S. Lynd and Helen Merrell Lynd, *Middletown: A Study in Modern Culture*, New York, 1929, pp. 263–71, 342–43.
2. Henry May, *The End of American Innocence*, Chicago, 1959; James R. McGovern, "The American Woman's Pre–World War I Freedom in Manners and Morals," *Journal of American History* 55, September 1968, pp. 315–33; John Higham, "The Reorientation of American Culture in the 1890s," in John Weiss, ed., *The Origins of Modern Consciousness*, Detroit, 1965, pp. 24–48.
3. Daniel Scott Smith, "The Dating of the American Sexual Revolution, Evidence and Interpretation," in Michael Gordon, ed., *The American Family in Social-Historical Perspective*, New York, 1973, pp. 321–35.
4. William O'Neill, "Divorce in the Progressive Era," in Gordon, ed., *The American Family*, pp. 251–66. Among a vast literature see Michael Gordon, "From an Unfortunate Necessity to a Cult of Mutual Orgasm: Sex in American Marital Education Literature, 1830–1940," in James Henslin, *Studies in the Sociology of Sex*, New York, 1971.
5. Richard Hofstadter, *The Age of Reform*, New York, 1955, pp. 217–18; C. Wright Mills, *White Collar: The American Middle Classes*, New York, 1956; Daniel Miller and Guy Swanson, *The Changing American Parent*, New York, 1958; Peter Filene, "Men and Manliness Before World War I," Address at the Convention of the Organization of American Historians, April 1972.

6. Hofstadter, *Age of Reform;* Arthur Link, *Woodrow Wilson and the Progressive Era, 1910–1917,* New York, 1954; George E. Mowry, *Theodore Roosevelt and the Progressive Movement,* New York, 1946.

7. Gabriel Kolko, *The Triumph of Conservatism,* New York, 1963; Robert Wiebe, *The Search for Order,* New York, 1967; Samuel P. Hays, *Conservation and the Gospel of Efficiency,* Cambridge, Massachusetts, 1959; James Weinstein, *The Corporate Ideal in the Liberal State,* Boston, 1968.

8. William E. Leuchtenberg, *The Perils of Prosperity, 1914–1932,* Chicago, 1958, pp. 158–203; Gilman M. Ostrander, *American Civilization in the First Machine Age, 1890–1940,* New York and Evanston, Ill., 1970; Paul Carter, *The Twenties in America,* New York, 1968; Leo Lowenthal, *Literature, Popular Culture and Society,* New York, 1961; David Riesman, *The Lonely Crowd,* New York, 1956; John Kenneth Galbraith, *The Affluent Society,* Boston, 1958.

9. Arthur S. Link, "What Happened to Progressivism in the 1920's?" *American Historical Review* 64, July 1959, pp. 842–44.

10. Probably no single facet of American life is surrounded with so much unreliable information. A few studies of note are Benjamin Hampton, *A History of the Movies,* New York, 1931, which has the advantage of being a first-hand account by an early executive; Lewis Jacob, *The Rise of the American Film: A Critical History,* New York, 1939, one of the few documented studies. A good first-hand journalistic account by a contemporary is Terry Ramsaye, *A Million and One Nights,* New York, 1926. A source for original interviews as well as the excitement of early film making is Kevin Brownlow, *The Parade's Gone By,* New York, 1969. A good sociological examination of Hollywood in the late teens is Leo Rosten, *Hollywood: The Movie Colony, the Movie Makers,* New York, 1941; and an intriguing psychological examination of films in the forties is Martha Wolfenstein and Nathan Leites, *Movies: A Psychological Study,* New York, 1950. Both of these studies suffer from an ahistorical perspective which mars their accuracy about the industry and American life.

11. Robert Sklar, *Movie-Made America: A Social History of American Movies,* New York, 1975; Garth Jowett, *Film, The Democratic Art,* Boston, 1976. See also Mary P. Ryan, "The Projection of a New Womanhood, The Movie Moderns in the 1920's," in Jean E. Friedman and William G. Shade, eds., *Our American Sisters: Women in American Life and Thought,* Boston, 1973, pp. 366–84; and William Everson, *The American Silent Film,* New York, 1978, which besides being an excellent study of aesthetics and film development, also includes a valuable appendix of film scholarship.

# INDEX

Adams, Henry, 19, 20
Addams, Jane, 38, 44, 47–50, 52–53, 82, 148–49
*The Affairs of Anatol*, 210, 224, 225, 229
Aitken, Harry, 65–66, 80, 110, 158, 180
*The Americano*, 117
*The American Woman's Home*, 11
Anderson, Gilbert, 101
Anthony, Susan B., 14
Arbuckle, Fatty, 104, 204–5
*The Arena*, 28, 35
Arvidson, Linda, 70
*The Avenging Conscience*, 78, 87

Balaban, A. J., 148–49, 157, 171, 177
Bara, Theda, 106–7, 127, 177, 214
*A Bedroom Blunder*, 104
Beecher, Catharine, 10–11
*Behind the Scenes*, 142
Belasco, David, 32, 120
Benton, Thomas Hart, 238
Bernhardt, Sarah, 176
Biograph Company, 27, 42, 66, 71, 80, 103, 192
*The Birth of a Nation*, 66, 80, 81, 84–85, 88, 89, 97, 99; aesthetics of, 81; Griffith's defense of, 83; public reaction to, 67, 82–83, 86
*Blind Husbands*, 208
Blythe, Betty, 230
Bow, Clara, 218–19
*Broken Blossoms*, 93
"Broncho Billy," 101, 118
*Broncho Billy's Bible*, 101
Broun, Heywood, 86
Bryan, William Jennings, 61
Burnham, Daniel, 22

Cahan, Abraham, 35, 173
California (*see* Hollywood, Los Angeles)
Camera (movie), 22–23, 25–27, 159
Canby, Henry Seidel, 3–7, 15, 18–21, 98
*The Candidate*, 37
Carnegie, Andrew, 5, 54

Castle, Irene and Vernon, 34
Catholics, 15, 174
Censorship: Anglo-Saxon assumptions about, 55; and *The Birth of a Nation*, 83, 86; and the family, 55; and Hays, William, 204–5; and legitimation of movies, 63, 64, 148; and the National Board of Review, 53–55; and Progressive reform, 55–58; and vice crusades, 53
Chandler, Alfred, 29
Chaplin, Charles, 104, 109, 113, 120, 129, 130, 154; background and films of, 105; and Los Angeles, quoted on, 185; and success, 190; and World War I effort, 195; Zukor, Adolph, 176
*The Cheat*, 207
Chicago Vice Commission, 51
Chicago World's Fair, 22, 150
*City Girl*, 221
*The Clansman*, 80
*The Clerk*, 102
Cohn, Harry, 254
Collier, John, 51
Committee of Fourteen, 45, 52, 54
Comstock, Anthony, 43, 54
Coney Island, 28
Consumerism, xi–xv, 145, 146, 197, 199, 200, 202–4, 213, 232–35; and Fairbanks and Pickford films, 111, 143; and the family, 142–46, 232–36, 190, 196–99, 206–13; and the modern economy, 117; and Progressive reform, 58; and the star system, 190, 234; and Victorian breakdown, 32, 34
Conwell, Russell, 5
Cooper, James Fenimore, 5
*Corner on Wheat*, 79
*The Crowd*, 216–17, 228
Culture change, 95, 168–69, 174, 196–201, 236–38; and economics, 96, 99, 165, 168–69; and Hollywood, 168–69, 190; and the home, 98, 194; and movie industry, 99–100, 165; and

Culture change *(continued)*
  new middle class, 97, 99, 168–69; and
  sex roles, 96, 109, 142–44, 146, 203,
  214–15; and theaters, 156, 166; and
  Victorianism, breakdown of, 21, 29,
  31–32, 49
Culver, Harry, 180

Daniels, Josephus, 61
de Koven Bowen, Louise, 49
DeMille, Cecil B., 175, 200, 219, 221,
  230, 236; early background of, 206; and
  censors, 205–6; and family, 206, 213;
  and film aesthetics, 221; themes and
  plots of, 205, 207, 209–14; and moral
  change in films of, 205, 209–11,
  219–20; and films of, 205, 207, 209,
  210, 219–20; and women, portrayal of,
  212–13
de Mille, William, 185, 189
*The Devil's Wheel*, 107
Dickson, William Laurie, 23–24, 41; and
  Edison, 22, 25–27
*The Disciple*, 102
Dixon, Thomas, 80, 82
*Dolly of the Dailies*, 107
*Don't Change Your Husband*, 209, 223, 224
*Down with Women*, 37
*Dream Street*, 93
Dreiser, Theodore, 20, 32
Dunbar, Olivia Harriet, 153
Duncan, Isadora, 34

Eaton, Walter P., 149
Economic change, 46, 51, 95, 197–98,
  202; and the corporate order, 29, 62,
  97–98, 116–17, 183, 201, 235; and the
  movie industry, 165, 178, 183, 187;
  and the nineteenth century, 6; and
  Progressive reform, 51; and Victorianism, and the breakdown of, 29;
  and women, 29–30, 201; and work, 27,
  29, 51, 116–17, 183
Edison, Thomas, 22, 39, 40, 41; as self-
  made man, 23–24; and the movie camera, 25–27; and selling out to J. P.
  Morgan, 29; and patent trust of, 62, 63,
  168, 250–51
Eisenstein, Sergei, 214, 231
Ely, Richard, 46
Essanay, 101
*The Eternal Grind*, 122, 136

Fairbanks, Douglas F., 130; and roles
  played, 110–15, 118, 129; and consumerism, 116–17, 145–46; and culture change, 96–97, 109, 146; and early
  background of, 109–10; and economic
  change, 116–17; films of, 110–18; and
  Griffith, D. W., 96, 110, 115; and
  leisure, 112–13, 116–17; and male role,
  114, 117–19; and modern home,
  144–45; and Pickford, Mary, 118–19,
  141, 142, 144–47, 154, 163, 198,
  204–05; and sports, 112–14, 131; and
  star system, 96, 132, 145, 163, 233; and
  women, 117–18, 142; and World War
  I, 144, 195; and youth culture, 114,
  124–25; and Zukor, Adolph, 176–
  77
Family; in the new corporate order, 144;
  and consumerism, 146; and culture
  change, 98; and Griffith, D. W., 75;
  and Hollywood, 167; and immigrants'
  structure of, 48; modern compared to
  Victorian, 202; and Progressive reform, 46, 48, 50, 51; and Victorianism,
  6, 48
Famous Players in Famous Plays, 175,
  185, 205
Farnum, Dustin, 176
Far Rockaway, 28
*Fatty and the Broadway Stars*, 104
Federal Council of Churches, 54
Fenton, Frank, 183, 184
Ferguson, Charles, 147
Filene, Peter, 244
Film Aesthetics, 123, 221; and acting
  techniques, 230, 231; and DeMille,
  221, 230; and Fairbanks, 115; and
  Griffith, 71–74, 76–77, 81, 85, 88, 89;
  and Pickford, 123
Fitzgerald, John F., 149
*Flesh and the Devil*, 219
*Foolish Wives*, 208, 222
*A Fool There Was*, 106
*Forbidden Fruit*, 209, 213, 225
Ford, John, 215
*The Four Horsemen of the Apocalypse*, 208,
  222
Fox Pictures, 238
Fox, William, 152, 177, 183
Frederic, Harold, 15, 30
Frohman, Charles, 32
Fulk, Joseph R., 40

Garbo, Greta, 219–21, 226, 231
Gaynor, William, 56–57, 108
Gianini, A. H., 176
Gish, Dorothy, 76, 126
Gish, Lillian, 75–76, 90, 126
Glyn, Elinor, 219
*Godey's Lady's Book*, 9
*The Godless Girl*, 212
Goldwyn, Samuel, 170–71, 177; early background of, 254; and Los Angeles, quoted on, 181
Gompers, Samuel, 54
*The Good Little Devil*, 120
Grauman, Sid, 163
Grauman's Chinese Theatre, 162, 163
*The Great Train Robbery*, 38, 43
Griffith, David Wark, 60, 96–97, 100, 103, 109, 154, 186, 205; and aims of, quoted on, 61; and attitudes toward movie audience, 77–78; and culture change, 99; declining popularity of, 93–94; and Charles Dickens, 73; early background of, 66–70; and economic change, 69–70, 95; and Fairbanks, Douglas, 110, 115, 146; and family values, 61; and film aesthetics of, 71–72, 74, 76–77; and films of, 66–67, 78–86, 92–93, 97; and film medium, conception of, 72–73; issues dramatized, 61; and monopolists, distrust of, 69; and Pickford, Mary, 118, 121, 146; and Progressive reform, 71–74, 80, 94; and racist attitudes of, 83; and themes of, 78–79; and theater design, 150–51; and vice crusades, 71; and Victorianism, 62, 80; and women, 69–70, 75–77; and World War I, 92; and youth, idealization of, 74–75
Griffith, Jacob, 67
Grimes, Alan, 13

Hale, Sara Josepha, 8–9
*Harper's*, 28, 39, 53, 153
Hart, William S., 101–2, 109, 118, 214–15, 233
Haymarket Saloon, 152
Hays, William Harrison, 179, 182–83, 204–5, 236, 244
*The Hazards of Helen*, 107
*Hearts Adrift*, 124
*Hearts of the World*, 92
*Hell's Hinges*, 101

Higham, John, 243
*His Majesty the American*, 110, 116–17
*His Picture in the Papers*, 116–17, 216
Hofstadter, Richard, 244
Hollywood, 240, 245; and consumerism, 167, 189, 197–99, 234–35; and corporate order, 197; cultural meaning of, 167, 169, 197–99, 235, 237–38, 240; and the Depression, 238–39; and "formula" of, 232–33; and popular image of, 196; and Hollywood "home," 234; and mythic image of, 189–90; and star system, 169, 196–97, 232–34; as urban mobility ideal, 188 (*see also* Los Angeles)
*Home Sweet Home*, 79
*The Hoodlum*, 137, 143
Howe, Frederic, 46–47, 50, 57, 82
Howells, William Dean, 30
Huntington, Henry, 184

*Intolerance*, 66, 84, 90, 91, 99; critical reception of, 86; failure of, 86; themes of, 85
*Iron Horse*, 215
*It*, 219

Jackson, Andrew, 5
James, Henry, 20
*The Jazz Singer*, 218
Jewish producers, 169–75
Jowett, Garth, 246

Katz, Michael, 14
Katz, Samuel, 148, 177
Keaton, Buster, 214
Kennedy, Jeremiah, 63
Kennedy, John Fitzgerald, 149
Kennedy, Joseph, 183
Kenney, Abbot, 184, 185
Keystone, 103
*The Kid*, 105
*The Kiss*, 219, 226
*Kleptomaniac*, 38
Kline, George, 63
*The Knickerbocker Buckaroo*, 115, 216

*The Ladies' World*, 124
Laemmle, Carl, 148, 155, 170–71, 177, 186, 254
Lang, Fritz, 221
Lasky, Jesse, 33, 175, 185, 205, 254